"If the election of Barack Obama signaled that Americans had embraced the idea of racial equality, it disguised the continuing hold of white sovereignty and subjection of black communities. Utz McKnight demonstrates the danger of accepting the common sense of the 'post-racial era' and offers a compelling alternative. Creatively interweaving continental political thought, critical theories of race, and African American fiction, *Race and the Politics of the Exception* paints a portrait of racial power, from slavery to the present, that demands our attention."

—Lawrie Balfour, *University of Virginia*

"McKnight is one of the most interesting and important writers on the question of race in democratic political theory. In this new book he turns to the actual status of race in the American political system. Importantly, he finds central resources in European thought, which he uses to show that even with the election of an African-American president, race cannot be understood as a matter increasingly of the past. For McKnight. the racial subject remains as a central concern in democratic theory. In *A Preface to Democratic Theory*, Robert Dahl argued that the path to overcoming racism lay in the attainment of formal juridical equality—McKnight shows us why that is not the case. This book is a new and important reconceptualization of the question of race in America."

—Tracy B. Strong, *UC San Diego*

Race and the Politics of the Exception

The traditional assumption today about race is that it is not political; that it has no political content and is a matter of individual beliefs and attitudes. In *Race and the Politics of the Exception*, Utz McKnight argues that race is in fact political and defines how it functions as a politics in the United States.

McKnight organizes his book into three sections, beginning with a theoretical section about racial politics in the United States. Using theorists such as Benjamin, Agamben, and Schmitt, McKnight discusses how the idea of racial communities went from being constituted through the idea of racial sovereignty and a politics of the exception that defined blacks as the internal enemy, to being constitutionally defined through the institutions of racial equal opportunity. In the second section, McKnight further develops his critical race theory by exploring in more detail the social use of race today. The election of President Obama has brought the politics of racial equality to a critical point. In spite of a very powerful set of political tools to define it as a thing of the past, race matters. In the final section, McKnight engages with important African American fiction from each of the three major periods of racial politics in the US. Earlier descriptions of political theory are used throughout these analyses to refine the argument for a new critical politics of race.

Scholars of political theory, identity politics, African American studies, and American Studies will find this work ground-breaking and relevant.

Utz McKnight is an Associate Professor in Political Science and Chair of the Department of Gender and Race Studies at the University of Alabama. His publications include *The Everyday Practice of Race in America* and *Political Liberalism and the Politics of Race*.

Routledge Series on Identity Politics

SERIES EDITOR: ALVIN B. TILLERY, Jr., *Rutgers University*

Group identities have been an important part of political life in America since the founding of the republic. For most of this long history, the central challenge for activists, politicians, and scholars concerned with the quality of U.S. democracy was the struggle to bring the treatment of ethnic and racial minorities and women in line with the creedal values spelled out in the nation's charters of freedom. We are now several decades from the key moments of the twentieth century when social movements fractured America's system of ascriptive hierarchy. The gains from these movements have been substantial. Women now move freely in all realms of civil society, hold high elective offices, and constitute more than 50 percent of the workforce. Most African-Americans have now attained middle class status, work in integrated job sites, and live in suburbs. Finally, people of color from nations in Latin America, Asia, and the Caribbean now constitute the majority of America's immigration pool.

In the midst of all of these positive changes, however, glaring inequalities between groups persist. Indeed, ethnic and racial minorities remain far more likely to be undereducated, unemployed, and incarcerated than their counterparts who identify as white. Similarly, both violence and work place discrimination against women remain rampant in U.S. society. The Routledge series on identity politics features works that seek to understand the tension between the great strides our society has made in promoting equality between groups and the residual effects of the ascriptive hierarchies in which the old order was rooted.

Some of the core questions that the series will address are: how meaningful are the traditional ethnic, gender, racial, and sexual identities to our understanding of inequality in the present historical moment? Do these identities remain important bases for group mobilization in American politics? To what extent can we expect the state to continue to work for a more level playing field among groups?

Black Politics Today
The Era of Socioeconomic Transition
Theodore J. Davis Jr.

Jim Crow Citizenship
Liberalism and the Southern Defense of Racial Hierarchy
Marek Steedman

The Politics of Race in Latino Communities
Walking the Color Line
Atiya Kai Stokes-Brown

Conservatism in the Black Community
To the Right and Misunderstood
Angela K. Lewis

The Post-Racial Society is Here
Recognition, Critics and the
Nation State
Wilbur C. Rich

Race and the Politics of the Exception
Equality, Sovereignty, and
American Democracy
Utz McKnight

Race and the Politics of the Exception
Equality, Sovereignty, and American Democracy

Utz McKnight

NEW YORK AND LONDON

First published 2013
by Routledge
711 Third Avenue, New York, NY 10017

Simultaneously published in the UK
by Routledge
2 Park Square, Milton Park, Abingdon, Oxfordshire OX14 4RN

First issued in paperback 2016

*Routledge is an imprint of the Taylor & Francis Group,
an informa business*

© 2013 Taylor & Francis

The right of Utz McKnight to be identified as author of this work has been asserted by him in accordance with sections 77 and 78 of the Copyright, Designs and Patents Act 1988.

All rights reserved. No part of this book may be reprinted or reproduced or utilised in any form or by any electronic, mechanical, or other means, now known or hereafter invented, including photocopying and recording, or in any information storage or retrieval system, without permission in writing from the publishers.

Trademark Notice: Product or corporate names may be trademarks or registered trademarks, and are used only for identification and explanation without intent to infringe.

Library of Congress Cataloging-in-Publication Data
McKnight, Utz Lars.
  Race and the politics of the exception : equality, sovereignty, and American democracy / Utz McKnight.
    pages cm.—(Routledge series on identity politics)
  Includes bibliographical references and index.
 1. United States—Race relations—Political aspects. 2. United States—Politics and government. 3. African Americans—Politics and government. 4. Racism—United States—History. 5. Race discrimination—United States. 6. United States—Race relations. I. Title.
  E185.61.M166 2013
  305.800973—dc23
  2012050556

ISBN 13: 978-1-138-68972-5 (pbk)
ISBN 13: 978-0-415-82760-7 (hbk)

Typeset in Sabon
by IBT Global.

Contents

Acknowledgments — xi

Introduction — 1

PART I
Defining Exceptions to Equality

1 The Racist and the Elite — 17

2 The New Normal — 36

PART II
Defining Racial Sovereignty

3 The Experience of Race — 51

4 Race and Community — 66

5 History and Politics — 91

PART III
Black Politics

6 Slavery and Its Aftermath — 119

7 Jim Crow — 159

8 Integration — 195

Conclusion — 217

Bibliography — 231
Index — 243

Acknowledgments

This manuscript was written while enjoying a generous sabbatical from teaching at the Department of Political Science at the University of Alabama. I owe special thanks to everyone involved in making that happen, as I do for the interest and support shown by several faculty in the department. I would like to thank Richard Fording, Barbara Chotiner, Emily Ritter, Dana Patton, Naomi Choi, Joe Smith, Doug Gibler, and Daniel Levine. Intellectual affirmation and advice in the last few years from the following were invaluable in making it all come together: Pal Ahluwalia, Paul Thomas, Amilcar Shabazz, David Lanoue, Cornel West, and Paul Gilroy. I would not be complete without my family. I thank Mogen, Onda, Yemi, Winona, and Adrian for each in turn making me love life in different ways, and my wife Elizabeth for believing in me.

Introduction

> The time of reading is always late . . . .
> —Nancy and Lacoue-Labarthe, *The Title of the Letter*

> "German" is not spoken to the world so that the world might be reformed through the German essence; rather, it is spoken to the Germans so that from a fateful belongingness to the nations they might become world-historical along with them. The homeland of this historical dwelling is nearness to being.
> —Heidegger, *Basic Writings*

The time has come for us to challenge the model of equality in the United States in order to achieve the goals of democratic progress and racial justice. The conceptual framework that allows for a politics of representation does not make the necessary changes in the social, economic, and political status of Blacks as a community. Instead, the institutional description of racial equality is constrained by the very political and conceptual limitations with which it was established as an alternative to Jim Crow racial segregation.

There has been progress. The election of a Black president can be seen as the culmination of a complex politics that privileges individual equal opportunity in the context of a description of race that is ongoing, even traditional, in the US. This era of integration has witnessed the selection of the first Black Supreme Court justice, a record number of Blacks entering corporate America, becoming presidents of majority White universities, the secretary of State, senators, and professionals at all walks of life. It is now possible to speak of Black individual success as a way to support the current politics of racial equality. This description of success is a result of changes in the law, a product of an evolution in the way race is used within political institutions in the US, from that of slavery through the period of Jim Crow to that of equal opportunity. It is very important to a critical political theory of race in the US that there have always been successful Blacks in the polity and that these persons are not eliminated historically in the political ambitions that define the current politics of the Black exception. As I will show below, however, this idea of political evolution is not the same thing as suggesting that race is a thing of the past, nor is the professional success of individual Blacks today a sign of the absence of race in their lives (King and Smith 2011: 267).

2 *Race and the Politics of the Exception*

ASSERTIONS

This book makes several contributions to a political theory of race in the United States. By providing a description of how race works within democratic political development, it critiques the current institutional apparatus of racial equality of opportunity. Within this apparatus race is defined as a specific object of politics that facilitates the constitutionality of White community political interests. This book asserts that the politics of the exception, made possible by equality legislation and its enforcement mechanisms, transferred the onus of racial social control from the White community under Jim Crow to the state. This transfer left intact the description of racial communities in conflict, a decision that can at least initially be explained through the description of racial friend and enemy as a central political conception of sovereignty in the society.

I claim that the idea of racial community within the new political apparatus of racial equality of opportunity is flawed. Instead of separating the social description of race from the problems of institutional development in the polity, the current development facilitates the reproduction of White community social cohesion while constraining claims of racial injustice as an institutional problem. The problem of race in America remains the problem of the social description of community. The theoretical difficulty lies in building a critique of the definition of community that makes the political basis for the current social description of race available to the transformative processes of democratic development.

This problem is explored in some detail as I discuss several different definitions of community in the literature to address how the White community in the US is able to ensure that its political interests remain those of the state through the institutions that define racial equality of opportunity. This discussion presents several assertions about how race is used to define a subject that is a member of a community distinct from others, and how this forms an important description in US democratic politics.

To develop a new direction for democracy in America, it is necessary to return to those historical descriptions that support the current conception of racial politics. As other scholars within the tradition of critical race theory have demonstrated through the study of the works of Du Bois, the writing of Baldwin, and the historical documentation available on the Jim Crow Era, there is something very important in the present to be gleaned from the critical attention to earlier work on race (Christian 1980, 1985; Balfour 2001, 2011; Kelley 2003; Olson 2004; Shelby 2005; Baum 2006; Blackmon 2009; Gooding-Williams 2009). In the final section of the book I look to works of African American fiction to refigure the community politics of race and argue that this allows for the critique of the current racial political apparatus and the coincident description of racial communities in conflict.

CHAPTER OVERVIEW

The theoretical arguments in the book build successively from within our considered convictions about race as a product of formal racial equality of opportunity. It is necessary to work from within this position to conceptualize a new politics of race. The text is divided into three distinct parts: a first section that defines a theory of racial politics, a second section that provides a critical race theory, and a third section that describes elements of a critical Black subjectivity.

Beyond our complicity in a politics of formal racial equality is a description of a Black subject that is fractured by the experience of race, a White subject that retains sovereign authority over both the state and local political practices, and a description of democracy that remains unfulfilled as a promise. I will argue that a particular definition of the exceptional African American, along with the definition of the racist as a constraint on the description of the substantive political claims of a White community subject, allows for the continuation of race as a central political principle in US society. In spite of a focus on formal racial equal opportunity, race is just as much a problem for a democratic US polity today as it was in both of the earlier periods in the history of race relations.

Unlike those who see the current growth of a Black middle and upper class as indicative of a society that has accepted that race no longer exists as a concept, I see the situation today for Blacks as still constrained by the same politics of race that has defined the US throughout its history. I want to address what allows for this bifurcated situation and to elaborate on the problem of race in the US today. In this introductory chapter I provide a general discussion of the current politics of race in order to clarify why it is important to consider a new approach.

In Part I, Chapters 1 and 2 discuss the work of Carl Schmitt. Schmitt's writings on sovereignty and the exception occupy a special place within a political theory concerned with the description of the state, sovereign authority, and the definition of politics. Applying Schmitt's reasoning on the nature of sovereignty, its definition through the determination of the exception, and the description of politics as that of delineating friend and enemy helps to explain the current structure of formal racial equality of opportunity. White sovereign political authority was able to maintain its control over racial politics through the transition from Jim Crow to formal racial equality because it was able to use the state to establish a space for conditional race neutrality that protected its interests. Two exceptions were defined to accomplish this goal: the White racist available to legal action and the African American able to take advantage of the resources available for social advancement. The normal description for Whites as a community became social rather than political as the basis for policing their authority over Blacks, and the description of racial difference was taken over by the institutional criteria for formal equality. That few African Americans were able to take advantage of this structure to become exceptional and therefore enjoy conditional equality was blamed on incapacities in the Black community. Under formal racial equality the normal Black population was defined as a problem of social order, crime, drugs, welfare, and poverty. Whites became color-blind, the society race neutral, and racism was defined as irrational behavior. The idea of White sovereign authority, described until that moment in the idea that the US was a White country first and foremost, disappeared with its constitutional investiture in the state.

The next part, comprising Chapters 3 through 5, develops a critique of this idea of race and community. In Chapter 3 I provide a basic phenomenological perspective on racial politics, that which arises from our perspective on being individually raced in coherent social communities of absolute difference. The definition of everyday racial practices as implying a gesture between a definition of being and Being is linked to a discussion of the problem Foucault identifies with the politics of origins and founding in the *Ion*. In Chapter 4 I further expose some of the limitations of a description of a politics of racial community by considering the critiques of community in the works of Blanchot and Nancy. The idea is to show the problem with an easy phenomenological postulation of racial community and the need for a politics, some form of authorizing event, to define absolute difference beyond the normal everyday plurality of human experience. In my opinion the current phenomenological description of race arises from our refusal to consider the limitations of equality of opportunity as a description of racial politics. To step outside and therefore around our subjectivity as exceptional Blacks, for example, demands the critique of the decision by which race persists as a problem in society. Chapters 4 and 5 provide the necessary background for a critique of this structure of racial equality. Chapter 5 uses the work of Santner, Esposito, and Foucault, respectively, to discuss issues of history, community, and truth.

After describing the problem of racial community and the definition of the individual citizen-subject in contemporary US politics and then developing a critical racial theory of community in the first two parts of the book, the third part, comprising Chapters 6 through 8, provides an argument for a different description of race in the US by exploring several texts written by Blacks in the three different eras of racial politics. This use of literature allows for a definition of a fractured Black subject and a racial subject that remains in spite of the current political desire to keep all discussion of race out of public discourse.

The development of a politics of racial equality in the larger sense has stopped expanding its purview and instead defines a politics of racial community that remains timeless if quintessentially American. This idea of racial communities as outside of history, immutable and absolute as descriptions of individual human types, remains a core political value in the construction of the democratic polity. Instead of interrogating this value and describing a politics that would challenge the idea of race itself, today the politics of racial equality coalesces around a series of ruptures that define Black life with Whites. The discussion of fiction allows for a description of aspects of racial politics that remain unaddressed by the current racial apparatus, and thereby have the potential to upset or resist its normalizing of yet another description of a false postracial society.

The use I make here of the concept of apparatus (*dispositif*) to identify the structure of racial politics is that developed first throughout the work of Michel Foucault. Foucault says of the apparatus that it is "a kind of formation, so to speak, that at a given historical moment has as its major function the response to an urgency ... a set of strategies of the relations of forces supporting, and supported by, certain types of knowledge" (1980: 194–96). An example of the importance of the idea in his work can be seen even in early studies, such as a *History of Madness,* when he writes:

> It is clear that confinement, in its primitive forms, worked as a social mechanism, and that the mechanism was extremely widespread, stretching from elementary economic regulation to the great bourgeois dream of a city where an authoritarian synthesis of nature and virtue reigned supreme. (Foucault 2009: 78)

This provides the general term for the complex set of political instruments that describes formal racial equality of opportunity.

Agamben usefully describes the Foucauldian apparatus as "a set of practices, bodies of knowledge, measures, and institutions that aim to manage, govern, control, and orient—in a way that purports to be useful—the behaviors, gestures, and thoughts of human beings" (2009: 12). It is important not to become so enamored with the reduction of these strategies to universal terms that we level out the political possibilities available to the subjects that are formed (Foucault 2008a: 2).

The sense of the *dispositif* I apply here is that given to describe a persistent political institutional development around a specific concept, and it is through this concept that it is important to describe societal evolution, not the proliferation of certain structures as a general problem. As Foucault discusses the idea of the *dispositif* in *Security, Territory Population*: "Under this name of a society of security, I would like simply to investigate whether there is a general economy of power which has the form [of], or which is at any rate dominated by, the technology of security" (2007:11). He then goes on to describe the apparatuses (*dispositifs*) of security. This is the limited use to which I put the idea of apparatus to discuss the current politics of race.

THE OWL OF MINERVA

The constant failure to resolve the problem of race as an absolute difference in the US historically has meant that a definition of race, of a community of persons, always contains within its purview the experience of the past as well as the future, the possibilities available to a politics of race. We need to resolve the problem first identified in the social construction of a Black community that could be enslaved in the late 1600s, just as we need to consider the effects of events throughout the turbulent and often vicious racial history of the US on the idea of a Black community.

The question is not why bring up the past, so much as how we can avoid addressing the formation of racial communities as a product of past conflict. The definition of a community of persons who are White, and who have retained an authority to determine Black life, a Black subject and community, has distorted the democratic political process in the US to such as extent that continued political development is impossible. There is no steady march of racial progress in US history; rather, there is a constant return to a fictive moment outside of time, a political decision that questions the place of Blacks in the US. This decision is defined by a collection of practices that are continuous across the formal periods of change in racial politics, from slavery and Jim Crow to integration.

The periodization of events that I use here of slavery, Jim Crow, and integration is a necessary shorthand for the larger developmental problems of race in the US. It is necessary because the standardized received history of racial progress in the US depends on the idea that 1) with the Civil War, Black slavery ended, 2) after a few decades of political activity Blacks were disenfranchised and Jim Crow policies held sway, and then 3) after World War Two the advent of the Civil Rights Movement led to the acceptance of racial equality in the society. In the discussion that follows I both acknowledge the importance of this myth of racial progress for the politics of racial integration today and reach around it, past it, to provide a description that privileges racial subjection as a continuing problem of political theory (Benjamin 1969b: 263).

RACIAL POLITICKING: THE RISE OF INDIVIDUALISM

The partial form of racial equality today, that of equal opportunity, is a function of hard-fought political struggle and the constant political crisis brought about due to racism, not of high-minded principled soul-searching by Whites wielding political authority in the 1960s. It is hard to contend that an individual is trying to engage in democratic deliberation, negotiation, reconciliation, and political debate about racial equality if what underlies his or her argument is the idea of the inferiority of a group of persons, where this group is defined not by the desire for specific goods but as a distinct racial community of absolute difference. It is likewise difficult to argue as an individual for further institutional change to reflect the political needs of the Black community if this idea of community is only defined within the discourse of absolute racial difference.

The idea that persons are defined by a human typology such that they are members of a group that is thought to deserve fewer resources and scant or indifferent political attention conflicts with a politics that is defined by individual equality of opportunity. It is common to see the answer to this problem in a politics that limits the impact of race on the demands of equality, but in fact in the US it is equality that has always been constrained by the demands of race, as a description of communities in conflict. The demand for formal equality arose out of racial politics, not from the evolution of democratic politics as an application of principles in the law.

It is no longer sufficient to engage in a politics that conceals White community sovereignty in the society behind the political structure in support of racial equality. It took several decades after the Civil War for racial politics to consolidate around the practices of Jim Crow. I believe something similar is happening today. In the contemporary period, race is bifurcated into a received idea of individual equality of opportunity and collective difference, and the terms that this political stability has demanded of institutions and persons.

The idea that a critique of President Obama could be based on his race is often met with contempt, the idea being that such a claim is "playing the race card," as though the claims of persons acting from the assumption of racial difference are to be seen always first as not only spurious but as requiring further proof as to the veracity of the claimant as well. The practices of verification rest at the center of racial politics today, and it is to provide for a new description of the problem of race that I turn to a discussion of African American fiction in Part III.

This resistance to the possibility that race is a factor in political discourse is itself a function of how race is viewed today as a concept, as something to be used to change the behavior of others, as a card that resonates so strongly in a discussion game that its use is always to be thought suspicious and purely political rather than as calling for a reassessment of the terms of the discussion. What would count as proof that race was a factor in individual resistance to and the critique of Obama's presidency? What is the presidency such that a critique is located in the actions of the person as contrasted with the office of the president? Would not the claim of race have to be about Obama as a Black person, of his person in ways that political debate today does not normally allow? How could any approach in this political discourse of racial equality to the idea of Barack Obama being Black impact how a person feels about his actions as president?

This seeming slippage between personal beliefs and public activity is a major problem in how we define race in the US today. Our current political discourse of race asks us to provide evidence, proof that race motivates a political discussion. What are the specific words or phrases that denote a racial description of the current policies of the administration or of the president as a person? At first glance it seems as though we need to define the language of race by studying how race was originally thought to pervade public discourse prior to the existence of racial-discrimination law. Then we would have a way to measure or assess how the current language of race is similar to that which existed at a time when it was considered relatively unproblematic and even unnecessary to express racial statements in public since race was defined as true.

Just as it was erroneous to measure the social progress of racial politics during Jim Crow by pointing to emancipation, it is wrong to use the practices of Jim Crow to judge the condition of racial politics in the US today. The political elements that resulted in a dramatic shift in the law and practice of racial difference in each era—emancipation and the end of the Civil War, the decision of *Brown v. Board of Education* (1954), and the passage of the Civil Rights Act of 1964—continue today to develop in the society. The idea that after conflict occurs things are resolved assumes that it is possible to end history. On the contrary, there are always survivors, and the resolution of a conflict always leads to further conflict, another level of interrogation between political ideas. To ignore what Derrida (2005) describes as sublation, or the process Hegel (1977) argues occurs in the wake of history, the movement of a conflict to another level as resolution seemingly occurs, is to create political theologies that find coherence only through purposefully concealing the truth of the elements that continue beyond the seeming resolution of difference. This is to argue for history as a series of discrete moments and not as a continuous evolution of society. It is time to challenge the efficacy of this covering over or concealment in the form of different historical stages of democratic development for the politics of racial justice in the US.

The measure in this book of the definition of three eras of racial politics is that of how the current antagonism is shaped, not whether the problem of race continues to exist between persons. People are grouped by social practices into racial communities that determine a major form of political subjection in US society. It is consistent with the continued evolution of the effects of race in the society that these social practices are both in some respects identical to and different from those used to define racial difference in the US for centuries past. I will return to this issue of the evolution of racial practices later in the second part of the book.

HOW RACE WORKS

The argument for racial communities in conflict that I think we are returning to in the US is in direct contrast to a description of the new individual citizen-subject able to take advantage of the equal opportunities for economic success available to everyone in the era of integration. The idea of racial equality as the equality of opportunity to compete in the marketplace for goods and services, in professional life, is also distinct from the definition of racial political equality established through the Voting Rights Act of 1965 and the controls placed on specific states by the federal government to ensure fair electoral procedures. Unlike equal opportunity in the market, which depends on the resources of individuals, the definition of the equivalency of the individual political subject able to vote is a precondition for the democratic polity, and therefore to the extent that voting is constrained this describes not a difference in political resources but the absence of individuals from the decisions made in politics (Griffin and Newman 2008; Soss, Fording, and Schram 2011).

As in the case of the Three-Fifths Compromise in the US Constitution and the finding that slaves were not citizens in *Dred Scott v. Sandford* (1857), the description of certain persons as counting for less than others for the politics of representation, or being designated as permanent noncitizens while living in a society is similar to that of constraining voting for a particular group. The implication of this differential political representation, of resistance to the idea of racial political equality and the Voting Rights Act, is that sovereignty in a democracy lies in the hands of one racial community rather than the general population. While this book will not discuss in detail how this defines a differential political structure, one that is only partially democratic, it is important to the larger point here that current popular political debates do not consider the problem of the numbers of African Americans that cannot vote or do not for various reasons, some of which are the result of barriers to voting, as critical to the health of US democracy. There is no more important question in a democracy than who can participate, and we must ensure that those who should can have a say in the design and functions of government.

Today the claim of racism and the turn to the explicit use of race really matters in politics. It threatens to upset the reconciliation in the 1960s of the explicit demands of the Civil Rights Movement and White sovereign authority. Any political claim that violates the precept of individualism with one of community or group preference has the potential to raise questions of how the community of Whites continues to ensure the subordination of Blacks. Seen in this light it makes sense that given the initial massive resistance to its redefinition in the 1960s the existing reconciliation of the desire for both equality and continued racial subordination has developed several instruments by which to deflect potential criticism.

A public claim of racism is first described as misplaced because it describes the use of racial social forms no longer required in the society. Second, a claim that race is being used is often defended as instead a byproduct of the political, economic, and social choices made by individuals from these defined racial communities. It is then merely a fact of individual difference, not the result of the social construction of racial difference. What matters today about the argument that race is being used to support political decisions in the US is that unaddressed it threatens to reveal, as did the Civil Rights Movement during Jim Crow, that Whites continue to wield the authority in society to describe a difference from others that is comprehensive and effective, even if it is also at one level arbitrary and antidemocratic (Olson 2004: 70).

How should we describe the flourishing or confluence of a racial typology that works directly below the received political debate, almost like a set of code words? But the question that must occur as well in light of the democratic political aspiration towards racial equality is, why use these ideas at all; why do we have need of these descriptions of community? I am not saying we should allow race to spill forth openly into public discussions, but it is important to realize that the perceived need to control social discourse, use code words, and obscure how we speak means racial difference is alive and well in the social practices of Americans. On the need of complicit silence as a precondition of this politics of race I follow Dominick LaCapra here in thinking there is no better source than Himmler's Posen address to the SS in 1943. To quote at length,

> I also want to make reference before you here, in complete frankness, to a really grave matter. Among ourselves, this once, it shall be uttered quite frankly; but in public we will never speak of it. Just as we did not hesitate on June 30, 1934, to do our duty as ordered, to stand up against the wall comrades who had transgressed, and shoot them, also we have never talked about this and never will. It was the tact which I am glad to say is a matter of course to us that made us never discuss it among ourselves, never talk about it.(LaCapra 1996: 107)

This is an example of what Derrida describes when he says, "The unavowable in community is also a sovereignty that cannot but posit itself and impose itself in silence" (Derrida 2005: 100). The definition of racial difference provides a description of when race should matter in human interaction. For example, today you can have an African American Republican presidential candidate, Herman Cain, discuss topics relating to African Americans, while Republican public figures never mention that he is Black. It is literally that which cannot be mentioned in the primary debates and public discussion of Cain's candidacy. It is as though in public Republicans agree that to speak of the race of Herman Cain is to make it important. The silence makes it something only his opponents can bring up, and as a result the complicity of those who see Cain as Black but will not speak about what that means for them in electoral politics signals to everyone that race is a central purpose with his candidacy (Harris 1999; Headley 1999: 199). What kind of situation is it when the most important thing, but not the only thing, about a primary candidate is something everyone must say is not important? Of course, we could take this silence as a sign that race is not visible to the general Republican politico, that they do not see Cain as African American but as a successful businessman and entrepreneur, a viable candidate for president with no experience in elected office.

The presumption of this racial politics, where a person can both benefit from the effects of an idea of racial equality in his or her personal life and then deny that race matters for others, must be that this idea of equality is comprehensive enough to address and negate the impact of race everywhere. The position of complicit silence takes the politics of race very seriously. What is going on theoretically when people say in public that race is not important, but simultaneously use a rich symbolic language and established social tools to convey that they work from a racial typology in determining how they act toward political issues? The prevailing definition of racism, the prohibited use of race, is that an individual targets other individuals with race-based social judgment and stereotyping. Clearly the idea is to make those who believe race is at work in a social practice have to prove that it exists as a problem, even as racial attribution is described as a belief system that cannot be demonstrated except indirectly through specific language and actions. If the politics of race today requires that a claim of racism has an individual target, that there is an identifiable victim, what does it means to be racist in a collective sense, against all Blacks, when there is no individual target?

To act with race towards all Blacks or an individual as a representative of his or her race requires a collective description, some way to define a group such that individuals are members. How should we conceptualize this idea of wickedness that can designate a person to stand in for, or represent, a human typology such as race? The best we can do currently is to provide the formal criteria for discrimination, indices that measure, for example, the degree of segregation or evidence of individual bias through attitudinal studies. If you believe Blacks are different from Whites, then this means you act towards all those defined as Black differently from those who are White. But this social differentiation is impossible to measure. It is not contained within a statistic nor is it available for empirical study; it is an absolute, qualitative difference of human type. To claim some action as racist is in this way universal but its proof is particular. As a result, it is easy to turn around and make a counterclaim that the beliefs are not there, that an action is not racist but individual, particular rather than typological.

I was recently at a large formal function in Birmingham, Alabama, where the hostess refused to shake my hand, and pointedly turned away rather than greet me. She did greet and shake hands with the rest of my party of ten both before and after me in line, all of whom were White. Since the family has been substantial benefactors of the society that was hosting the event, her behavior was noticed by others in our party. It made some of the family uncomfortable, and they became demonstrative in their association with me throughout the events of the evening. To make things more complicated, the gathering was at a normally racially segregated country club. In the audience there were only two other African Americans of the three hundred or so guests in attendance. Since I was sitting at a reserved table immediately in front of the stage, I was the object of curiosity for many attending. However, except for the moment when I was rudely disregarded, nothing was obviously racial, and even that can be attributed to any number of factors, many of which could be innocuous. You can see the problem. How could I or anyone in my party have said to the hostess that she was being racist? Why would I say something, and what would it accomplish? Should I think of her as the exception or the rule in that moment regarding the other participants at the event? The current perspective on racial politics would be to see her actions as not representative of the other Whites at the event, but a case of the racist in an otherwise neutral environment, if we could even figure out how to establish that race was indeed involved in her actions. I think we can measure the lack of progress with racial politics in the US based on how similar this event was to what Du Bois describes in his childhood when the young White woman refuses his greeting card, his first experience with race (Du Bois 2012b).

CONCLUSION: THE PROMISE AND THE PROBLEM OF EQUALITY

Do we seek with our current politics of racial equality merely to ensure that a person does not use specific language and actions that would trigger a claim of racism in its formal description? The era of integration has developed a politics where race is something that cannot be addressed except when defining the importance of individualism and self-help in connection to the idea of the relative deprivation of Blacks, of a difference in Black community resources that disadvantage its members in the competition for goods and services.

What is consistently going wrong in US politics is an approach to race that says that the democratic exhortation to good behavior is in everyone's interest, that since to be a racist is bad, we should then want to do good. Many people see racism as bad, but believe that race exists and the categories of difference it describes are a true reflection of the human population. For these people, doing good with regard to the use of race is not connected with their holding the idea that race is a social construction. For years after the Voting Rights Act, the sit-ins, the marches by the SCLC (Southern Christian Leadership Conference) and others, it was believed that there was the possibility for something to develop in the democratic institutional framework of government that would definitively change the racial values of people. That not only would formal segregation collapse into the integration of Blacks and Whites in housing, education, and employment, but that something new would come that impacted those beliefs in Black inferiority and difference held by White Americans. No such thing occurred. This failure was not the result of the relative resource deprivation of Blacks at the time and up to the present day. The political changes necessary to dissolve the descriptions of racial communities are available without reference to the reproduction of economic or social differences between Blacks and Whites. These differences instead reflect the distinction of race, how we choose to persist in its use, and are not the cause of the description of racial community.

The promise that our parents gave us, as Blacks and Whites who grew up after the marches, was that now we would have chances to live as our parents did not. My father spoke of having to avoid addressing Whites directly as a boy on the streets of Richmond, Virginia, in the 1940s and 50s. He used his stint in a largely segregated Navy to leave Virginia and settle in the Bay Area, where race was different enough for him that he could escape some constraints on his ability to make a living. I remember Angela Davis saying somewhat the same thing some years ago when I told her I was about to take a job as an assistant professor in political science at the University of Alabama. In answer to a question about how she viewed the area she grew up in, she said, "Why would I ever want to go back there?" I and so many others of the generation after the civil-rights protests felt that things would be different, that things had to change. But what changed was simply the arena in which formal racism, institutionalized and indelible, developed. It shifted in response to a renewed sense of social pressure to act with formal racial equality of opportunity; it changed in response to legal pressure.

The expectation of being able to work, study, and live anywhere remained the obvious fruit of the movement's politics, but the reality was that little was done to allow Blacks to compete or otherwise live as equals with Whites. To do that would demand some type of principle of equality beyond that of a formal market principle that all are given an equal chance with what resources they can bring to bear on the exchange of specific goods. This would be a claim for a corrective function of democratic government, a reparative function beyond that of the mere reconciliation of the two competing ideals of formal equality and racial difference. We would have to allow for a politics that would move beyond the discrete event to explore the problem of the continuous ability in the US to form communities that can alienate important parts of society from other persons and groups.

In a representative democracy such as the US, it is difficult to repair inequities that involve the deleterious actions of a large group of people. The argument for minority rights is not strong or comprehensive enough to force institutional change unless coupled with a claim to a universally applicable principle, something that reveals the inconsistent application of a procedure or politics. Such a principle creates very real limits to the political claims that can be made on behalf of groups in the society. In the US the change from Jim Crow to formal racial equality required only that enough was done to control Black political activity. It is not a coincidence that it is always the threat of Black political protest that still, decades later, motivates the everyday assessment of the treatment of race in a specific event.

We need to explore further the problem of racism itself, and argue for a politics of the subject that incorporates the conception of a racial community; we need to take on the struggle for racial equality ourselves, in this generation. It is in this moment of racial dehiscence, when the reelection of Barack Obama to the presidency reveals the inadequacy of the contemporary politics of racial integration, that we can determine a new direction for critical race theory.

The argument of the chapters that follow is that, to understand contemporary racial politics, we must develop a conception of the type of community of race that can exist alongside a description of racial equality. There are several descriptions of community that have the potential to persist in what is a bifurcated situation. Exploring these will allow us to consider more seriously the type of problem race creates for democracy today in the US.

Part I
Defining Exceptions to Equality

1 The Racist and the Elite

> But all mythical, lawmaking violence, which we may call executive, is pernicious. Pernicious, too, is the law-preserving, administrative violence that serves it. Divine violence, which is the sign and seal but never the means of sacred execution, may be called sovereign violence.
>
> —Benjamin, "Critique of Violence"

> But less well known are the interpretations that arose in the Middle Ages, in which the unique, totally abnormal condition and attitude of the Jewish people toward all other people became discernible, a condition that cannot be compared with that of any other people.
>
> —Schmitt, *The Leviathan in the State Theory of Thomas Hobbes*

THE STUDY OF RACE

Bruce Baum describes the complexity of the problem of determining when the idea of race changed historically; his assessment is that the definition of race as scientific fact changed by the 1950s as a result of egalitarian assumptions on the part of scientists (Baum 2006: 189). At the same time, did the assumption, the supposedly well-developed and scientifically proven settled social truth of the inferiority of Blacks, change in the US?

Only to the extent that the factual definition of race was dependent upon rather than expressed in the legal structure of Jim Crow and specific forms of legal discrimination in housing, employment, and education. Race is not first a rights problem, but a problem of how we describe persons. The description of race, and the inequality that defines it, has been explicitly developed since the mid-1600s in the political institutions of first the colonies of the North American New World and then the United States (Baum 2006: 50). That is, it is present in a wide range of social practices we take for granted today. What matters is not its origin in a decision that is metaphysical but in the ability of persons today to persist in its development as a political concept. This is not to say that specific people are responsible for its definition, even though prior to the changing racial politics in the 1960s it was more obvious that individuals were invested in race in particular ways that impacted their social activities.

One of the arguments I want to make is that the refusal of a personal investment in race is a specific attribute of the current political structure of race today. It has become necessary to question the salience of race as a way to continue to use it on a regular basis in our lives. This is not a novel claim.

In fact, an argument could be made, which Ralph Ellison does, for example, that the ability to avoid personal attribution is one of the strengths, unfortunately, of the concept (Ellison 1965: 12). To be both indeterminate and determinate, isn't that what informs Du Bois's famous argument for double consciousness, as an exploration of how we address our racial subjection and the potential of subjectivity simultaneously (Du Bois 2012b)? I will argue that the application of the concept of race changes, how we use it not what we use it for, with the shift in the political apparatus of race in the post–civil rights period. In this chapter I identify four distinct racial subjects that I believe have been developed from within the institutional construction of formal racial equality.

I think it has been important to erase from memory, from political and social theory, what it was like with regard to race in the US until the 1960s. Many of the academics working in political theory today were young adults or born during the transition from Jim Crow to the current period of formal equality of opportunity, what I call the period of integration. The idea of racial segregation is therefore not something those older than forty-five in the US see as ancient history or outside of our personal experience. Race remains defined as it was during the period of Jim Crow, as a problem of different communities in conflict, and the current apparatus of institutional development reflects a solution of one community rather than a politics of pluralism.

What accounts for the shift in use? Was it not the Soviet Union pointing out our complicity in racial practices developed to their extreme under the National Socialists that gave the SCLC and King leverage to get a hearing from the White House in the early 1960s (Branch 1989; Olson 2004: 97; Blackmon 2009; Wilkerson 2011)? It is often said that the Cold War was instrumental in the success of the aims of the Civil Rights Movement (Woodward 1966: 131). Even a cursory glance at the headlines of newspapers about the racism in the American South in the 1950s and 1960s shows how important this was for framing the international image of the US. The US was a substantial target in the post–World War Two global struggle against government-sanctioned racial politics (Baum 2006: 170). The movement created a substantial political crisis. When force did not move Blacks and their complaint, the only choice was to change the way that racial difference was applied throughout society by removing the basis for the complaint (Rawls 1972; Dworkin 1978).

This is not the same thing as doing away with the importance of the distinction of race. Unable to ignore White sovereign authority as a political force, the state could only seek to resolve the situation by changing the political basis of Black community organization (Schmitt 1996: 59). It is because of this problem that I think it is efficacious to use the writing of Schmitt to explore how White America developed the current structure of formal racial equality of opportunity and the consequences this has for developing a critical race politics today. Schmitt describes a people that have become a political entity: "When it no longer possesses the capacity or the will to make this distinction, it ceases to exist politically. If it permits this decision to be made by another, then it is no longer a politically free people and is absorbed into another political system" (1996: 49). This was the intention of the change in the racial apparatus from Jim Crow to formal racial equality.

The importance of research on integration and assimilation in the period arose out of this perception by the government of political vulnerability (Gordon 1964; Glazer and Moynihan 1970; Dahl 1972). Solving the race problem as an issue of equality became a central element of US national politics. The science of race was replaced by the argument for tolerance and pluralism and the idea of diversity (Rawls 1972; Dworkin 1985; Baum 2006: 179).

This politics defined a specific place for race in the work of most political theorists. The political concerns of Blacks were described as the function of the role of civil disobedience and rights discourse, and as a problem for the resolution of the tension in a procedural democracy between liberty and equality (Rawls 1972; Walzer 1982, 1984; Shklar 1998). Racism was supposedly giving way to a new political individualism by creating the legal structure to safeguard racial equal opportunity and the protection of Black voting rights (Boxill 1992).

The idea of White sovereign authority and the importance of racial communities in US political development that had been such an obvious element during Jim Crow literally no longer had a place as a description of democratic politics in the new era of integration, and so remained unaddressed as a continuing problem for political theory (Mills 1997). That this politics coincided with African Americans coming into White academic environments in greater numbers was seen as further proof that race was no longer important (Bell 1996).

Race was no longer considered a legitimate subject of academic study. Instead, African American history, culture, and community development could be the subject of research as this normalized the description of race without conflict, as a social identity without political effects. All this and more were possible to support the new politics of racial equality. Marek Steedman has written on how liberal paternalism and White supremacy were able to coexist in Jim Crow society (Steedman 2012: 106). Such remains the case today.

POLITICS

How did the US go from the description of an absolute difference of human type that allows for exceptional politics on the part of a socially affirmed and reproduced community, a politics that works to substantiate the subordination of those in another community during Jim Crow, to a condition of formal racial equality? There was no political mandate for a change in the idea of a racial absolute difference and there was no politics addressing the decision of race itself in the 1960s. The collective ambitions of the movement, even if described too simply above, addressed instead how to create a racially neutral public space where previously none had existed. It did not challenge the reproduction of racial subjects from within their discrete communities; it did not challenge Whiteness as a concept of community.

In response to this political demand for change, White authorities created the political *dispositif* or apparatus of equality of opportunity in public space. The only way to do this while retaining the importance of race as a political distinction in the society was to create two exceptions. One was the racist and the other was the exceptional Black. Both social subjects were reifications of social practices and rules already in place in both the period of slavery and Jim Crow, and so therefore did not require changing the definition of White community political authority. What was done was to elevate both descriptions of persons and the practices of their development to the level of political exceptions. In doing so, this changed the description of White sovereignty as something constituted as a political force coincident with government that could establish exceptions to the latter's authority to preserve racial social order under Jim Crow, to a sovereignty fully within the constitutional politics of the US government under formal racial equality (Schmitt 1988: 27, 43). The tensions that had been present within the description of White sovereignty since before the Civil War were finally integrated fully within the institutional development of the state. As Tracy Strong suggests in his discussion of Schmitt, "The sovereign delineates the realm in which political action takes place" (2012: 233). It was White sovereign authority and not the Civil Rights movement that defined this space for formal racial equality.

THE FIRST EXCEPTION: THE RACIST

One of the most powerful, and problematic, ideas to come out of this period of change from Jim Crow was the political redefinition of the traditional idea of "the racist." This conception of the racist did not come from the events of the Civil Rights Movement but from the discourse made available to Whites to explain the way their authority was to be asserted against Blacks. This politics of the exception defined racists as those who resisted the changing racial politics, had enabled Jim Crow prior to its collapse, and did not agree that all races were due formal equality of opportunity. By applying the concept politically it was possible to absolve the remainder of the White community of culpability in ongoing social descriptions of racial inferiority. The racist became the label for those White people "over there" who are not like the rest of Whites who can accept racial equality

(Olson 2004: 73). This became the description of one part of a new bifurcated White subject who was capable of both policing the social difference of race and engaging in the professional activities that supported racial equal opportunity.

This resolved the problem of the responsibility of individual Whites for the actions that occurred during Jim Crow; it was all done by racists unlike the normal White person who now could openly abjure such activity in the post–civil rights period. The question of guilt and responsibility for the past was thereby severed for the current "normal" White population, who often began describing themselves as liberal. The traditional role during Jim Crow for individual Whites of ensuring the social difference and control of Blacks was in the new politics of equality no longer the purview of individuals but of the state. Of course nothing stopped the White person from having to engage in traditional forms of racial social control if the state of exception that described the racist and formal equality collapsed or was attenuated to an extent that challenged the sovereign authority of Whites as a community in the society. This is one reason racial public discourse again became common with the presidential election campaign of 2012. The apparatus was established by Whites, not Blacks, and the exception of the racist could therefore easily be withdrawn as a political description to include all Whites once more. With this option always held in abeyance, the White community could distance itself from a racist subject, sacrificing once more some Whites to resolve the immediate political problems caused by the effects of race in the society.

This was a dramatic difference from what occurred during Jim Crow, when government, private companies, and individual Whites could openly discriminate against Blacks. A shift in how race was used, not its importance, was accomplished with the redefinition of "the racist." This was a way to distinguish between actions that were available to legal challenge and those that were defined as not racial, as though Whites could decide, in spite of their complicity in racial politics during Jim Crow, what was racial and prohibited and what was acceptable as a way to differentiate between people. To ask Whites to define what actions should count as racial after Jim Crow is possible only if the problem of racism is described as marginal to community practices rather than the basis of the definition of Whiteness. Without the racist to differentiate good from bad Whites, the idea of Whiteness and the community politics it elaborates in the society could potentially come under criticism from within a description of formal racial equality. Today the importance of racial community in US democratic society is obscured by the racial politics of the exception defined in the subject of the racist.

The solution for Whites was to use the government to change the laws and formal practices, and thereby change the relationship of Blacks to the state, the private sector, and to individual Whites. The question became, is it possible to absorb the persistent discontent of Blacks with the institutions of government such that the fact of the decision itself, that race matters, is left intact (Morrison 1993; West 2001)? Crudely put, since there was no revaluation on the part of the White community as a collective of the place of race, the state had to find a way to absorb the continuing discontent of Blacks with segregation without threatening the social order. This explains the conundrum of how first the decision in *Brown* and later laws of racial equal opportunity came to be applied and enforced so slowly throughout the society. This was done with an interest in preserving the status quo wherever possible, since the majority of White citizens were against a change in the description of race in their lives.

Over time it was discovered that, similar to the decades following emancipation, Whites could retain their status as a community with respect to Blacks in the new regime. As Walter Benjamin writes, " . . . the law's interest in the monopoly of violence vis-à-vis individuals is not explained by the intention of preserving legal ends but, rather, by that of preserving law itself" (1986a: 281). The racist is sacrificed; the local Southern sheriff, the perpetrator of the ugly hate crime, the unthinking coworker, as well as the idea of integration and equal opportunity, all serve to displace the location where race is decided upon as a part of the new social order. In colloquial terms, the former friend becomes the enemy so as to form new alliances across the old divide. The racist is offered up in sacrifice as an example of reconciliation in a public arena without race, where formal equality of opportunity can be legally sustained.

This requires the absence of the traditional discursive elements of race used in the formal legal structure of Jim Crow. This new structure repeats the moment in the Civil War when the conflict between Whites was realized as requiring the description of Black slaves as contraband and important to the success of the war for Whites in the North. The wound this creates by defining the White community as also containing the enemy, now the racist, is a constant requirement of the limitless politics of friend and enemy.

Under integration, Whiteness remained important as a private organizing concept, but was described as the result of ethnicity, or as the retention of cultural and social practices that individuals wished to hold on to as qualifiers of difference and where these differences should not impact the availability of opportunities for those of other races for success with life plans in the society. Whiteness became synonymous with merely wanting to choose one's neighbors, friends, and family, not a decision of absolute difference and social hierarchy. This model of social integration, multiculturalism, depends on the absence of anything that points to race as a difference that still makes a difference in the economic or political achievements of an individual.

The use of the racist to suture in this way the conflict between distinct racial communities as a problem of individual beliefs and equal opportunity defines a community of difference that conceals the persistent decision of racial distinction that remains an abiding political concern in the

US. The concept establishes a political space of rules, norms, and legal structures whereby Whites are able and willing to cede their control of the institutions of society to those Blacks able, as African Americans, to achieve the exceptional status allowed by this description of equality. This space is supposed to be sustainable while retaining the idea of race as one of the most important social elements in a person's life. The concept of the racist allows Whites to literally use this subject as an exception to the rule of racial equality. Pointing at the racist as holding onto the idea of racial difference conceals the way the description of Whiteness remains a salient description of social community and important in society.

THE SECOND EXCEPTION: THE EXCEPTIONAL BLACK

Schmitt would explain the current lack of legitimacy of the president of the US with certain sectors of the population who are themselves considered important to the description of the nation as due to Obama's inability to represent the unitary, sovereign will of the people (Kalyvas 2008: 158). That this could be the case points to the second suture necessary to allow for the stability of the current *dispositif* or political apparatus of racial equality. This is the description of the exceptional Black subject.

To maintain the distinction of racial difference within a society of formal racial equality, in addition to the racist subject, it was necessary to create the exceptional Black subject. This was a person who is able to use the opportunity for success and to distinguish him- or herself from a Black community that still experiences the effects of race. The key points in this are the idea of individual success and the creation of a distinction of the person from the normal Black community. Historically it has always been the case that some Black people were able to accumulate wealth, social success, and political prominence. What makes this status a focus of politics now is that the individual, and therefore a particular conception of individualism, is taken as proof of the success of racial equality in the US and of the change in society that has occurred since Jim Crow.

This is the definition of the suture, to return to the metaphor of the wound of race on the democratic body politics, allowing a covering over or a closure to take place for the remaining politics of race to persist in its traditional hierarchical absolutist form. The exceptional Black is not responsible for the political effectiveness of the device, nor its application upon the Black community. This was a case of incorporating a nascent or marginal Black subject into the political apparatus necessary to define racial equality, to define what equality would look like and what criteria determined a Black subject available to its institutional practices. Through this capture it became possible to often use the classically representative leader of the Black community and the established forms of educational and social success as a buffer between the normal everyday racial descriptions of difference still operating as it has historically in the US to define a subordinated Black population. The capacity for the Black community to create organic intellectuals able to mobilize the claims to injustice that would otherwise arise as an organizational politics was severely curtailed by this deepening of Black incorporation into professional life with Whites. That to succeed in improving conditions for the Black community now required becoming incorporated into the structure of exceptional Black subjectivity is at least in part therefore aporetic.

To create the idea of exceptional Blacks who could rise above their supposed qualitative difference from Whites has been taken as a mark of the success in public discourse of both equality legislation and of the aims of the Civil Rights Movement, a living counterexample from within the subordinated community to the otherwise continuous claims arising of the inefficacy of the current institutional structure to define racial equality more broadly. The person becomes an example of the supposed limits of the effects of racial difference in society; the success of individual Blacks is literally taken as the measure of racial equality. This is true even in the face of statistical information that reveals a persistent gap in material wealth between the Black and White communities (Conley 1999; Oliver and Shapiro 2006). This difference between the exceptional African American subject and the community places the responsibility for any relative deprivation and material differences with Whites on the normal members of the Black community. This is typically a characterization of political, social, cultural, and moral incapacity, a construction of difference as a community that then stands in for individual differences as a category of human types, as a description of racial difference. The Black subject is always defined today as having to prove access to material resources and personal qualities that can allow for a conditional equality with Whites. The traditional idea of racial difference in the US historically is thereby reproduced in the very moment of designating someone as an exceptional Black. This is our contemporary racism.

THE NEW NORMAL

The exceptional White racist is used to separate the existing racial White community from the onus of the past practices of Jim Crow. The exceptional racist also signals for Whites that their sovereign position is unthreatened in society, since the community is still able to determine the politics of the exception. The exceptional Black is used to squelch arguments that the politics of racial equality is insufficient today. He or she is used to fracture the potential for the type of political mobilization of the Black community that had occurred during the Civil Rights Movement. The Black exception also masks the reality of the normal everyday social practices of race by juxtaposing this with a promise of escape, equality, and success conditional on their conformity to a set of social standards and measures of performance. Like the racist, the exceptional Black is a rare figure by definition, an exception to the rules of race, someone who can stand outside the prevailing social and political pressures that continue to work through the designation of racial communities to create substantial inequalities without his or her person also challenging this sutural aspect of their subjectivity.

Together the application of these two exceptions as political concepts have allowed for the two traditional descriptions of racial communities derived from the racial decision of Black inferiority to continue past the moment of crisis brought on by the convergence of political events around the Civil Rights Movement. The White community can continue to form its subjects while engaging in political processes that support formal racial equality. The political sovereignty of the White community continues to be enmeshed in the description of state political processes, but this occurs without having to engage in racial practices at the individual or collective level such as was the case during Jim Crow. Instead, the mechanisms of equality of opportunity reflect for both Black and White individuals the different material and political resources that have developed historically through Jim Crow for each community. The point I want to make here is that even if some form of equality of resources could be effectuated across the two communities, this would not address the social mechanisms that still reproduce the hierarchy of race as a function of the definition of racial communities of difference through the equality apparatus.

The larger White community, many of whom describe themselves as liberal or socially progressive, are the primary beneficiaries of this apparatus. In fact, as a consequence of the apparatus it is possible to understand something that otherwise is difficult to figure out in everyday social situations in the US today; the claim by Whites of not being racist suggests in most cases that they agree with the structure of the apparatus, which is explicitly a racial political construction. Similarly color-blind reasoning, race neutrality, and other descriptions that use the exceptions within the apparatus to claim that race is absent are false, even if the possibility of pointing out the elements of racial definition are not immediately apparent. It is not that everyone still uses race, but that race as an idea structures the basic descriptions of social achievement and sense of choices in the society. It is only the White "nonracist," the normal White subject that says race does not exist as a problem in their lives, a position that is itself comprehensively racial.

This description of the apparatus of formal racial equality has implications for how we view electoral politics. Since White community interests lie in reinforcing the distinction between the racist and the normal color-blind or race neutral White individual as concepts within the apparatus, political elites have to recognize that successful campaigns have to be designed to appeal to this distinction. While moving to the right on issues of race, or on symbolic issues related to race, does garner attention, there are limits to its appeal. If White community interests again become explicitly synonymous with state interests, as during Jim Crow, then this threatens the model of formal equality. At a minimum this risks generating the very political mobilization of African Americans, and other non-White groups who also find themselves within the apparatus, that it was designed to inhibit.

What also happens, which I think was evident in the election of 2012, is this drift rightward also risks splitting the White community, leading to a crisis in the definition of political sovereignty in the society. For electoral success a political party with conservative interests would appeal to those who benefit from the development of the apparatus, while a socially progressive party would bring into question the normalizing of racial subordination that occurs for African Americans, Latinos, Native Americans, and Asian American and Pacific Islanders who do not become indifferent on balance with the political needs of their communities through the appeal of the material and social benefits of formal equal opportunity. Without spending more time on the subject, it is easy to see how using the theoretical claims made here of the characterization of the racial *dispositif* provide an important way to understand the recent developments in electoral politics in US society.

Without having to reproduce racial political differentiation, Whiteness can retreat from exercising political force and describe race as merely a social difference, a social construction. However, the practical elaboration of the social in the form of distinct communities of color of course contain the very instruments Black and White individuals need to make effective choices and use existing institutional resources in order to succeed. So long as Blacks do not have access to White community's description of institutional processes, processes that continue to be defined societally by the political needs of this community, it is very difficult to make use of the resources hypothetically available to Blacks in this paradigm of racial equality (Oliver and Shapiro 2006; Alexander 2012). Since everything except the racist and exceptional Black is defined as race neutral, the first as prohibited and the second as an indicator of racial equality, individuals are unable to critique social practices for their racial content. Challenging the transfer of racial meaning to the exception, as a description of privately held beliefs, is made difficult because the location of racial content, the reproduction of the hierarchy of absolute difference does not originate in the local social practice but as a consequence of the decision displaced onto the racist as a subject. It becomes almost impossible to claim that an institution, rather than an individual, is using race in its processes.

It should be remembered that in the 1960s and into the 1970s very few Blacks were in positions of professional or political prominence. Schools were in the process of desegregating, and the refusal to address the effects of the distinction of race in forming communities meant that to ensure the viability of the new normal, potentially "equal" Black subjects had to be created by the political process. Without a politics and policies that address the persistent resource gap between Whites and Blacks there is no racial equality in the US; there is only the individual Black success story and the continued salience of a White community that does not have to account for how Whiteness continues to impact life in the US. Legal controls of hate speech, racial discrimination, and racial violence were put in place to distinguish between normal, race-neutral apolitical Whiteness, usually popularly described as "liberals," and racists (King and Smith 2011: 93). The evolution of the current politics of law enforcement, prison sentencing, and race is well documented in this period, as is the reproduction of historical patterns of housing and education inequality without the explicit reference to racial difference within institutions (Kozol 1992; Massey and Denton 1993; Bell 2004; Parenti 2008; King and Smith 2011: 137–67). The combination of the two exceptions and the new normal of institutional practices in this apparatus of racial equality eliminate any space for Black political protest and a discourse of societal injustice.

It has become convenient to ignore the possibility, in our new racial ordering, where explicit expressions of racial hatred are unnecessary to preserve the social impact of the decision to define races, that the liberalism that Schmitt critiques is fully capable of existing alongside a full-fledged racial ordering of the human population (Steedman 2012). Liberalism must depend for its coherence on some basic social unit, some definition of the normal, and this can just as effectively conceal as well as make explicit a decision of the place of race in determining human difference. This is the point of the statement by Benjamin above: something has to determine the direction of the law, while its force is inherent. The politics of race and not the law is the problem in US society today.

The ideas of hierarchy and difference are not antithetical to liberalism. Slavery is acceptable for those defined as absolutely different to the extent that they are not considered equal citizens. The ongoing question of whether Barack Obama is a natural-born citizen is an example of the continued salience of this idea. The decision of race negates all claims to anything but a common humanity. That the liberal state stops short of extermination is small consolation for those impacted by this decision.

It is not possible to equate the consequences of the racial policies of different regimes. The Holocaust was a unique and terrible example of allowing extermination as a description of the politics of the exception, while the terrible practices of slavery in the US, convict leasing, and the current impoverishment and marginalization of Blacks in the US are predicated on the subordination and subsequent definition of the value of the Black community for the economic and political development of the society. Schmitt's critique of liberalism is that sovereignty becomes a problem in a government divided against itself by function and law. I believe that it was not a divided government that allowed for a change from racial segregation for the Civil Rights Movement to have an impact on the law and government policies.

Instead, the collapse of order was threatened and the use of violence as the everyday exception was countered by visions on TV and in newspapers of young children being sprayed by fire hoses, young students being beaten, and buses being burned. The normal effects of segregation came into question through legal cases like *Brown*, such that the political decision of Black inferiority and role of White sovereignty as an element of segregated facilities were made apparent. This made this politics also a statement about the nature of the US democratic polity and became a question of national security and foreign policy and a problem for the political ambitions of the US abroad in the aftermath of World War Two. It was not an accident that the decisions handed down in *Brown* did not immediately realize significant changes in the society. The political changes were the result of a calculation as to maintaining the racial social order, not a signal of its collapse.

Race at the time was described as given by specific practices of place and order that were accepted by Whites, since these were given by what it meant to be White. This is the problem with the multiculturalism model of integration. It assumes that it is possible to displace by fiat the place of White authority in determining the political and social institutions in the society. It assumes, in spite of evidence to the contrary in such legal decisions as *Dred Scott v. Sandford*, that the government was not itself formed primarily in the US to facilitate the reproduction of the social, economic, and political progress of what we today describe as the White community. The change in the racial institutions of US society occurred only because the existing social order was directly threatened, not because of largess or guilt connected to ideals of liberalism that were already adopted to facilitate White community development. It has similarly become convenient and necessary to minimize the current perception of the threat that was posed at the time by the Civil Rights Movement to a racial order that allowed for segregation and explicit social expressions of racial inferiority and superiority. Couple this constant Black political organizational effort with the politics of the Cold War, the post–World War Two redevelopment of Europe, the collapse of the European colonial empires and a new role for the US in the global market, and the tensions arising from postindustrial development in the US and it becomes easier to understand the need by the state to ameliorate the political vulnerability that was caused by the public claims of racial injustice associated with Jim Crow policies (King and Smith 2011: 67).

In the US, the state is unable to define its content in the absence of the explicit connection to White sovereignty, and therefore all politics becomes possible. Since the 1960s, the US has entered a period where the decision of race may be threatened by politics. What would signal the dissolution of state sovereignty in the US, if not the separation of Whiteness from the law? Today we must decide if the US will become another new country or remain tied to the idea of race (Olson 2004: 127). This is our crisis, this inability to accept a state sovereignty absent the racial content of its politics. As Schmitt writes, "What matters for the reality of legal life is who decides" (2005: 35). What I am afraid of is that we have reached the limit of the democratic practices of this particular description of racial equality in the US.

I am more pessimistic in my approach to racial politics here than Desmond King and Rogers Smith, for example, who argue that changes in racial politics should be viewed as examples of successful pluralist political activity (King and Smith 2011). I do not see in the US today a serious challenge to the idea of racial communities in conflict where the outcome is determined by White community interests. I believe that the current political construction of formal racial equality is inadequate to address the problems that Blacks continue to experience in the US today.

LOOKING FOR A CRITICAL RACE THEORY

The political structure of a racial polity is well rehearsed at present: formal and informal rules for controlling the type of social contact between races, a description of racial difference that cannot be challenged or changed in practice, a decision always already in place outside of the purview of an individual to posit race as that difference to address the difference between persons. This is the depiction of races as communities of ideas, values, and material circumstances in opposition to one another, a politics of friend and enemy described by racial subjection. As Schmitt writes,

> The enemy is not merely any competitor or just any partner of a conflict in general. He is also not the private adversary whom one hates. An enemy exists only when, at least potentially, one fighting collectivity of people confronts similar collectivity. (1996: 28)

This last, of a necessary opposition as a definition of the political, is evident in everyday social interaction today if even the slightest reference is made to race. I will take issue with the distinction of friend/enemy in Schmitt's writing as it applies to racial politics later in Chapter 5, but for now it serves as a convenient starting point from which to begin discussing the current way that we use race as a politics in the US today.

The idea of collectivities in conflict described above initially seems to suggest equality between groups, rather than a description of the inferiority of one community in relation to another, a condition which, in addition to the idea of absolute difference, is the hallmark of racial social practices. It is in the context of the importance of sovereignty in Schmitt's writing that the hierarchical value of this description of race develops. The danger was, as Schmitt writes of the problem of sovereignty,

> The real friend-enemy distinction is existentially so strong and decisive ... is always the decisive human grouping, the political entity. If such

an entity exists at all, it is always the decisive entity, and it is sovereign in the sense that the decision about the critical situation, even if it is the exception, must always necessarily reside there. (1996: 38)

A person asked what race he or she is immediately realizes the burden of the political, the consequences of a decision that has profound and lasting effects on his or her prospects, person, and relationships. The fact is, in a comprehensive racial polity, there is no need to discuss race, nor does it require references directly in political theory, as it is a given fact of the definition of the human. This allows us to read Carl Schmitt as though he is not speaking about race when he suggests that liberalism deprives a society of the political (1996: 70; Strong 2012: 259). He does not need to, for the idea of friend and enemy as a necessary component of what it is to be human must describe a distinction between persons, for which race, along with the foreigner, the stranger, is a paradigmatic concept (1996: 27).

The consequences of accepting the idea of sovereignty as the ability to describe the state of exception are that we describe our lives in terms of death, struggle, and hate. We concede the description of our desires as coincident with the absolutism of race, a struggle of the one community, a "we" against all "others." The political distinction is reduced to that of the direction of our decision of difference, the ability to inspire loyalty and cultivate disdain against those described as outside our community. This direction defines difference as inferiority, as marginal, or coincidence, as something derivative of the original and normal (Gilman 1985).

Anything is then possible as slavery, violence, and death all arise in the melee that is a politics of friend and enemy (Nancy 2000: 151). This perspective even allows the argument, provided by Schmitt and repeated by contemporary political theorists, that liberal universalism similarly opposes all who claim another conception of the human, that it in fact also lays the groundwork for a war against an enemy in the name of humanity (Schmitt 1996: 54, 79; Mouffe 2006, 2009). This is to engage in that common hubristic move within a conflict, of saying that your opponent adopts the same view implicitly in his or her argument, to enlist your enemy in the justification of the decision. To exterminate in the name of a universal humanity is to deny the very idea of the human; and, in fact, the common complaint, also shared by Schmitt, is instead that liberalism leaves intact the basis for a continuous struggle of all against all, rather than a removal of the Other (Schmitt 1996: 70).

Since liberalism is about limits, about placing constraints on the political, the elimination of the Other is impossible. Rather these communities are put to work for the greater good of the sovereign authority. The limits on sovereignty this creates if described within Schmitt's conceptual framing force a constant return to the question of sovereign authority, and therefore of the place of African Americans in US society. This is one reason why, in spite of a terrifying difference between the Shoah and racial politics in the

US at the time, I want to equate theoretical work in Germany prior to and during World War Two and the state of racial politics today in the US liberal democratic society, and consider what it means if we do not see a radical break from the description of race that was inherent then in the political development of the US in the 1960s. Beneath the veneer of liberal racial pluralism today lurks the racial sovereign authority that was expressed in the legal codes of Jim Crow society (Hooker 2009).

Tracy Strong's description of Schmitt, allowing "his notion of enemy to too easily define his idea of friend" (Strong 2005: xxxi), accurately describes the emphasis of Schmitt's decision to create groups against which all must contend (1996: 24). Schmitt's work is what a racial political theory, in contrast to racial science or sociology, looks like. This is how we use race uncritically today as a politics. It is important to keep in mind my assumption that we lack a fully developed theory of race and still question the future of race in our democracy.

I am not suggesting that Schmitt or his work is racist; that is another claim entirely and not relevant once we begin to break through the procrustean political structure of how we use race today. I will address the idea of the racist as a conceptual problem later in this chapter. I believe Schmitt approached as closely as possible to a justification for a distinction between humans that would ground the polity, its institutions, governance, and the description of the citizen. This coincidence of community with government is what many find attractive in his work.

The political crisis in the US in the 1960s did require that the tradition of political theory come up with a way to explain the development of racial politics in the society and its own implication in this development. The temptation today is to continue as usual, merely adopting the theoretical solution found by researchers at the time, by suggesting that the problem does not lie in anything Whites do as a community, but in the description of Black incapacities. For example, this accepts the theoretical assumptions of culture, diversity, and individualism that provide the parameters of the debates on racial integration and assimilation described by Glazer and Moynihan (1970), and Milton Gordon (1964). The definition of what types of issues arise with regard to Black economic and social life in the US and the solutions to problems of racial inequality depend on a politics of race. If this is described as a problem of sociology or psychology due to the difference between Blacks and Whites as types of humans, this merely reproduces the traditional descriptions of community racial differences in the society. If culture or social values, history, or socioeconomic status is used to define a difference in communities, this does the same thing. The difficulty with defining race as a political concept within this tradition can be seen in the work by liberal theorists (Rawls 1972, 1993; Taylor 1994; Appiah and Gutmann 1996; Gutmann and Thompson 1996; Kymlicka 1996, 1998).

That a critical definition of race continues to be an issue today in political theory means that the use of Schmitt's writings is not seen as more or less provocative than that of Rawls, with regards to race and racism (Boxill 1992; Honig 1993; McKnight 1996; Mills 1997, 2003; Scheuerman 1999). On the other hand, without a better description of how race persists as a problem in the US we are left with this unfortunate comparison of two scholars with otherwise very different agendas (Dyzenhaus 1999: 83). The question is exactly what these disparate political theories say with regard to race and racism; are we using a conception of racial politics that is merely a product of the resolution, rather than a critique, of the problem of race within the law today? If so, then I would argue we are not confronting racial injustice, but rather accepting the ideas given by the continued efficacy of White sovereignty in US politics.

CARL SCHMITT TODAY

Applying Schmitt's ideas to US society in the 1930s in terms of racial politics is relatively straightforward, and without obvious discordance since there was little distinction between the state and the ambitions of Whites as a community. Schmitt writes, for example,

> The political can derive its energy from the most varied human endeavors, from the religious, economic, moral, and other antitheses. It does not describe its own substance, but only the intensity of an association or dissociation of human beings whose motives can be religious, national (in the ethnic or cultural sense), economic, or of another kind and can effect at different times different coalitions and separations. (1996: 38)

Today things are a bit different. US contemporary politics recognizes that, prior to the mid-1960s, the state was "the specific entity of a people," but that this appellation was applied to Whites to the exclusion of the contributions of other racial groups (Schmitt 1996: 19). In theoretical terms this means that the last fifty years have been an experiment in consolidating a new definition in the US of the people, of the state, and its scope with regard to racial group politics. How do we address a fractured state interest that is represented by the need to create a space for racial equality without simultaneously constraining the importance of the community of Whites in the determination of the development of the polity?

One approach is to suggest that there has been a change in the relationship between state and racial communities with the decision of *Brown*, the passage of the Voting Rights Act of 1965, the Civil Rights Act of 1964, and similar legislative changes and legal developments from the period of the 1950s to 1970s. This idea of racial political development would argue that White community interests and those of the state are no longer coincident, but in fact increasingly at odds given the importance of racial equality of opportunity as a principled position of the government. In this case, the current period in US political development has laid a foundation for a new politics of race and governance, a new state entity, which continues to develop in tension with a racial state structure which preexisted it for more than two hundred years.

In support of this hypothesis is the ability of African Americans to increasingly find professional employment, the increases in the standard of living of the community as a whole, the expression of racial social equality between persons in public, and the successful representation of African Americans in all walks of life in the society, including now the president of the United States. This is the argument that says that given the baseline of African American life in the US historically, the resources of the community have improved tremendously in the last fifty years.

This argument would suggest that the state has created a form of racial equality apparatus that gradually brings about the erosion of the social, economic, and political distinction between races. The state in this description would be developing in spite of White community resistance to its authority to determine specific rules and norms in the society. If this were true, then we could possibly say that the state was now allied with the interests of Blacks instead of Whites, as it seeks to secure and further evolve the social space for racial equality. Instead, we see resistance to this idea of the continued political development of racial equality (King and Smith 2011). Unfortunately there is no political structure that facilitates continuing US political development beyond what already exists regarding racial equality of opportunity. I don't see any diminution of the importance of the social distinction of race in the society outside of the space for formal equality, and so I think we have to reject this possibility.

The alternative, which I am arguing here, is that what occurred in the transition from Jim Crow was not a continuing process of progressive change but instead the establishment of procedural elements of racial equality of opportunity as a one-off moment defined by limited political changes to which the state and racial communities are then responding constantly decades later. Once in place this apparatus of racial equality was designed to control the impact of the racial hierarchy on economic and social development. The political problem of race was "solved." To my mind this matches the experience that Blacks had as well after the Civil War, where the absence of obstacles initially allowed for the rapid social and economic development of the resources of the community.

This second description of the development of racial equality accurately reflects the fact that African Americans as a community have not experienced a dramatic change in their relative resource position compared to European Americans, even though until the recent Great Recession the proportion of Blacks at middle-class income levels has increased within the community (Shapiro 2004; Oliver and Shapiro 2006; Collins 2009; Conley

1999; Alexander 2012). For a large portion of the Black community their status relative to Whites remains the same as it was in Jim Crow. This contrasting information occurs because through the institutional structure of formal racial equality the larger Black community is defined by practices of social and material subordination.

Schmitt would see a problem with this importance of the social with regard to the claims made by African Americans and others as something that should instead be a political decision for the state (1996: 22). However, the state in the US has never been in a position to make a decision regarding Black equality without the acquiescence of the White community, and so the social is political with respect to race. The distinction of friend and enemy that Schmitt offers for a definition of the political relies on a description of the social that I believe is flawed (26). The problem is in his assumption of politics describing the relationship to a person as an Other, something alien. As Schmitt puts it, "But he is, nevertheless, the other, the stranger; and it is sufficient for his nature that he is, in a specially intense way, existentially something different and alien, so that in the extreme case conflicts with him are possible" (27).

In this definition, the enemy is a public enemy, a description of a collective subject in opposition to another collective subject. As Schmitt writes, "An enemy exists only when, at least potentially, one fighting collectivity of people confronts a similar collectivity" (28). His explicit distinction between politics and social, collective and individual, is similar to the way race is addressed today in the US as a problem of a politics of simultaneity where the private description of racial beliefs and that of racial communities are described in conflict and collusion with one another. This is a political description of social communities where there is no practical distinction between persons and communities, and where the description of race moves between the material distinctions of individual persons and the idea of discrete racial communities (Schmitt 2005: 45).

Schmitt was advocating for just the situation we find ourselves in within the US today, and the idea of a difference between races was openly recognized through legal segregation in the US at the time he wrote his major works. The problem from this perspective today is that, to the extent that racial equality is true, it places the state in a position of no longer determining the friend-enemy distinction, but instead requires that race be described as a problem of equality. The state is unable to establish the political apparatus to enable racial equality since it no longer represents the sovereign interests of the White community. In Schmitt's terms, this fracturing of state interest from its pure political function leaves us without a clear political order within which to govern (1996: 44). In effect the state would be acting to negate the former decision of the friend-enemy definition for race and the categories of racial difference as a part of the basic social organization of the society without the ability to move beyond its purview in the law for the description of equality.

For Schmitt, a community is a political entity when it can prohibit the enemy distinction of a certain adversary (37). The friend-enemy distinction is so strong existentially that everything devolves into this relationship at a moment's notice. All other distinctions fade against the moment of the decision of community. So, rather than see the dissolution of White racial sovereignty with the change to the politics of racial integration, this shift could be viewed as an expression of the authority that is retained in the act of being able to redefine the relationship between racial communities. The capability to define the scope of racial equality while retaining the social description of White community difference, that Whiteness still matters, is a demonstration not of the loss of control over state interests but of its further entrenchment in the political structure. Contrast this idea of politics with that of Rawls's (1972) idea of reflective equilibrium, where persons arrive at a common position, a community, through a process of sharing perspectives. For Rawls the question of race must be left to future generations to deliberate since it cannot be addressed as a politics within the principled parameters of political liberalism. For Schmitt the answer is to instead make a decision from within the sovereign authority of the democratic public to redefine how to address the enemy.

2 The New Normal

> And then some unjust God leaned, laughing, over the ramparts of heaven and dropped a black man in the midst.
> —Du Bois, *Black Reconstruction in America*

> The tradition of the oppressed teaches us that the "state of emergency" in which we live is not the exception but the rule. We must attain to a conception of history that is in keeping with this insight.
> —Benjamin, "Philosophy of History"

Today the easiest way to defeat the attempt to integrate Blacks and other non-Whites into the polity is to deny the state the ability to answer the needs of these groups. Will the US remain a racial polity as it was under Jim Crow, except that, instead of formal segregation, under integration we substitute other mechanisms? What better way to ensure the inability of anyone to organize against a policy than to link racism to a vague, theoretically inadequate idea of class, to suggest it is all a problem of socioeconomic differences even if coincident with the traditional description of racial groups (Wilson 1980, 1999). A lot of thought has gone into how to continue to treat Blacks as inferior in order to avoid addressing the problem of a continued assumption of White superiority; how can *we* ensure *they* do not change our society and then only in peripheral ways like in select forms of entertainment and sports. The election of Obama can be seen as a potential setback in this struggle for stasis because it raises the possibility of African Americans developing a counternarrative as the community comes to the existential limit of the promise of equality.

Schmitt's idea of politics described a potential, the capability of social relations to devolve into a basic relationship between friend and enemy, not that this situation was required (1996: 29). This is exactly how race functions in the US today, as a distinction usually held in abeyance, at a distance from what occurs every day, except when the political primacy of the White community is brought into question. The gestural aspect of race today becomes important to mitigate any claim that White sovereign authority remains in the policies of the state. Obama's presidency is just such a gesture. It allows for the illusion of a necessary conflict of all against all, of no priority given to any one group in society in the midst of developing liberal pluralism, even though the political efficacy of the White community remains unaddressed as a problem after the collapse of the Civil Rights Movement. If this is correct, then in this era of integration, race as an associative description of community could continue as a political entity without requiring the state to mediate the application of a racial description of the social practices of friend and enemy (44).

For Schmitt, "every state provides . . . some kind of formula for the declaration of an internal enemy" (46). This idea allows us to see the wound of the American Civil War and its constant reenactment as a reminder in the relationship between the South and North, of the inability to reconcile the actual conflict with the idea that Whites are not the enemy while those not White are. In this perspective there is no way to apologize to other Whites for the treachery of a war that included as one of its several major premises a conflict over how to resolve the race question. How does the community of Whites apologize to itself for allowing for internal sacrifice on behalf of an external enemy? This was only possible with the move by Southern states to secede. This allowed for a new moment of founding, of defining a sovereign community of persons, all White, which was distinct from the Northerner. Once established, the reunification of the White community with the end of the Civil War did not erase this definition of a difference within Whiteness.

This idea of a wound that cannot be addressed would explain how the White North could only acquiesce to the increasing demands over the course of several decades after the war by White Southerners for a return of the legal means to subordinate Blacks (Woodward 1966; Blackmon 2009). The character of Jim Crow subordination, its scope, and duration were necessary as a constant attempt to unify White sovereign authority within the state, a necessary gesture made by sacrificing Blacks (Roediger 2006, 2007; Ignatiev 2008). The desire for unity across this decision of difference made it impossible to push for further racial reforms to improve the place of African Americans in the society. This same dynamic would also explain the reluctance to force further changes in racial practices in the society after the legislative achievements of the 1960s. The African American remains the internal enemy of the state, the essential adversary to which all others are compared. This description of history of course does not match how we want to see ourselves today in the US with regard to race. For Schmitt, the existential threat, not an economic or religious threat, justifies the elimination of others, the public enemy.

It is therefore a political entity that determines the degree of sacrifice necessary to preserve the ultimate definition of community. Without the ability to determine the enemy, the community is no longer free but part of another, larger description of community; a limit on the violence toward and sacrifice of the enemy would demonstrate a lack of authority. With the Civil Rights Movement the only option was to acquiesce in such a way that White sovereign authority was retained. This was accomplished by a combination of violence, intimidation, and the availability of the structure of equal opportunity. For Schmitt, war does not permit the idea of justice, so that if we stick to this framing of racial politics to argue for racial justice this misunderstands the nature of the conflict between White and Black communities in the US (1996: 49). Kalyvas defends Schmitt against the wrong charge with respect to racial politics when he writes in Hegelian terms, "In real life, however, absolute homogeneity also means that a permanent elimination of the enemy 'is a fiction' (*fingiert wird*)" (2008: 155). The primacy of the struggle against others means that the defeat of one merely leads to the formulation of another, but the elimination of the opponent is always the ultimate desired outcome of Schmitt's politics. Accordingly, within this description of racial politics there is no just war.

War is here then defined as a conflict over the freedom to determine the nature of the enemy by a political entity. That this entity decided to allow for formal racial equality of opportunity rather than further address the basis for the institutions of formal segregation and custom of Jim Crow is a testament to the depth of the continuing conflict today. Rather than a lack or absence of a concern for the role of race within the polity, the state was mobilized to create a space for equality that allowed the value of the concept to persist everywhere else. This perspective helps explain the popular framing of racial equality of opportunity as a way for the White community to continue to develop according to its own ideals of equality and justice; that the changes in the 1960s were a measure of democratic social progress. The basis of politics is protection and obedience (Schmitt 1996: 52). It is this conception of the political that describes race in the US (62). The shift to a politics in support of the equal opportunity for Blacks was not an evocation of White authority in the polity; it was an act of immunization that purported to signal both the coming of the end of the history of race in America and a new democracy of equal rights (Esposito 2008: 56). This is why it is not an assertive racial social description but rather a constant process of obfuscation and concealment of the decision. As Esposito argues, "Immunity is a *process* that always involves an open system of self-definition that consistently produces self and other" (Esposito 2011: 169).

SOVEREIGNTY AND THE EXCEPTION

Sovereignty is that which defines the politics of the exception (Schmitt 2005: 5). If we accept that, as numerous studies of soldiers and citizens who participated in the pogroms and mass killings under the National Socialist regime have shown, great evil was possible for ordinary people, then we can easily compare these conditions to life under Jim Crow for White Americans (Goldhagen 1997: 101). There is something going on when people can casually lynch, rape, and commit atrocious acts amidst the steady continuous beat of their daily lives (DuRocher 2011; Wood 2011). Blacks certainly had to accept this as a regular part of their experience (Wells-Barnett 2002). What allowed this condition of a constant exceptional politics to exist without disturbing the lives of Whites? What relationship should we describe between these actions and those Whites who never had any contact with Blacks, and if so only in their duties as the help or in menial professional capacities?

It is very important to understand that the availability of Blacks to exceptional politics during Jim Crow meant that race was a central part of the political for them, whereas for Whites social instruments were available when Blacks did not conform to their stated place in society, as an exception to regular and normal social practices. For Whites, race was important when its hierarchical features were not adhered to by Blacks but otherwise was an invisible social element of their lives; it was just right.

Race is used constantly today in the US. How is this use defined such that persons are able to sleep at night, feel they are good people, and lead the society? This question is so provocative and strong that the response is to immediately move away from what seems a too easy description of US society as a racial polity. What must be the case instead is that the polity is defined so that certain actions that describe race are justified under certain conditions. The state of exception, the decision of the exception, and its delineation of conditionality lie at the center of the politics of race. It is important to remember that what matters today is that we accept this description of racial equality and the political, that we do not question the ease with which a racial distinction can be made between a collective friend and enemy. If this idea is not at the center of politics, then the entire theoretical approach changes.

The argument here is that in the US it is common to accept the conception of racial politics as that of defining an enemy in common. In *Political Theology*, Schmitt writes, "The decision on the exception is a decision in the true sense of the word" (2005: 6). The exception arises in situations of extreme peril to the public interest. For Schmitt, this idea of conflict and danger need not be codified in the law, and remains always a function of the interpretation of the community that defines the sovereign, the authority to define friend and enemy. This raises the question of who or what holds this interest such that it requires race. To what is the African American a threat, if not to the community of persons defined in opposition, Whites and Whiteness?

What description of sovereignty allowed for a decision about race during Jim Crow, that which allowed for the most seemingly insignificant action on the part of African Americans in daily life to be defined as a potential threat to the entire edifice of social practices that defined the community of Whites? Race was until recently perceived as in the national interest, synonymous with social order and democratic politics until very recently. This new political structure is predicated on the recognition by Whites as a community of the necessary ability to respond to the nascent threat to public order and security represented by African American social activity that challenges persistent racial inequality. This is activity that tries to define a new valuation of race, whether this would lead to its eventual dissolution as a concept or the possibility of equality in distinction.

I believe that confusing a past of unlimited authority and exceptional politics during Jim Crow and the illusion of limits on that authority today, the idea of a current limit to the sovereignty of the White community within the US, is the basis for the contemporary claim that a racial equality exists in the US.

That it is an illusion may not be obvious for some. Today there is a structure of institutional practices that allows, as did formal racial segregation, for the majority of decisions on the exception to White rule to be taken out of an individual White person's purview. It is no longer necessary for race to be invoked explicitly as often, as in when someone Black or White threatens the racial order of the polity, because the law is in place with which to punish those who resist this shift in how the racial order has evolved. Since events are no longer described as racial, the sovereignty of this situation is no longer available for a counterargument. There is nothing to protest against.

I think Schmitt is correct when he states that in the everyday the decision recedes to the background. In this case the racial distinction is obscured, while the exception, when race has to be reintroduced explicitly, is a sign of the collapse of the normal (2005: 15). The temptation is to ascribe the lack of codification of the exception as extrajuridical, as sociological. Schmitt suggests that since the norm and decision are juridical, the exception remains juridical (13). As Agamben writes, the state of exception is "the place where the opposition between the norm and its realization reaches its greatest intensity" (2005: 36). This is the case with the description of the racist today. It "reveals . . . the decision in absolute purity" (Schmitt 2005:13).

A PARADIGM CRISIS?

For Schmitt, liberalism defines the moral decision as evil. While he deemed the decision necessary to preserve the sovereignty of the state against the variety of interests that arise in the society, the problem for liberalism lies in the metaphysical description of the decision being suggested within the former's view of politics (2005: 65). If the decision of friend and enemy is brought into the realm of democratic deliberation, it immediately becomes available to the claims of justice. "The essence of liberalism is negotiation," writes Schmitt (63). If the decision is defined instead as derived from a discrete social environment, history, and unique circumstance that establish the necessary structure for the constant move from ontic to ontology required to support the use of race politically, then this absolute description of difference devolves into the definition of these elements instead. As Schmitt writes, "The friend and enemy concepts are to be understood in their concrete and existential sense" (1996: 27).

The threat to Schmitt's vision of liberalism as all and nothing, a politics of the many and none, is that we realize that there is no description of friend and enemy that is not already social. It confounds the critique of liberalism in his model of politics to suggest that the act of the decision is evil, instead of suggesting that it is the idea of absolute authority that is the problem. An authority that cannot be questioned in a democracy is a sovereignty that lies outside of time and space, something that is defined against the potential future demands of individuals in the society. It suggests that not every person has equal political weight (Santner 2011: 4). The liberal concept of equal concern and respect developed from within the Rawlsian project would be opposed to the idea that specific descriptions of individual persons could be derived such that friends and enemies would encompass descriptions not of persons but of collectives. For liberal theory this is the problem of the intolerant, something adequately rehearsed in the literature. At the same time, what Schmitt is doing is not a solution to this problem but suggesting that obscuring the reality of the political decision of friend and enemy in liberalism, through the practice of a gestural politics, will allow us to avoid the need for addressing the issue of White sovereignty and the problem of the exception. This is a problem as it builds into politics a necessity to conceal the illegitimacy of a metaphysical claim to authority, in this case that race is an arbitrary concept.

That race would arise as a result of struggle, of pluralism, is the classic definition of racial politics, not that it exists as an organic or natural concept prior to politics. The latter is a measure of the ability to place the decision outside of politics, not the reality of the politics of the distinction that race makes. Kalyvas makes the point that Schmitt was not a racist in the classic sense, with an idea of ethnic or racial communities which would found a society (2008: 122). He is correct of course, in the sense that the racist subject position today describes exceptional racial political activity. Once we get past the idea that sacrifice is necessary to ensure normalcy, that this idea of the normal juxtaposed with the racist is itself a construction of the need to conceal the decision of race and its place in society, we can often avoid worrying about this problem of personal implication in works of political theory. Everyone is implicated in racial politics.

Race can be thought of as the perfect political concept for a theory such as Schmitt's, social all the way down, and with final consequences for everyone. To say that race is a social construction is merely to accept Schmitt's characterization of politics as about the distinction, not to refute the efficacy of his vision of a constituency before there is a constituency, the illegitimacy of paradox that defines the arbitrariness of the distinction. There was no friend prior to the struggle, nor did a sovereign, even when viewed across country borders, define itself prior to the idea of a border. This means that the justification and definition of friendship are always both post hoc and open to challenge. The result is a society in which violence is always justified and always questioned in the name of a decision about difference.

The answer to the query of the legitimacy of violence refounds or reestablishes the basis for the government even as the justification for violence that is done in its name. It had to be done and therefore it is just. This political formula is framed as a matter of survival, the violence enacted by the state the only alternative to the dissolution of the community. This avoids the possibility of a challenge to the arbitrariness of the decision that defines those on the side of the government, our friends. The enemy always questions the use of violence by the state; friends never do. So the decision doubly defines friends, and loyalty to the authorizing moment becomes also the basis for sovereignty. Or as Kalyvas puts it while trying to absolve Schmitt of theoretical complicity in the development of the Nazi regime, "Legitimacy overpowers legality . . . legality then overpowers legitimacy" (2008: 128). The problem is again this description of politics when set against the distinction between natural and social human differences which were taking place politically during the time of Schmitt's writings of the period. There was little public discourse in Germany or the US in the 1920s, except in radical political circles, that would have considered race as problematic for the friend-and-enemy distinction Schmitt describes as the basis for politics. In fact it is only in the context of how we today resolve the problem of Nazi activity that gives us a working definition of a critique of race with regard to Schmitt, and Heidegger for that matter. It is on this point that Faye (2009), Ott (1994), and Farias (1991) are vulnerable in their critique of Heidegger. Today we use a similarly contentious description of racism developed in light of the events in the 1960s to justify the claim that racism is a thing of the past.

The problem with this is the idea of a required conflict while leaving unexplored the requirements used to determine those differences between persons and communities that define friends and enemies. To value competition in and across communities as a way to resolve what we wish to be is to take for granted the forms available to us rather than challenge our subjection within communities that subordinate others (Schmitt 1988: 35). Tracy Strong suggests that it is in this way that Schmitt misunderstands the nature of friend and enemy (2005: xxxi). Schmitt's theory is really about how we define enemies, since he has no definition of friendship beyond that of a vague description of the people. Schmitt needs instead a description of friendship, how it is assigned, and of what it consists. "How do we make friends?" is the simple query that I would argue should lie behind this otherwise elaborate definition of constitutional politics (Derrida 1997). I will return to this problem in the chapters that follow when I discuss what race requires as a definition of community politics in the US. I now want to spend some time discussing the consequences of this description of the new politics of the exception with regard the politics of the Obama presidency. What does this reconsideration of racial politics mean for the way we look at the election and tenure of the first Black president of the United States?

PRESIDENT OBAMA

The move from constituted sovereignty to constitutional sovereignty created by the legal changes of the 1960s did not thereby remove the problem of a distinction of race between persons (Schmitt 1988: 27, 43). I think Schmitt would find it ironic that the US today is in racial terms the type of successful constitutional democracy he would find appealing. Of course, other aspects of governance today he would abjure as threatening the rule of law and the social order. It is in this context that Obama's election is particularly interesting. It suggests that the distinction of race and the description of popular sovereignty in the US are once again coming into conflict with one another. This time it is not a protest on the street, but instead the electoral organizations that brought Obama into office and his presidency, the democratic political process itself.

The Tea Party movement of 2010 and the subsequent rightward drift of the Republican Party in the election of 2012, seen in this light, are in part an affirmation of this thesis of the threat to a sovereign Whiteness and the idea of the distinction of race posed by Obama's election. What would constitute proof of this in our current definition of racial politics? When a movement arises upon Obama's election that takes as its symbol the history of a successful revolt against a constitutional monarch, one that serves as a political marker for the founding of the process by which the US came to be, and when this same movement expressly claims that Obama in his person is the source of the problem with politics, that anyone else will do as president, Schmitt's reasoning about politics becomes important. When Sarah Palin is able to pronounce on national TV, for example, that Obama is bringing us back to pre–Civil War days, and have this make sense to commentators, it is a disturbing confirmation of this impending crisis (*Huffington Post* 2012). In this perspective, President Obama stands as a threat to an American state that argues that popular sovereignty is destabilizing and dangerous for US economic and political development. It is similarly telling that Mitt Romney's campaign slogan when running against President Obama was to return us to The Promise of America and thereby seems to limn the elements of this racial narrative of a White community sovereign authority in the US.

The members of the Tea Party movement in 2010 were not available to the exception, to investigation, and legal instruments as ways to control and limit its activity in the same way as African Americans or racists are; its members were popularly viewed as core constituents of the nation, of what it is to be American. This should warn us of the ease with which it is possible, using the complex racial equality apparatus, to tap into the continued salience of race for Whites as a central organizing political force in US society and how we continue to categorize friend and enemy in Schmittian terms alongside the liberal political state in which we also exist. Protests by members of the Tea Party were viewed as a central element of the definition of a specific, but not popular, sovereignty in the society. The political importance of this distinction between popular sovereignty and White sovereign interests is captured in the constant evocation of the phrase "majority of Americans" rather than "Americans of all walks of life" or "America" to justify support for political hostility to many of the positions of the Obama administration. The former phrase has little to do with a majoritarian democratic impulse on the part of its adherents and is rather an explicit call to mobilize those who believe they had reason to fear the reelection of Obama as president.

That this Tea Party movement and those described as right wing are described as having failed in the bid to elect Romney as president instead of Obama, that they are somehow responsible for this loss in contrast to a moderate GOP politics, merely repeats the division between the prohibited and the accepted political description of a sovereign Whiteness, the exception and the normal. Neither the now-ascendant liberal nor the newly abject right wing White subject addresses the bifurcation of either the White or Black community as a function of the construction of institutions of formal racial equality; poverty, imprisonment, educational disparity, and underemployment remain unaddressed as a problem for the development of the democracy (Shipler 2005). The election of 2012, while important as an indication of the institutional policies available in the next four years, threatens to ensure the consolidation of the racial apparatus without addressing the problem of defining a normal Black subject available to traditional forms of racial subordination.

What remains available to exceptional politics is the Occupy Wall Street protests and the equivalent constant always possible threat of African American political mobilization as occurred during the Jim Crow Era. What we see today is a strange moment where in fact the president of the United States is himself subject to the potential use of exceptional politics, if he does not acquiesce to the place of the decision of race as a description of sovereignty. His very birthplace is questioned, his grades in school are requested for public scrutiny, his person is reviled and interrogated as alien, as an always possible enemy. At what point do we realize that this degree of investigation of his person and his life is not the normal inspection given to a sitting president of the United States? Is the idea to merely remind everyone that the election of a Black person is exceptional and not normal, or do people really think that it is important to find some way to dismiss his contributions as president to the polity and that this is crucial to the health of the democracy?

So what does this description of two racial communities whose politics is sutured by the racist and the Black exceptional individual mean for the assessment of the election of Obama as president? I think this is a good example of the politics of integration that has occurred since the 1960s. To be Black is to be one thing; the new requirement is that to succeed you now have to become something else as well. Not White of course, because that is not possible, but also not Black like those others. That President Obama can be described as possibly African by the "birther" discourse serves another purpose from the attempt to curtail his ability to occupy the office; it also makes it harder to make his success indicative to Whites of the potential held by all African Americans for success in the society; he is explicitly always the exception and not the rule.

The most important economic resources for the individual in this political institutionalization of racial equality of opportunity are acceptable personal attributes such that the person is not a threat to the hierarchy of race. The description of hierarchy is not something as simple as the need for authority or specific roles in the workplace, but instead the idea that the individual does not bring into question the right of Whites to determine the conditions for this hierarchy. This does not preclude critical race theory or the personal critical engagement in popular political discourse, or someone Black being the boss at work over Whites, merely that whatever is said or accomplished does not threaten the existing racial hierarchy as defined by the White community. So what does this mean for a Black president? Certainly he and Michelle Obama can remark on the racism they have experienced growing up in the society, as their overcoming of this supports the elements of the exceptional Black.

The political choices available to Barack Obama are identical to those for any Black person who has succeeded through the mechanism of a Black exceptionalism that differentiates him or her from the Black community as such. You can see how even the idea of asking the question of how a particular successful Black person is connected to the Black community, the idea of requirements of authenticity and diversity as a problem for being Black and successful, is a function of this particular post–Jim Crow politics. Why couldn't every Black person's success be a statement of the possibility for success inherent in every member of the community? Instead, successful Black individuals cannot represent the community without addressing the politics separating them from the community, a political conversation for which there is no space.

This is why I use the term *suture* to describe the concept of the exceptional Black. It is impossible for the individual to address what is in fact an artificial construct that depends for its efficacy on the inability to address the continuing effects of race in society. It is possible only through dehiscence, the incomplete concealment of the wound of race by the suture of the concept that a problem is revealed for the individual. The criticism he or she encounters from a normal, still racialized traditional description of the Black community or the persistent racial effects of still being Black in America allows the exceptional Black individual to realize that something is not right and that racism as a problem is not resolved merely through the life they live as a television producer, public intellectual, academic, or president. The very efficacy of the distinction of individual exception and community deprivation as a way to define racial equality ensures that individuals are given little opportunity to impact the politics of community as it defines racial difference.

Like every other Black successful person in the US, Barack Obama can only work within the confines of his particular subjection. The limits to this subjection are given by the historical legacy of physical threat, intimidation, and social exclusion by a White community that is always both immanent locally and comprehensive socially, described as the majority, as sovereign in the society. A challenge to the institutional structure of racial equality of opportunity is met with social ostracism, economic deprivation, and political marginalization; the consequences are dire for the Black subject who makes what are considered poor choices within this racial politics.

The problem is that the description of threat, of an acceptable act by Blacks in the new integration, is given by the White community. The definition of threat is something any White person can bring up as a possibility regarding any one Black individual. It does not take more than one to question the nature of the Black person's success in the society. Fanon's description still holds true, of a young White boy able to call out the Black person for who he or she is, an oddity, an alien, a threat (2008: 111–12). The new racist is someone reviled, and rightly punished, as upsetting the politics of integration even as the same problem continues in the ability of any White person no matter how liberal to police the borders of the decision to create the hierarchy of race (Ayo 2005). The racial politics of the exception remains the same as in the past; the necessity of extralegal action, the permission to do so, merely is exercised differently within the strictures of the new laws of equality. The description of racial violence has changed, but its source has not.

OBAMA'S CHALLENGE

Obama's presidency challenges the racial equality apparatus in three ways. First, the role of the president defines an individual who has equals only in the collective sense in the US political process, the Congress, and Supreme Court. There is no higher authority within the political structure of government. Clearly having someone Black in this position would cause a political challenge to the idea of White sovereign government. Professional promotion must be accompanied by increased levels of control to ensure the Black person does not begin to change the ability of the racial hierarchy to function properly. The election of Obama reveals the limit condition throughout the apparatus for Black exceptionalism as a means of supporting White sovereignty.

The second difficulty for White sovereign political authority caused by Obama's election to the presidency is that the organizational forces that supported his election are in part a product of a desire to challenge the political efficacy of the decision itself. It took forty years, but the Black community was able to bring forward someone who could use the instruments available within the very limited description of formal racial equality to become president. How do you keep these organizational forces in play from becoming a new form of Civil Rights Movement that challenges the status quo? In this interpretation, the Black community was finally able to make its political ambitions coincident with the subjectivization of the Black exception used in the 1960s to ameliorate its broad demand for the dissolution of the decision of race. From within this organizational frame it becomes very important to put pressure on Obama's administration to fulfill the political desire for a reassessment of the conditions for formal racial equality in the society as a problem for both the normal Black community and those Whites who also find themselves unable to take advantage of the material and social promise given within the apparatus. Political pressure on the problems of persistent poverty, underemployment, the growing prison-industrial complex, a concern with the environment, housing policies, and education all are necessary to overcome the pressure on the Obama administration to further entrench the discursive practices of the apparatus of formal racial equality (King and Smith 2011; Edelman 2012; Smiley and West 2012)

The persistent political claim as to President Obama's political radicalism arises from the concern that he is a threat to a general idea of the liberal welfare state in the same way that earlier Civil Rights Movement politics was perceived in the 1950s and 1960s. That he is somehow as president also in the vanguard of a new political movement for racial justice. When popular political discourse suggests counterfactually that the president of the United States is a socialist, or a Muslim, it is obvious that something more than normal political rhetoric is taking place. Instead of being unimportant, this way of speaking about President Obama and the fact that this is a discourse directed exclusively to Whites, that such a direction is still possible today, demonstrate how important the current construction of formal racial equality is for White sovereign authority. What this rhetoric does is gradually erode the suture of the racist as distinct from a White community that is merely social. It brings the political needs of this community into public discourse for the first time in several decades, and therefore it gradually erodes the ability of its members to dissociate themselves from the definition of the individual racist; this discourse gives political substance to Whiteness. As one half of the structure that undergirds formal racial equality of opportunity in the US, to attenuate the importance of the racist is also to return to the question of the way Whites as a community should police racial difference; it returns US society to the possibility of slavery and Jim Crow. It is alarming therefore rather than amusing that Sarah Palin can suggest in an interview with Sean Hannity on Fox News,

> Now, it has taken all these years for many Americans to understand that that gravity, that mistake, took place before the Civil War and why the Civil War had to really start changing America. What Barack

Obama seems to want to do is go back to before those days when we were in different classes based on income, based on color of skin. (*Huffington Post* 2012)

To accuse someone Black of inciting race hatred, of being racist merely by insisting on the opportunities available to Whites, of causing Whites to coalesce as a political community to protect their interests is a traditional device from the argument for White sovereign authority in the US (Wright 2008). That this way of speaking is not prohibited reveals how cogent the interest of Whites as a community remains in the US.

The third problem is that Obama's election also brings into focus a problem with the idea of exceptional individual progress and the Black normal community, the relationship that defines the other half of the political structure of racial equality in the US. This is an incredible individual accomplishment, to be elected president. At the same time, for all of us who have negotiated the politics of race as an individual pursuit, for those of us who have always tried to be "exceptional," this election more than anything else brings attention to the fact that the conditions of our success are always measured in relationship to a Black community that suffers under difficult material and political circumstances. That the price of success as the exceptional Black is to accept a politics of representation, and to often mistakenly confuse this with challenging the status quo, becomes obvious when a Black individual is able to become president even as Blacks as a community face substantial barriers to economic and political success (Cohen 1991; Tate 2003; Shapiro 2004; Alexander 2012; Smiley and West 2012). What has happened to the idea of improving the entire community, of "racial uplift," as a clarion call for Black professionals historically in the US? Even this connection between rich and poor Blacks as a community was sacrificed to the idea of racial equality of individual opportunity, a contradiction between the idea of a racial politics of community and that of an individual that contains the economic and political impact of racial subjection in their lives. The idea of the racist and the exceptional Black were concepts necessary to the construction of a space for this idea of racial equality. As we will see later when discussing the problem of nonviolence and the object of critical race politics, as important as it is, "racial uplift" is itself limited as a strategy to providing for social change within rather than against a specific description of racial politics (Balfour 2011: 84).

If Black individuals begins to view their success as dependent on conditions in the Black community, this vitiates the entire conceptual structure of racial equality of individual opportunity. It is not a coincidence that there is a constant popular political discourse on the relationship of President Obama to the Black community. Discussions about President Obama's personal knowledge of the Black community, and a resort to the traditional politics of Black authenticity, often conceals the larger political concessions that Blacks have been forced to accept as the price of the ticket to this description of equality.

Part II
Defining Racial Sovereignty

3 The Experience of Race

> We do not know where thinking will lead us. Where we believe we know, we only believe we think. For, then it would not be a "standing" under the challenge that strikes us and which we do not choose. Thinking challenges us, and we have to stand or fall. Standing, however, means to stand fast, to correspond, to answer—and not to play, in a calculating manner, with possibilities.
>
> —Gadamer, *Heidegger's Ways*

> An imagination trained in the play of language(s) may undo the truth-claims of national identity, thus unmooring the cultural nationalism that disguises the workings of the state—disguises the loss of civil liberties, for example, in the name of the American 'nation' threatened by terror.
>
> —Spivak, *Nationalism and the Imagination*

In this chapter I provide a first critical description of race. I do this by defining the basic phenomenological description of race for individuals. This is seen as a problem of racial subjectivity within language. From the position of the structure of formal racial equality this has to be the initial perspective on race, that race arises as personal beliefs and culture rather than as a product of a politics. The idea that race is a product of reflection on the part of an individual has to be resolved as a particular historical moment that has to be overcome (Gadamer 1994: 58). In the next chapter I will argue against the intersubjective reproduction of racial community, and suggest that it cannot exist unless some type of coercive force is applied to the social activity of persons. We have to be forced to race one another, and to have this recur demands a type of decision or other form of imperative to exist as a political mechanism. For now it is best to begin with a simple form of community and intentionality.

Outside of the most abstract conceptions of political membership, that of the American citizen-subject or perhaps resident, US society does not define itself as a single social community of persons. In fact, the idea of community is usually described in terms of desires for material or social resources held in common by a limited number of persons. For example, some people really like coffee or cats, and the group of persons that do so comprises communities of coffee or cat lovers. These communities need not be mutually exclusive, for someone can both love coffee and cats. There is therefore a distinction between what can be called distributive values of community, where persons can be a member of many or several such groups without contradiction, and an absolute description of community.

Race, on the other hand, is an absolute difference between persons. A community created out of a definition of racial difference is not derived from individual desires but through something I want to call a political decision. This decision is political in that it exists outside of any one person's definitional purview, instead arising from a construction of authority that distinguishes between races and thereby defines them. This authority is located in the description of social existential forms which exist as a space by which to contain the essence of man, and its development is a description of human nature and of archetypes against which persons measure themselves (Marx 1971: 88, 219; Heidegger and Fink 1993: 76). The person as subject who belongs in this way to a racial community cannot also belong to another. This is a particular political construction developed as a way to insulate the sovereignty that derives from forming a White community with political authority in the society from the forces of democratic politics. It is not a true description of race, as in a natural or real effect of racial difference, which is a social construction. It is politically efficacious to posit a receding metaphysical decision point unavailable to any one White person but instead a product of community interests. The actual decision is something that can be addressed as a result of institutional political developments from the 1960s in US society. If we choose to do so it is possible to erode the salience of racial community descriptions by focusing on addressing the salience of race for the normal White person within the apparatus, and the reduction in practices of subordination on the larger Black community. Politically progressive attention to the two normal subject definitions in the apparatus would alter the parameters of formal equality.

To return to the theoretical argument, this particular thinking of being and Being, of a decision and its universal application, allows for conceptual unity even as it erases ethical responsibility for a subject that is raced. The decision to create this subject first must define what I call a politics, a description of communities of racial human types. That the authorizing subject is White is important; the idea of race collapses if it must be created by the Black subject. This necessary direction of thinking as a description of being occurs because once White exists it must remain a true expression of ontological difference defined from us to them, a particular reification of the requirement to address an Other.

This contrasts with the assumption that it is through a realization of an Other, that the Other first creates race for us as a description of that which we are not, cannot ever be coincident with. This would make the Other responsible for their own racialization. Instead, we put off the reconciliation of a difference with an Other for a definition of similarity, of a singularity that is not one. It is this assumption of the being of singular plurality that Derrida critiques in Nancy's work (Derrida 2005: 58). After the moment of identification, of the coincidence of origin and decision on the part of a person, this singularity collapses into plurality, a realization of an Other that is not our One. A decision to return, to reproduce this originary moment of singularity in the presence of Others allows for race to develop as a definition of communities of differences that are absolute because they derive from the decision itself. In this way racial difference is both timeless and in time, a product of our immediate desire to be complete, whole again.

As a way to defend this continued use, it is often felt that if this idea of Whiteness could be taken out of political context it would be harmless; if it could be described without the necessary subordination of the Other as its central directive, it would then be unattached to the idea of absolute difference and exist as a concept of pure representation. This illusion of the absence of direction, of the absence of a desire to subordinate and control an Other person, however, does not hold up. In its political and social use as a representation of human types, race is instead substantial enough in the direction of this temporal movement between ideal and subjection to define communities with terrifying implications for a democratic society.

The decision to race is as easy as defining any ideal typology against which human difference is measured. This ideal of Whiteness is then given as true and the excess of perception that otherwise describes the social impact of human idealization is limited by the subordination of the Other that is required to support its practice. The other person is only Black, just as all Others are not White (Ngai 2005). The initial perceptual event, and its reproduction, is contained within a horizon given by the historical development of the racial communities that form around the subjects defined therein, communities that must be true. The substance of race is given by that initial event. It is the decision to make a type out of the difference that exists because of the apparent separateness of human beings from each other. As Heidegger writes, "Seeing means having disposal over beings *as* they show themselves and must show themselves, therefore over *how* they are manifest and unhidden" (2009: 117). Race is not a social construction in the sense of arising out of real differences between persons, but an idealization of perception in the picture of the world (Heidegger 1977; Villa 1996: 182). Since race is a decision of perception, it always attempts to conceal what is an arbitrary definition, a decision of difference that is inaccessible to the Other.

From within the description of discrete racial communities that we experience today, race has to be true; even when in the process of denouncing its essence as based in natural science, the idea itself must be true because the historical communities of race provide a definition of singularities that determine how we want to relate and care for other persons. How do we remove an ideal that has become a central element of the language we are given to describe ourselves and of how we care for each other? In other words, the communities that have formed through the application of race in US society have a life of their own. It is not enough to argue that race is a social construction or an idealization of the fact of human difference.

The direction of subordination that necessitates two distinct racial subjects is supported by a similar movement from perception to ontology, a movement towards a metaphysics. This association, a form of constant gesturing or pointing to as a way to shore up the coherence of racial difference, is analogous to referring to human nature as a way to legitimate an idea of the human. That it is natural and therefore true. Because this is self-referential it is possible to call this social constructionism, yet doing so does nothing to critique the ability to move from ontic to ontological as a constant mobilization and defense of the decision to race human beings. An example of this is given when in the essay "The Friend," Agamben describes "friend" as nonpredicative, while assigning "White" as predicative (2009: 29). As he writes, "Calling someone 'friend' is not the same as calling him 'white,' 'Italian,' or 'hot,' since friendship is neither a property nor a quality of a subject" (31). The possibility that White can be used as a definition of being, just as the friend for Agamben, that they could come to mean the same thing is given both by his definition of friendship as "a proximity that resists both representation and conceptualization" (31) and his acceptance of Aristotle's (1999: 1170a28–1171b35) description of friendship in *Nicomachean Ethics* as defining a community. Does not Whiteness serve as a description, an ineffable proximity, and a community at the same time? It is this characteristic of race I wish to bring forth by describing it as susceptible to a movement as a social concept from the ontic to ontology, where it almost but not quite becomes a type of human being.

There is an inexorable need to affirm the truth of the idealization of race, that humans are raced, but the movement from the experience of social events up to but not including the point of a self-referential metaphysics is normally enough to dissuade resistance to the efficacy of the conception. The idea of the social construction therefore assists in this strategy of deflecting the political heft of a critique of the possibility of races. The challenge in this framing of the problem of race is how to arrest this movement from the ontic, "comporting towards beings," to the attempt at the "pure, rational . . . knowledge of the specific wholeness of its principle divisions" (Heidegger 1997: 6) without merely reproducing the circular gesture in the argument about racial human nature.

This model of racial politics accepts the premise that self-referentiality is enough to found a community, that there is no critique of strong evaluations, personal preferences, or desires that can break this circularity that ends in perception. From this invention and application of an idea of human difference comes the decision to develop its importance throughout society as a way to define something akin to "human nature"; a typology of human distinctions that are important enough to be learned is a form of politics. The social coherence of the community of raced subjects is a function of this gestural aspect of race; it is unaffected by claims of equality at the level of normal human social interaction. Try this as a way to understand what I mean here. Ask a room full of persons to raise their hands if they are White. The result is an example of the gesture that defies the argument for human particularity and diversity across and within racial typologies. It is as though in the impropriety of the query the raised hands no longer belong to the bodies of the persons who simultaneously must deny that race matters, politically and socially. The ease with which we want this gesture to merely imply the existence of an Other rather than their subordination is a result of this constant movement between ontic and ontology as a way to justify the initial decision of sameness in difference (Said 1979; Stallybrass and White 1986; Grosrichard 1998; LaCapra 1998).

We can therefore not defeat the idea of race by claiming that it is merely "social." Unable to halt the forward movement towards the idea, we are left addressing its actualization in the possibility of racial communities, of an essence that if not "true," is argued to be almost, maybe, nearly so, across discrete populations of persons in US society. Again, to dissolve the perception of race it is not enough to say it is not true, not scientific, or a social construction, since the constant movement forward from ontic to ontology, from perception to knowledge that the politics of race allows, makes this critique meaningless. This movement, the possibility of a gesture from *bios* to *zoe*, of acting from an idea of human difference that depends on discrete anchor points of the body on the one hand and the truth of the human on the other hand, makes race so effective as an idea of community. In this politics of establishing and reproducing race its veridication is never quite the physical nor that of human natural types. This allows for action since this contingent truth defines the perceptions of others that we use to make sense of our world. This is not a justificatory politics, the racial hierarchy that is created.

What I am trying to get at here is that our use of race today is not confined to a simple static description of difference, nor is it limited to removing and switching the language we use to designate Blackness or Whiteness, such as using the N word instead of another slur. Instead, race defines a subject for which it is also possible to switch symbols, to speak of welfare recipients while meaning Blacks in discourse, and never even mention race, and still have this be understood as one of many ways that connect the racial hierarchy to specific social practices. This metonymic development of racial practices in effect means that it exists outside of individual language use as a designation of human difference. Its reproduction is the purview of communities of persons and its definition is unavailable to individual critique or change. To develop a critical theory of race we need to work from how it is used today, our perception of it from within the apparatus of racial equality.

THE PERSONAL IS POLITICAL

That this can never be what a person just is, physically White or Black, and that we cannot approach the truth of human existence and our true nature does not mitigate against the facility of its application; race maps itself onto the basic desire to impose our perceptions onto the world around us, and as such is perceived as an indelible part of the social environment. From phenotype to behavior, the idea of racial difference defines a special type of social element, one that recognizes the indeterminacy of the problem of other minds as a political effect. Race cannot be alone in this role. The racial subjection of the person is exposed as constantly moving from *bios* to *politia*, as limning and informing the discursive elements that define many of the social practices of the society.

So, how is it taught and what are the boundaries of the discrete communities of race? Instead of cats and coffee, it may help to think of it in terms of the way advertising works, or more specifically, the way McDonald's corporation has marketed their products over several decades. The current commercials for the Big Mac depend upon those used previously. The narrative of Ronald McDonald has evolved with the needs of the market to promote the company's products. What we see today on TV, under the golden arches, is a product of this historical evolution as a function of market decisions, each done with the aim of preserving the products as ideas. In exactly this fashion, race is not merely a desire for subordination, for marking or typing humans, for hedging one's bets and predicting behavior; it is an idea that depends on the history of its evolution in society. At any moment we only receive the immediate description of race, but have available to view many of the discourses and elements by which it was applied in the past. These exist within the repository that is the racial community, since it is the confirmation of this evolution that allows for their definition. McDonald's corporation has survived and exists because it continues to define a collection of things as a product for consumers.

Of course, race and human beings are not burgers and fictional clown figures. Instead of the marketplace as a determinant of success or of survival, race describes a community of persons such that this allows for the subordination of entire groups of persons by others. Race is not an internalization of the idea within persons, but a description of communities of persons such that it is possible to define a polity that is stable enough to be defined as a democracy. A racial community is not a corporation working within the marketplace for goods and services in a democratic polity. But it is useful to think in these terms since today the corporation is described by many as a collective entity that is also similar to that of a person, a unified body with specific goals. It has political status and is perceived in its general description as important to the health and welfare of US democracy. At the same time it is important to differentiate a racial community from that of an economic corporation. While, for example, Whites are consumers of Whiteness, the determination of participation is not only given by the constant availability of goods for exchange. Race describes for persons a legacy of practices of difference, a threshold of origination or birth that is the affirmation of a decision to race. Once determined, a person is always just that race, a participant in a community defined by this designation. That race is a way to ensure or mark the subordination of other persons is always described as incidental to what could be called an onto-theological process that defines racial origin and community membership. Race does this with the same tenacity with which a corporation desires to survive and thrive, but does so as a force in the arena of societal goals, that which defines the direction and development of the polity itself. To critique this description of racial politics in the US we need to address the problem of community, how racial communities define racial subjects, and the politics that supports their description. We need to come up with a way to show that the assumptions of difference used to form racial community practices are false.

As Jean-Luc Nancy observes, community in the US today is today pre-political; it is a form of interiority and not realized at the level of politics (2010: 40). To express the idea of a racial community politically as a public act is to potentially threaten to reproduce the Jim Crow laws and the racist legislation of the state constitutions of the last two hundred years. US democratic society was able to create political stability initially only by describing the political theology of race's origin, a form of mythical ontology of the polity, using race as a founding principle of the society's political organization (Mills 1997).

Nancy identifies the absence or refusal of a continued reliance on a particular political theological conceptual apparatus as the necessary test for European democracy today. In the US, the major political apparatus is that described in the last chapter, that which defines racial politics. The difference between the countries in Europe and the US has been that the US was until recently always an explicitly racial polity, in ways similar to that described by White Australia policies or South Africa under apartheid. Nazi Germany was an aberration for Europe in this case of slightly more than a decade. This European racial political-theological position was exported to the colonies but thought unnecessary until recently as a main organizing political principle for countries in Europe. What existed in the US was a racial state, not a state that represented the entire population, but one that represented the interests of a select community of people, those who were White. The US was begun and thrived as a nation on the idea of different categories of membership, based initially on wealth, gender, race, and later on ethnicity as well. It is difficult to reconcile this political model of differential membership with the description of equality otherwise thought necessary to maintain social order within democratic political institutions.

The idea of race assumes several communities, and one of the important questions today in the US is how important these definitional boundaries of racial community are in the context of larger societal goals. I believe we are in a period of racial turmoil and conflict similar to that experienced in the immediate aftermath of the Civil War, the collapse of the Jim Crow Era, and the forced capitulation of the Civil Rights Movement. It has taken four decades of steady local conflict over the scope of civil-rights legislation and the concomitant description of racial equality for the problem of race to return to the center of American national politics. We can see our current political situation as bracketed in this sense by the two Nobel Peace Prizes of Martin Luther King Jr. and Barack Obama.

PLURALISM AND DEMOCRACY

The idea of racial communities in conflict mirrors that conception of plurality and division, that idea in the US of federal contra state and local government, which many political theorists argue is the foundation of representative democratic society. The importance of race in housing, education, employment, and in social life establishes the role of a community as a racial idea empirically. What does it take, on the other hand, by way of a community experience for someone to say, or act on the idea, that he or she prefers not to live around someone of a different race?

Race must be very important if living next to someone of a different race somehow impacts how you live in your own home. What is the sense of community that is threatened by the neighbor, such that it can readily be turned into a concern over changing property values? What is it that has us identify with persons who hesitate to move into a neighborhood because Blacks live there? The form of statistical assumption or argument often brought forward as a justification for social choices is normally viewed as being racial if it involves a store owner following around a Black individual in the store, or the police profiling someone Black driving in a car. People are not normally viewed as statistics or general popular stereotypes; they are individuals. Something must occur for Blacks to be first seen as representations, subjects derived from a description of racial communities in conflict. As representations they are available to statistics that depend on similar classifications of difference. To speak of "those Blacks who live across the street" addresses a different politics in the US than to speak of "the people who live across the street," where the subjection remains that of location and not human type.

Even though you rarely hear someone speak of the White community as a unified conception, it exists in ways that mirror those that enable someone to speak of the Black community, or to use the term *Blacks*. The same empirical factors that define the economic and social parameters of Blackness also define Whiteness. A common experience of discrimination does not make a community, however, but rather a class of victims. Segregation establishes common social practices and expectations across several categories for a group, and in this way we can speak of a community of persons who are similar through their experiences with how they use race. In their respective communities Blacks and Whites have inherited practices and social narratives that reflect hundreds of years of the description of race.

This history is not merely the subtle, nuanced language of social discrimination, but until recently included the creation of racial social difference by force; this force included lynchings, beatings, rape, formal government policies, and economic campaigns to make sure that Blacks did not acquire wealth, influence, and status. These practices delineated the separation of the races into communities through a politics of representation. Individual persons were described as representative of their race, as confined by it in ways that superseded personal character. This use gave race substance in the descriptions of human lives; it became real. While lynching and race riots no longer occur, the social practice of distinguishing between racial categories of persons persists, as do economic and political practices that, while they may not always violate the letter of the current law regarding racial equality, reproduce racial segregation in housing, lending practices to businesses, conditions of employment, and education.

A part of the politics of race today is accounted for by the way we inherit race, how the description of racial communities has evolved. Why is the novel *To Kill a Mockingbird* still taught in American high schools today, or why do movies like *Precious* or novels such as *The Help* have such a popular following? We don't have the ability to assess the way that others experience race based on our own individual situation, so instead we use a type of politics of community to discern this, to make judgments as to what race still means today. The discursive practices of racial difference operate using concepts derived from the economic market for resources, from popular ideas of multiculturalism and diversity, and within the legal language of antidiscrimination politics, as well as from traditional descriptions of racial difference in society. The absence of formal segregation has not made the importance and social viability of these racial communities less salient; it has merely shifted the way we speak of them.

But what is the idea of community at work here if not merely the purposeful coincidence of the different practices of segregation to give empirical substance to racial typologies? How is this description of community then related to the definition of an ideal community, of language and of ideas that arrange social practices to the benefit of its members, rather than shared trauma? Today, on the one hand, you have a Black community that describes a political efficacy derived from the status of its members as victims of racism, and on the other you have a community of Whites that requires that each of its members deny its political efficacy as a racial community that unfairly oppresses other groups. In the way that has been discussed above, this dual description of community along the lines of race is appropriate; Black/White communities are reflections of each other. Returning to an example above, if you ask a room full of Whites to raise their hands if they are White, there is no hesitation in knowing what is being asked, and they do not need to inquire of others in the room as to what is meant. Everyone knows what Whiteness means, but the politics of its expression and the impact of this community on the polity is what needs to be brought into focus.

It is possible to nuance this idea of racial community to suggest that over time the multiplicity of race has led to the creation of cultures, ways of acting that also define the attribution of race beyond that of this duality of discrimination. One might say that the presence of these communities has led to a social and cultural description for each. These descriptions of culture today resist their definition as derived from the pernicious distinction of race, of being the result of identifying victims and perpetrators of claims of absolute human typologies. At the same time, the problem with the description of a racial community is exactly this dilemma, how to define it in ways that do not merely reflect this dual description of difference, metaphysical and real, White and Black.

It is important to apply the concept of community here because it allows for a description of how race would be used beyond the attribution of individual prejudice. As Foucault points out in relation to the imperative expressed by Socrates to care for oneself, in a community it is possible to learn to work together to define values and actions (2008b: 110, 273). This provides an explanation for how someone who is White would live without conscious individual racial animus towards Blacks as an explicit set of beliefs, and yet act with the social practices learned from within the idea of the White community, as a collective set of ideas and behaviors that then discriminate against Blacks as an individual representative of a group.

To repudiate this form of Whiteness would require a rejection of the norms and activities of the community that depends on this duality of belief and unconscious learned behavior for coherence. This is difficult because today the possibility of a politics of racial community is denied *prima facie* as a precondition for normal White subjection. This is something the racist does, not the normal White person. It becomes important for Whites to refuse to address the role that race plays in society in determining housing, education, and employment opportunities because otherwise this brings into question the substance of White subjection. The persistence of racial segregation throughout the society is instead described as coincidental or a function of class dynamics. The idea of racial communities in conflict gets at the problem today of establishing collective definitions of racial difference through resource distribution rather than legal decision, and also includes in its purview the study of the possible cultural and social practices that exist as a consequence of the recent history of defining racial communities outside the law.

THE CRISIS OF DEMOCRACY

Since the presidential election in 2008, the standard of living of African Americans has deteriorated significantly, due principally to the impact of the Great Recession, but also because of the steady erosion of community political efficacy since the 1970s (Tate 2003). The election of Obama has not resulted in similar electoral gains for Blacks elsewhere in the political landscape. Instead, there has been a huge backlash against the organization of support that led to the election of the first Black president. This backlash has created a new identity for many, specifically for those opposed to his success, and to any potential significance his presidency may otherwise have for Blacks and the struggle for racial equality. That the same group of people would say they believe that it is important to support the president of United States of America as a symbol of the American political experiment in democracy is not viewed as a contradiction, simply because the status of Blacks in US society remains a salient political question. To many, Obama is not an American; the controversy over the birth certificate exemplifies how important it is to define his status as not threatening the way we look at our American experiment, as one that is first and foremost for a community of persons who are White.

There is little parity beyond the principled application of formal equality of opportunity between White and Black in the US. If we strip away the euphoria of the immediate post–civil rights period, as we must do the after the 2008 election, the absence of instruments and policies to create more substantive forms of racial equality in US society is striking. What happened to all of those people born before the mid-1950s? Where did their experience and beliefs concerning racial segregation and formal inequality go with the advent of new laws of antidiscrimination in the 1960s and 1970s? Changing their actions to conform to the new requirements for formal racial equality, the description of racial difference was pushed down by individuals into the social elements that could establish distinct racial communities, overdetermining rather than eliminating the coherence of absolute racial social differences. The question that has to be asked is how effective has this current politics of racial equality been in changing the social practices of racial segregation taught to everyone? And what of the children born in the 1960s and 1970s? Have they given up the idea of superiority that Whiteness brought them, the sense of community and purpose, of direction and status?

Consider how a group of persons establishes a set of rules by which to determine how they should act towards one another. Several things are important: 1) the goal or task to which the group is collectively oriented (why they are together in the first place), 2) the type of resources available to the activities they participate in, and 3) how they communicate their ideas to one another. The assumption in a constitutional democracy is that there is a common purpose, for example, to form a more perfect union of individuals and their activities within a defined polity or geographical area, or to foster the development of a specific type of person. Typically, the government is formed by the people to represent their development of diverse interests over time, to define a purpose that always meets and exceeds the ambitions of its participants.

Out of many, one society. As more than the sum of its parts, a democracy provides something more than what each person contributes. But what happens if the excess, that which society produces as a collective enterprise, requires that individuals change their actions, change how they act towards other persons in the society? Or, in reverse, what happens if the description of the society has always been that some must suffer for the good of others, that specific people should be sacrificed to ensure the prosperity of some others?

To what extent is the goal of US democratic society to ensure that race remains a central organizing principle? It would be difficult to figure out the importance of race early on in determining the growth of a community of Americans in the new US. We know it was a critical social and political factor in many people's lives, and we know that at the time of independence there were millions of Black slaves living in the US. The formal legal status of African slaves and free Blacks as American citizens was settled in the late 1800s.

Barack Obama's election in 2008 and reelection in 2012 therefore reveal how membership in the polity continues to be connected to the importance of race as communities that distribute resources and communicate ideas in the society. The dilemma for US democratic politics is to determine what it means that a member of the Black community has obtained the highest political office in the country.

To what extent is it possible to establish politically that his election still leaves something unavailable to Blacks as individuals and continues to deprive the Black community of something important in the society? Barack Obama's election in 2008 could be viewed as signaling the final end of Jim Crow almost fifty years after the political changes of the 1960s. After his election what remains as an exclusively White occupation or office? It is only in the moment of his election that the political consequences of racial equal opportunity are finally available to all Whites as a community.

Prior to this event in 2008, no Black person could represent America, in ways that allow for a member of this community to become the leader of the political institutions of the society. This is not in turn an issue with the role of the presidency, but that race defines who leads, who defines the agenda, and which person should be considered first for scarce resources in the society. It is still considered wrong somehow if a Black person receives something important if someone White does not already have it. Traditionally in a division of goods, Blacks in America get a "fair" share so long as Whites are also getting an "equal" share. Under equality of opportunity, individuals can have different levels of resources across the racial divide so long as Whites retain superior access to the political, economic, and social resources collectively, as a community. To what extent can it be said that this hierarchy is still in effect if a Black man can be elected president in the US? At one level of course this is not a threat for Whites. All the presidents until now have been White.

The problem is that this idea of race dividing people into groups in the US is so accepted that it seems natural to argue over the distributive definition of fairness between members of each community. Does the election of a Black person to the presidency initiate a political crisis that requires constitutional remedies so that the ability of the office of the president to make substantial changes in the society is curtailed? What happens if Barack Obama uses the powers of the office to address the problem of racial inequality in the US? The political problem is that the White guy lost, even if it cannot be said openly, as this raises the question of how a White person could lose to someone Black, and whether this is indicative of a new and undiscovered threat to the White community posed by the political assumptions of racial equality.

It is in this moment the society is confronting its continuing legacy of racism. The heated antipathy in popular discourse that surrounds the Obamas reveals this more than anything else. The disclaimer of the Tea Party movement as to the racism of its members is a case in point but is not itself more than symptomatic as a political movement of the unease of the larger White community. The problem of race in America is not located in the idea of recognition or equality, but in the definition of ineffability, of something outside the human and yet derived from the body, that makes certain people superior. What we are facing here is not a day-to-day struggle between a sheriff and a group of protesters. Instead, we are in the middle of a new Civil Rights Movement, one that until now has not been acknowledged and that involves how we describe the hierarchy of race in spite of a politics that defines racial equality as equal opportunity.

CONCLUSION: MISTAKING FORMAL EQUALITY FOR SUBSTANTIAL RACIAL PROGRESS

The mistake we have made in recent decades is to focus on strengthening the availability of opportunities even as research has shown that the possibility of getting a job, attending college, or becoming president has not appreciably changed the role of race to distinguish resource distribution and political efficacy in the society. We bemoan the inability of Blacks to take advantage of opportunities without addressing the fact that racism is about hierarchy, not equality. A young Black person experiences this description of values, even as formal equality is stated in terms that often seem just out of reach. It is common to hear a young Black child say, "Yes, I know I can be anybody I want, even president," but the unstated question in his or her mind is "but how do I get there from here?" White supremacy, the explicit hierarchical distribution of important resources in the society based on a racial typology in which Whiteness is the highest category, is not threatened directly by the political demands of equal opportunity. What we need in the US, to borrow a phrase from Nancy, is a Nietzschean democracy, a change in the description of values that make up the table of values in the social world (2010: 22). This is easier said than done.

How do we leave behind the idea of race and suggest that someone who otherwise would be defined as Black could have a role conceptualizing the values of society explicitly for Whites? As a partner who may in fact have better ideas, as a person? How do we set aside a difference that currently prohibits a person from directing, defining, or leading where a society will go? This condition is only partially met by having someone Black lead a company or group of Whites while moving the plot forward for them. The criterion of a new politics of race is that it is no longer important in the group, that the fact of Blackness no longer disqualifies the person from having a say in all aspects of the society. We have to be free not only to fail, but to succeed, to win. For some areas of a market-driven economy, in a competitive social and political environment, only by winning in a zero-sum game, in any game, is it possible to begin to say that race does not matter in American society.

To pretend that consolation prizes are also okay, even welcomed, in a situation where Whiteness is defined by victory over others, by superiority, is to be disingenuous. Obama's re/election offers the potential therefore to bring into question how we address the idea that Blackness could disappear as a conception of difference from Whiteness, that the resource hierarchies based on race could dissolve. The fact that many people openly spoke of the worry that Blacks would take Obama's election victory in 2008 to think more of themselves, that there was open concern that now the status of being White was under threat, indicates how racial narratives are not changed merely by the election of one person to a position of status. For that is what the office of the president is in the US, the position of commander in chief, the self-described leader of the Free World, and the final authority for executive political power in US society.

Now, of course, we could select a leader who while Black allows for, or gives cover to, the continued racial practices that occur elsewhere in society. But this argument also assumes that merely occupying an executive office gives the person political omniscience, rather than having his or her actions limited by the functions of the office. This is not the case. I don't think it matters very much what views President Obama has about racial politics given the constraints of the office. No matter what Obama believes, his presidency will nominally provide support for a claim that racism is a thing of the past because that is the political discourse of racial equality. But his presidency is a form of retreat from the idea of a coextensive segregation of the races; it is a loss of White sovereign authority in the US even if as an individual President Obama has little impact on the sheer scale of racial practices in the society. The problem is that we have reached the limit of the political efficacy of Black exceptionalism and the description of the White racist as a way to conceal the continued importance of race in the society. I will develop this argument more in the coming chapters.

4 Race and Community

> Silent and unavowable like sovereignty itself.
>
> —Derrida, *Rogues*

> The other is the form the self takes where inside intersects with outside, the proper with the common, immunity with community.
>
> —Esposito, *Immunitas*

Without some way to avoid the force of legal equality on everyday practices, the distinction of race would quickly disappear. People obey the law when possible, so the attenuation of the formal description of racial equality occurs because something else exists that makes it possible to describe racial distinctions as permissible. From this it is easy to see the importance today of describing a racial community in terms of culture or history, behavior, or custom. It is almost as though from the findings of *Brown v. Board of Education* in 1954 to the successes of the Civil Rights Movement of the 1960s there was an attempt to shift the onus of race as something defined for Blacks to something defined for Whites, with the latter community then working to resist the consequences of formal equality once in place. For those who disagreed with the new change in legal racial practices, Whites could say that they were the ones who were unable to exercise their way of looking at the world. Their view as Whites that some people were inferior due to their race was now prohibited in public. If the person was Black, a claim of racial legal injustice was no longer appropriate since the individualism of the market replaced the formal racial distinctions of Jim Crow.

While it is easy to see how there would be an initial *ressentiment* on the part of Whites in the 1960s to the changes in their formal status, it is harder to figure out why this did not fade away with time. It is now almost fifty years since the Voting Rights Act, and politicians still try to undermine the substance of its provisions. Why has the idea of denying Blacks the vote not disappeared over time? It certainly is not as simple as saying that African Americans traditionally vote with the Democratic Party. It is an attempt to control the political demands made by Blacks.

In the midst of this politics of determining an institutional framework for racial equality, how do we assign authority for the truth of the experience of racism (Balfour 2011: 90)? Certainly for most people today, race is something that if possible we avoid speaking of; we expect to act within the law or when the law cannot apply to us according to the social practices of race that we have learned as members of a racial community. For many people this means that they have social behaviors, learned norms of action towards others, and use race without knowing or acknowledging it. As racial subjects in this way, how is race to be criticized?

I find myself in sympathy here with Foucault's description of the *parrhesiast* (2008b; 2010). He describes how the person of the philosopher should develop his or her thinking parallel to that of the needs of government, to offer ideas so as to make better decisions without directly advocating policy positions. That only through the actions of someone able to tell the truth to government and to act as a critic can just governance occur. An important function of the truth teller is therefore to speak truth to power, as the weak can avail themselves of their position to appeal to the stronger. If the state is amenable, the truth is a way for those most vulnerable in society to provide an alternative voice from that of the language of rights and obligations (Foucault 2010: 163). It is a way to challenge authority while accepting the relationship between persons as that of difference.

In contrast to this in the US today, African Americans are not seen as in a position of defining the truth of racism. This is not because they are collectively weak economically, socially, or politically, but because they are described as a group in such a way as to prohibit a critique of the continued use of race to define their lives (Foucault 2008b: 318). Instead of giving the racially subordinate the ability to judge the actions against them, this judgment is withheld by obfuscating the location of the power used to differentiate racially between persons; they are unable to find a person or persons responsible for their condition except themselves. Truth and the law are confused in the state of exception defined by the politics of racial equality (Agamben 1998: 65).

As an African American what one can do is to acknowledge that this is a position where the only option is to appeal as during the Civil Rights Movement to a politics outside of the law and reason, that Whiteness through the application of formal racial equality of opportunity precludes a discourse of criticism by Blacks. While racism is messy and vague in its defense, it is not in its application. We do not address the problem by being close to it, as in being one of the elite who then is able to illicit a response from our peers. For example, Clarence Thomas has been silent on the bench of the Supreme Court since 2006. The last time he spoke he made a case for the harm of cross burning, as describing a position where First Amendment protections do not apply: to burn a cross is not a political statement but an act of terror (Sacks 2011). This argument failed to move the other justices. The problem is not his silence, but that Justice Thomas was unable to convince the other justices, even in his authority as an African American from Georgia who grew up in the period when cross burning was practiced regularly as a way to intimidate the Black community.

To become successful as an African American is to be used to facilitate the discourse of tolerance, as an instrument in the cause of formal racial equality, not of racial justice. To expect otherwise is to misunderstand the truth being described by the other community. Whites are not giving up their assumption of superiority; it is what Whiteness is for them. In order for change to occur, the authority being told the truth has to be receptive to what you are saying. They have to be willing to engage the difference you represent as a potential critique; they have to be able to listen. That this is impossible for Whiteness does not thereby obviate the importance for Blacks in describing the truth of race in the society.

LOOKING FOR TRUTH IN ALL THE WRONG PLACES

What is the truth of Blackness? From within the tradition of African American studies, this statement initially brings to mind a convergence of several ideas: James Baldwin's stricture that you know where the bottom is, for there you find the Black man; Frantz Fanon's query as to the impossible possibility of the Negro in our midst; and the movement from *bios* to *politia* evident in the resistance to forms of Black subjection found in the works of Toni Morrison and Zora Neal Hurston. These are all truths that describe the recent Black experience in America. In this chapter I want to explicitly invoke Foucault's (2010) use of the concept of truth telling in his later public lectures to explore the possibility of a Blackness that can speak its name today.

It is difficult to become a subject that can tell the truth about the facts of racism in America. The circumstances of Black subjectivity make it difficult to imagine let alone establish a venue for critical expression. In part this is because it has become increasingly difficult in the academy to provide social concepts that are critical of how race is used. This is in turn a problem of audience and subjection, how people describe others as raced differently, as much as it is an effect of how the politics of race has developed into something that people must avoid rather than confront.

We want the race question, how we are to use race, to be settled and no longer be open to political negotiation. To do otherwise is to remain vulnerable, to take risks, to have to question how we each use race constantly. If we can't be racist, how are we supposed to act? An example of this problem is when another professor suggests to me that they do not find it easy to help Black students because they worry that it will be seen as a form of racism. The professor is unsure how the student will take the professor's interest and solicitude and worries that the student will perceive the help of the professor as condescending. Implicit in this justification is uncertainty as to what racism is and how to develop a critical perspective to the use of race.

What does it mean to treat everyone equally in the face of a tension between what is really two competing political ideals? The idea of a universal application of the law to every citizen is found throughout the institutional fabric of US government. The idea of meeting the needs of individual citizens, as individuals or members of groups, is also central to democratic government, even if disguised by the process of assigning representatives for specific geographical areas and the support for the rights of minorities in a majoritarian system. This simple construction of two ideals makes it easy to see how the conflict over how race is used in the US would lead to a series of universal prescriptions as to what racial equality means in public life. Some idea of racial difference is permitted so long as this does not impinge on the rights of everyone to form appropriate life plans.

Even with this simple model of racial equality we can see that it depends on the ability to define race as a good and not a description of a hierarchy of types of persons. Race has to be a cultural or social good without subordinating social consequences. It is here that this model collapses, since the description of race prior to the application of the model was always a description of types and social hierarchy. The inability to effect a caesura or complete cut from the social description of race in the past, to redefine the racial communities from the period of Jim Crow into something merely cultural, is what obviates the efficacy of the institutional construction of formal racial equality. The question of the truth of race today is even more important given this desire to obscure its political effects beyond the space of formal racial equality.

OEDIPUS AND ION

Using examples from *Oedipus Rex* and the *Ion*, Foucault, in his lectures from 1982 to 1983, titled *The Government of Self and Others*, argues for the importance of truth, *parrhesia*, as a tool to engage political reason in democratic society. The difficulty Foucault faces is how to explain the means by which a subject can halt or bring into question, irrupt, the normal flow of values and processes that describe others in society. *Alethurgy*, or truth telling, fills a gap in his analysis of the problem of subjection in contemporary society. The truth that he describes via Oedipus Rex and Ion is one of origin (Grene and Lattimore 1958; Sophocles 2002). Both are tales of the origin of Greek society, and the truth is only revealed in the progress of each play through a struggle for understanding the self as a part of the description of the polity. In each we are reminded that we are to learn about ourselves through the acts ascribed to us by others. Whites in the US today understand that the description of themselves by Blacks is the surest sign of a problem with race in the society.

In Foucault's analysis, the protagonist only learns the truth through the risks that others take to bring this knowledge. This process can be seen by the difficulty by which a succession of persons try to enlighten Oedipus to the truth of his situation (Sophocles 2002). *Parrhesia* or truth telling is a requirement for the description of a self that is able to participate in the conversation about the development of society. As such it is more than citizenship status for those who have access to it, those who are allowed have the right to question the structure of society and its ethos. This is true for race as well in the US today. It is more than citizenship since it describes those able to determine the political direction of the society. This explains the constant return by the media and political organizations to the perceived problem of Obama's birth certificate, even when he has sought to shift their attention to something less obviously about his place as an African American in the society. The question of the place of Blacks in society must remain available to White interpretation, even when the Black person is the president of the United States.

In both plays, *Oedipus* and *Ion*, *parrhesia* is defined by family and societal origin as well as through explicitly acknowledging a responsibility for the welfare of the polity itself. The subject able to speak the truth does so because its knowledge is the foundation upon which the society rests. At the same time there is a distinction between the legal right to speak, as citizenship, and the ability to speak such that one's statements direct the development of the society.

Foucault distinguishes between three types of *parrhesia*. It is political *parrhesia* to which Blacks do not have access. Blacks in the US can, at considerable personal risk, speak truth to power, but cannot themselves be the audience of the powerful; they do not make up the front rank of individuals in society (Foucault 2010: 163). This can be observed in the ability to detach the office of the presidency from its racial authority such that Obama can be elected, just as has occurred for Clarence Thomas and other African Americans who achieve positions of stature and potential influence in the society. The position of authority to design the polity is not located in any one political position; instead, the president serves at the behest of others, and it is this representative quality that is criticized by Whites who feel that even the idea that a Black person can achieve the office is inappropriate to their sense of political development in the US. The key here is of course that the texts Foucault is referring to in the lectures are plays, fictions and not historical facts themselves. We use literature like this today, in this case to bring the truth of the origins of the polity and the role of the individual as leader into focus for the audience.

My interest is in how Foucault uses each play to support the idea of *parrhesia* while ignoring the role of difference, of the fate of those of different origins and those unable to speak the truth in the moment of law giving. I believe that today in the US we similarly ignore the inability to include Blacks in a description of the society, as a part of society such that they determine its direction. The figures of Ion and Oedipus in each play represent their societies as both recipients and assayers of *parrhesia*. Their struggles are those of working out the role of truth in the polity. Whites represent, and expect to do so as members of a specific type of community, the important political truths of US society.

As in the example above of my professor colleague, this tension between our discomfort with race and its everyday importance is resolved by defaulting to whatever status quo exists as to the public definition of racial politics today. The assumption is that while not comprehensive in its assessment of the important social aspects of racism, the status quo is currently the best that we can do in the law and in our everyday social practices. There are two problems with this process. First it relies on a specific conception of how the use of race changes over time or what racism is as a phenomenon, and second it depends on the availability of legal recourse and legislative arrangements to an extent that threatens the importance of other institutional processes in society that potentially address the use of race by individuals. The difficulty here is again in how we look at race within a public discourse about equality and the importance of human difference in social life. If race is something that is defined and used within a special set of bad practices, the prohibition of these acts on the part of individuals would eliminate this definition of racism. If, on the other hand, this set of actions, be they speech or other practice, are merely a subset or the result of social ideals that find coherence in several areas of everyday life in America, then we need to explore of what these ideals consist.

Today the Black subject still cannot tell the truth of its existence. By this I mean that the problem of race in America is that of denying the ability of the Black individual subject to witness for itself, its own experience, and to have that experience of racism accepted as equally important to that of the racial experiences of Whites. The changes in racial politics that we have seen in recent decades are a result of a collective political statement that impacted the law and society. It was not enough for one Black person to protest sitting in the back of a bus, or to refuse to enter the rear of a restaurant, or to dare to speak to a White person while looking him or her in the face. This did not change the widespread use of race segregation since the confrontation by the individual was not directed at the location where the definition of race as a social concept was developed. Instead, it took social protest and unrest, a collective claim to suffering and injustice, and the suffering of Whites alongside those of Blacks to change the perception of racial justice from that during the Jim Crow period.

This is still true today. To be not merely heard but understood, the Black subjects must not only develop a critical capacity for self-discovery but wait for someone White to tell them who they are, and give them their particular racial subjectivity. This demands a similar critical capacity on the part of Whites. This argument for recognition is incoherent, in that to be defined as Black is to be a subject that does not have the ability to speak the truth of race without prior White understanding. The Black subject can only appeal for clemency or mercy for one's own abjection. To do otherwise would be to threaten or repudiate the definition of Whiteness. Foucault describes in his lectures situations where a person speaks of the injustice of the society, but he does not take up the problem of when the person is a subject that is defined as not speaking the truth, as unable to do so because, unlike Ion or Oedipus, he or she is not given the status to do so.

For much of the history of race relations in the US, this problem was explicit. African Americans could not witness against Whites in court, could not speak in their own defense, and were not accepted as credible speakers of the truth of their experience as humans. The Black subject, the slave, or free Black person defined against that of the slave, was unable to provide a description in the law other than that which defined Blackness as infrahuman.

This was demonstrated by speaking of African Americans as a group, using collective terms to describe the individual trying to speak. This is the legacy contained in the use of the N word, for example, and a simple explanation for why it should not be used. The social products of Blacks were the property of Whiteness. Only those things undesirable for Whites were ceded to Blacks as their own, and so the definition of race was always that of facilitating White community development. Those who were White were able to appropriate the persons and productive activity of Blacks within a contractual system of property rights between Whites and free Blacks.

To be free for Blacks did not mean that the status as potential property was vitiated, but instead strengthened the conception of Blackness, of its content, as something always under inspection by Whites. The exceptional status of some confirmed the subordinate status of the many. Black slaves were emancipated, but the idea of Blackness as the property of Whites, the salience of a definition of Whiteness that allows for the capacity to own the social life and activity of someone defined as Black, was not abolished. To free Blacks and remove the legal basis for enslavement shifted the social burden of this idea of Blackness and Whiteness onto that of the definition of citizenship in America. It created a distinction between those designated as citizens and that social community that determines sovereign authority. This is the difference made by Foucault between the framework, or *isogoria*, and the truth, or *parrhesia* (2010: 71, 154–63). In this case the apparatus of racial equality of opportunity provides the social and political context for the *parrhesiast*. As Foucault points out, however, "in democratic equality *parrhesia* was a principle of differentiation, a caesura" (2010: 203).

I want to use this idea, that of the Black subject as always lacking the claim to veracity, of still being suspect as a source of truth, to unpack a problem central to the use of race today. The current political structure does not allow us to speak the truth of racism (Foucault 2010: 89). Race in America functions similarly to the place of birth in the two plays Foucault describes, and race disallows the speaking Black subject from determining the practice of the law. America does not have a politics that dissolves the location of where you are from by race, be it defined by blood, hypodescent, community, or tradition, as in those who fly the Confederate flag to support their heritage against those who could not do so. As Foucault points out in the *Ion*, the problem for Ion is not that his matrilineal descent would disallow him *parrhesia* in Athenian society, but that he must be from Athens, and his purported father is not. He must be able to claim a specific type of connection to be an heir to the nation or society, to be its guide. Such is the case with race with America.

For Foucault, the truth is a reproach of the indifference of fate; it stands against the vicissitudes of daily life, the random interpretations of events, as a statement of what has occurred for the subject, his or her experience (2010: 126). That the interpretation of the truth takes the form of the discourses available to the subject is clear in his lecture, as Foucault develops a triple convergence of remonstrance, gold, and fertility that he identifies as important in the *Ion*. It is this that structures the form of the complaint by Creusa to Apollo in the *Ion*, a specific cry against injustice given the truth of her situation (133). To govern justly requires that the practice of governing allow for a critique of government as well as reason. For Foucault, public reason stands against private reason, and both are required for good governance.

While we cannot ignore the difference between our public description of racial equality and those beliefs we use every day, this model of *parrhesia* by Foucault is inadequate to the problem of intercommunity assessments of truth where the interrogative by the *parrhesiast* is to an individual that represents a group. The problem of racial injustice for society is not first a problem of individual rights and protections from harm, but an issue of the relationship of the event in question with the individuals and the description of the racial communities to which they belong.

How we approach the problem of race depends on where we place the emphasis in this situation. If we investigate the event where there is a specific use for race that is always suspect, this means that the larger description of racial community and typology that allows for both this specific use and the definition of racism in society to be left unaddressed. Such is the case if in our exploration of the problem of race in US society we merely focus on the problem of racial discrimination within institutions, the use of race as a criterion in hiring, for example, or evidence of racial prejudice in social interactions between persons such as in the use of the N word in discourse. By the time the event has occurred it is too late theoretically; the situation is already determined by the descriptions of racial community of which the person is a member. This means that to explore race we need to look at the idea of community upon which it depends.

RACIAL COMMUNITIES?

I describe here the idea of two distinct racial communities, one White and the other Black. This gets us away from the idea of the racial prejudice of the individual as a location for the study of racial politics and into the problem of racial subjection generally. It resolves the tension that otherwise occurs between an individual and racial subjection, the relationship persons have to the social practices of race that persist in US society.

Until 1865, Blacks were enslaved in the US (Blackmon 2009). In the period of Jim Crow that rapidly followed emancipation, segregation of the races was the law and social custom. Today there are still considerable problems with racial segregation, even if people speak of it now in terms of choice or class. For example, it is still very unusual to see a mixed Black and White couple, and it is common to speak of them socially that way, as "mixed" in racial terms, without reflecting on what this says about the importance we place on race in our everyday lives.

It is only in the context of the contemporary legal interpretation assigning responsibility for racism as located in an individual subject, that of the racist, that the conception of distinct racial communities was set aside as a popular idea. "Be true to your race," "do not be a race traitor," was, up until the 1960s, a common phraseology with which to define socially acceptable behavior across this community divide. The initial impetus for antidiscrimination law from the 1950s was to address the problem of the segregation of a community, and not the specific problem of individual racial discrimination. Without a definition of a community against which to define racism, for the collective culpability of Whites was exactly what had to avoided, vacated from its central place in the Jim Crow social and political inscription of racial difference on the entire society, the use of institutional segregation was replaced in the 1960s with a focus on the individual, without accounting for where the ideas of race were developed, how they were defined as a result of communication between persons, or as a product of communities that retained their force in everyone's lives. I will return to this idea in more detail later.

Traditionally democratic political theory conflates society and community, and does not consider the problem of multiple communities of persons, where these descriptions of community do not dissolve in the face of democratic governance (Rawls 1972). The individualism otherwise identifying the American, the US citizen-subject, is insufficiently robust; it is unable to exclude the pull of a definition of racial community (Kateb 1994). In spite of our best efforts, instead of countering the effects of race, the politics of democratic individualism facilitates the retreat of the reproduction of race behind the walls of discrete communities, seemingly concealed within the inviolate circumspection of the idea of privacy and personal choice. It is common to hear social scientists discuss resource differences in society in racial terms without a theory that addresses what is wrong with the idea of race being used. The normal assumption is to suggest that the description of race violates the conditions for the equal concern and respect necessary between persons in the liberal democratic political process. But there is not a description of what this then means for the process, to have a definition of a group that remains important yet does not meet this standard. This contradiction cannot be addressed at the level of the individual, because it is a problem at the level of the collective. As Nancy writes, "Community, far from being what society has crushed or lost, is what happens to us-question, waiting, event, imperative—in the wake of society (1991: 11). What would it mean to seek to dissolve the impact of one's racial community on persons in US society? The idea of racial equality merely moves around the application of the conception of the racial community within social practices; it does not erode the ability of the racial community to reaffirm itself. To see the extent of the political problem posed by race for US democratic development, it is useful to explore further some different descriptions of political community.

BLANCHOT AND THE DISAVOWAL OF COMMUNITY

Blanchot describes how it is in the moment of the removal of another individual, his or her death, that a community is realized for a person (1988: 9). This realization is matched by the birth of an individual into a relationship with the person. It is in the loss and acquisition of individuals that people find themselves confronted with their ideals, their descriptions of self that carry on beyond a specific relationship. We thereby, in the death and birth of another, take on a responsibility for the other. This is what founds community for Blanchot. The idea of a continuing relationship beyond death, the advent of one with birth, creates the community by defining its outside, its contingency (10). The White community exists as a force that defines persons who are White, against those who are defined as Black, as well as those other groups described in contrast to, or alongside, Whiteness.

Discussing the case of the death of the subject first, the definition of a White community would be described in that moment when someone ceases to be White, when he or she acts contrary to the definition of Whiteness, or when someone is sacrificed as a way to found community. The sacrifice of the other, the steady constant pressure on members to conform, and the need to disavow membership even as this act cements a person's status, comprise one way to describe Whiteness (Blanchot 1988: 15; DeMott 1996; Lipsitz 2006; Wise 2011). In this definition, to be able to act as a White person, to be a member of the community, would require the denial of the effects of race on individuals in society.

Denial of the prevalence of the values of Whiteness and racial hierarchy is a necessary but not sufficient condition for membership. It is not sufficient because it does not address the requirement of birth into the ongoing definition of Whiteness as a community with members that can be taught the meaning, as in limitations and possibilities, of race for individuals in the society. This is the opposite of the idea that community happens to individuals. Instead, with race the singularity of being is given by a description of community that resists application to certain persons, but simultaneously defines a type of person (Nancy 1991: 7).

In this perspective, Whiteness has always been about the sacrifice of the other to found a membership both stronger and more salient than mere American citizenship, but also coincident with what it means to be a founder of the nation and to be able to pass on the values that define one aspect of America. What matters today, then, is the ability to sacrifice others and to disavow responsibility for these acts. This would be the inability to be held accountable or to be punished for actions as Whites in such a way that the person or persons are forced to be sacrificed in turn and abjured by the community; immunity is a requirement of Whiteness. The lack of accountability and the need to make an other as an outsider define a community that defends itself. However, this is not the entirety of the definition of Whiteness. Really this describes only the upper limits, if you will, of Whiteness. Not its substance, but how it defines the ability to sacrifice another person to race as a decision.

Some type of reprieve must be possible through the selective disavowal of racism on the part of the White subject; otherwise, this political description of difference, the act of using race to define community, must be constant, always at work. As long as the racial hierarchy is unchallenged, in this approach to community by Blanchot, its operation is literally ignored; the presence of a community defined by race is easily disavowed in such a way that the individual who is White is able to pretend that this has no concrete value in the social practices developed with others who are White. The disavowal of the necessary sacrifice of the non-White other is harder when racism is addressed critically. This occurs when someone questions the need for sacrifice, tries to change the requirements for membership in the White community, and/or argues for expanding the description of formal racial equality. In this context it is obvious that flying the Confederate flag as a symbol of a tradition is about race; it is about a racial community able to take pride in a specific set of historical practices that defined racial activity. So is cross burning, a covenant made by neighbors not to sell their house to African Americans, redlining by banks, and the moment when a teacher confides in another White peer that she or he just does not know how to reach a specific Black student.

This is the moment of community for Whites, as sacrifice, as denoting a required hierarchy of values wherein some persons are described as in another community, as nonmembers. In this definition of death and birth all members of the community share responsibility for the actions of the other members. To be White is to share Whiteness not just in name but in deed. It is also something that cannot take place alone; racism requires a community. Therefore a part of the disavowal of the operation of racism is to ascribe to it the character of individual prejudicial actions without recourse to a larger community in which these actions are affirmed as necessary (Blanchot 1988: 17, 19).

In his description of community, Blanchot references the infamous case of Bataille and Le Coupable, where a willing victim was murdered by a group of individuals seeking to experience the moment, the cause, of death without dying (1988: 24). Is this, however, the same as the act of racism, which simulates a subjective death of an unwilling person from membership in a community, but also has within its action the possibility for the literal death, the potential act of violence that is completed in the naming of a difference? To talk of a Black community is to describe something outside the community of Whiteness, to thereby reaffirm the limit given by the sacrifice. But it is also to realize the importance of relationships outside this community definition, the need to turn towards something else with the denial of status that race embodies and figures. It is here that the relationship between friends and lovers comes to the fore of the discussion for Blanchot, as a way to reconvene a community beyond that of race, but which is made up of those who have been denied access and sacrificed in the founding of Whiteness (1988: 24). If we follow this application of Blanchot's thinking of an unavowable community beyond race, this suggests that Schmitt's description of the politics as the description of friend and enemy gets it wrong. If friendship only can occur outside of the relationship of necessary sacrifice and immunity and is described in the absence of the decision, then there are no friends in Schmitt's politics, only enemies.

To address the difference between the sacrifice enacted by Bataille and that of racism we need therefore to look at the problem of birth, how a person joins a community. The emphasis for Bataille was not on who was selected to sacrifice the other, but on how they accomplished this, what community they hoped to create in doing so (Blanchot 1988: 15). The substance of race, as contrasted with its limits and the creation of boundaries against the other, is defined in how persons are allowed to join or how they become members. As Blanchot writes, "The existence of every being thus summons the other or plurality of others" (1988: 6). Persons are born into Whiteness, and this is thought often to be the only way to join. Of course, many people also cross over into Whiteness, deciding to "pass" or having been accepted inside the community barrier. In doing so they are required to attest to their birthright and to conceal the truth of their birth elsewhere.

The definition of community as a way to define a White subject, as a collection of social practices, is not fixed naturally, as a product of a household, except as an ideal. This measure of purity drives the interrogation of its members, demanding an accountability throughout a person's life that can never be met, but also should never need to be asked. How can we really know that a person is White? We can't, except through the irruption of birth into the community. The physical racial community of persons is defined thereby in the foreground of a community of ideas, of decisions about the value of specific social practices, economic relationships, and political truths.

The individual person must learn to become White as a special collection of ideas and values, and he or she must then learn to use these to assert his or her membership; this raises the question of how someone could fall out of Whiteness as though its substance could be unlearned. To make it impossible to become American except by birth is to state that what it means to become an American is fixed. To make this idea of the American as then also described as White is to collapse the definition of membership for the society as a whole into that of the antidemocratic community of race, of hierarchy and human typologies, where the idea of birth certificates and bloodlines become important for the perpetuation of the nation.

This is the *Ion* described by Foucault, but by no stretch of the imagination could we call it democratic with regard to entrance requirements and membership. So in the US today we have a political quandary created by the idea of race and democracy, which is resolved by permitting several racial communities to exist with regard to one another, while also in a relationship to the larger conception of a polity defined by a representative democratic society. It is not enough to ignore this ongoing relationship between race and democracy. To what extent is Whiteness coincident with being an American or "All-American"? To get at this question we need to turn the idea of community against itself, to refute the idea of community as something to be preserved and protected. To critically address Whiteness as a community requires that we turn against the assumption that an individual is a part of, and defined by, community in the terms described by Blanchot (Nancy 1991: 5).

NANCY AND THE INOPERATIVE COMMUNITY

In *Being Singular Plural* (2000), Nancy discusses the problem of racism. Nancy suggests that race is false because humans are always already identified by the melee or constant exchange that occurs between humans; we already are mixed and a mélange in our communities, never pure (2000: 154). For Nancy, race is merely the desire for the ascendance of one household over another, of one community over another. It is not just described across the boundaries of the importance of a racial community in the practices with the polity, but neither is it already written in the exchange between parents that establish a child. It comes from a definition of community that is larger than the wishes and desires of an individual. To suggest, as Nancy does, that "all racism is stupid, obtuse, and fearful" is to concede the value of the construction of race even as it is seemingly resisted.

This cavalier use of identity politics by Nancy is important because it points to a larger problem with how he thinks of the relationship between evil and freedom. Identity politics is not a critique of racism. What if the freedom resulting from assignment of community membership, used to describe a subject, is a representation that constrains the ability of the other to choose who they are (Nancy 1993: 161)? If a value is not assigned to this gesture of authenticity the definition of Whiteness is only the ability to control the social values placed on other persons. The description of difference between persons matters explicitly only when confronting the person of the opposite race. It has no content of its own, no source but the other. It matters implicitly in requiring a person to identify, to represent, a race to everyone else, every other person, even those who are of the same race. This approach confuses the border with the social practices that exist within the community to define it; the attention is on a difference from other persons, as members of communities that affirm the idea of absolute differences of race.

Nancy argues for a freedom that must be free from itself and its position as caused or derived from either side of the Hegelian dialectic: *phenomena* and *noumena* (1993: 159). The *clinamen* he argues for, that of "The free opening of the 'there is' in general," is unattainable because the intervention of the idea of race prohibits the apperception of the "there is" by any person within these racial communities (159). Nancy misunderstands the nature of the problem, that the advent of race prohibits a sense of a self outside or a subject external to racial decisions.

You are either already White or Black in this game. Or you play multiple games with Whiteness, defining more races and inventing the potential for ethnicity against the idea of Whiteness. The person remains in the same position of having made a decision seemingly without volition. The problem is this founding of the thing of race against the absence of any thing, the abyss of nothingness (Nancy 1993: 84). Race is a thing that prohibits and works to control this description of something beyond its purview; everything is race, except that which is not.

Once it is settled, the race of a person, experience can begin. This is the explanation for why race can be a social construction and have meaning, and at the same time its operation be dismissed or ignored once established. Its positing allows for difference; its content is in the decision to apply it to our experience. From there, it can be used at will, as a seeming initial decision to be racial, racist. Yet the founding moment is already done. Race requires this formation, this collective subjectivization, and then persons live alongside it and through it, making false, because these are already designated, decisions of when or if to apply its description of a typology of the human to others and one's self. The fiction of choice here is revealed as a way to avoid the onus of seeming to engage in the terrible movement that is even then occurring from the movement of the physical identification of racial difference to that of a natural distinction of human type.

The original act of race was a gesture founding a community against all else, a desire for a collective in place because of the lack of connection with other individual persons. It is in this sense that race is a reaching across the abyss to the other; it is an attempt to make oneself in another, to bridge the problem of other minds (McKnight 2010).

That it fails to achieve a cohesive community except at the expense of some persons, who are described as outside the community, is a result of its failure to capture the truth of the human being. Race does not exist except as an imposition on the decisions we would otherwise make socially. In this sense Nancy is correct about the melee. While the effects of this imposition are devastating to the formation of society, at a personal level race is lived as an experience of inclusion or exclusion. The problem of how to speak this truth to racism, across the impact of racial communities on the polity, is therefore central to the resolution of racism.

Nancy's description of racism is typical of an approach that says the solution is to identify how race is not logical, that it does not fit the *logos* of the person in modernity. But what if racism appeals to those areas of the polity that accommodate our affections, our need for neighbors and human companionship? I would argue that race is the opposite of bowling alone, of the *anomie* of modern life. This is what makes it so dangerous, as it can be referenced and given substance at will to create a sense of community, a connection to other persons supported by sets of social practices. It has its own logic, that of the community. At the same time I am not suggesting that race is merely a way to fill up the absence of belonging experienced by individuals today, that therefore it is justified in some way or at least explained by other societal forces.

I am saying that race is its own creation, a thing that persists regardless of the situation for an individual. People learn to race not as a part of insulating themselves from the world but as a way to make sense of the world. Race is described as almost natural, almost real, and so it exists alongside the values of personal fortune and fate in determining life plans. It is a decision, not a desire, and as such masks its importance to the general description of human desire and the social practices that people use with other persons (Nancy 1993: 27). In this vein it is possible to see the impact or political effect of the Civil Rights Movement as an attempt to separate the authority of the White community from the polity. The demise of formal legal segregation is the separation of the definition of Whiteness as coincident with that of American governance. This is true unless the idea of governance changes as well from that of an expanding liberal constitutionalism to one of circumscribed responsibilities. I believe that what happened in the 1960s and 1970s was a political apotheosis. The forms of political reconciliation by government with the Civil Rights Movement and the persecution and erasure of the Black Power movement no longer made it necessary to ensure the collective sacrifice of Blacks to a White community; an explicit social and political demarcation of race was no longer necessary to ensure the latter's coherence. In this, Blanchot's description of community is partially correct as a description of race. That the decision to race could be concealed behind the idea of formal racial equality while the distinction of hierarchy this allows was transferred to Blacks, as a community that was to experience sacrifice and loss, a finitude as self-inflicted was merely the evolution of the apparatus of racial politics of Jim Crow. This new normal of racial subordination by institutions was now described as brought on by the individual choices made in the context of a politics of equal opportunity. Whiteness no longer demanded a gesture, but could retreat from the political while making Blackness, the Black subject, the location of its own subordination.

This transformation of the apparatus that describes racial politics is a dramatic event, since it potentially detaches the definition of the community of Whites from the necessary responsibilities of government, from what it means to govern the polity. At the same time, so long as the new government functions do not impinge on the ability of the White community to reproduce itself, economically, socially, and politically, the change in sacrifice of exceptional racial politics to that within formal racial equality of opportunity is advantageous. Thus it is possible to elect a Black president in the US, without necessarily impacting the political sovereignty of Whites as a community. So long as the politics of race remains constrained within the parameters of a definition of equality of opportunity, the success of exceptional Black individuals merely confirms the justice of the democratic process. This idea of race as a community of persons with specific social practices would explain why there is still, some four decades from the events of the Civil Rights Movement, a regressive politics to reconnect governance to Whiteness. It would explain why being White in contrast to being Black still matters in every human interaction even where equal rights and antidiscrimination law hold sway.

Only if there is something that persists beyond the individual person, that resists it dissolution as an idea based in many social practices, as a community, would this continued use of race make sense. Issues of personal racial relationships, Black housing integration, educational attainment, private-sector employment, wealth accumulation, and religious segregation are just as prevalent now as they were in the 1960s. Race endures because it is described as an individual problem but is actually a collective decision. This decision is constantly being affirmed and remade as an act of freedom when in fact it is everything but that. At the same time this decision is made by all, not by one, in this way, as found in the continual acceptance of the definition of race throughout social practices, so its dissolution requires a collective gesture, not an individual one (Nancy 2000: 26).

The need for a collective decision reveals the extent to which persons desire their collective experiences, that they must have limits to remain who they wish to be, White or Black. In Nancy's language, race is a decision about the singularity that will be used to erase the multiplicity of origin that comprises the one to the other of our lives (2000: 6). We substitute for the discrete spacing between us as persons, an Other which is made to bear our name (19). It stands for our nature and thereby obscures the circulation that goes through each person to an Other, a singular plurality connected to others (6). Nancy points out that this conception of race is irrational.

But at the same time, this observation that race is irrational obscures the need to work out a way to remove this decision from its central role in US society. It returns to a description of the use of race as irrational, as derived from the actions of someone without reason, which has today allowed a traditional rights-based logic to identify individuals who are racist while leaving the idea of race and Whiteness at the center of social politics in the US. What Nancy should argue is that race is logical to the extent that the society we wish to create is one where the "being-with" other persons is based on racial communities, not a reflection of our common plural origins. In other words, using race allowed and allows for a society in which a group of persons can define a direction for the social resolution of original human difference, something that, while harmful to the actual plurality of everyone, allows for the creation of communities of putative origin.

The difficulty here is in the description of this logic as individual rather than collectively derived, created through the circulation between persons of ideas and practices in common. To get past race we have to ask the question again that Nancy does, of what it means to be with others, without replacing it with something else, some potentially unifying collective expression, except that of an admission of our plural origins and a description of how we want to live in common (Nancy 2000: 26). This is not an obvious solution.

The destruction of this description of the singularity of race is not accomplished by referring to equality as an abstract idea, but neither is this achieved through the concrete application of the idea of a plurality of human origins. It was not the principle of racial equality that changed Jim Crow law, but the political application of a new way to conceive of the relationship between racial communities and of having something in common with other persons by reconciling on the idea of equal opportunity. The consensus seems to have been that at least more Blacks will now potentially get bread and chocolate, and in return Whites will receive acceptance of the means of exchange of goods in the society. Whites will be able to continue to define the norms for success.

The Civil Rights Movement changed America in 1960s by allowing persons to join together across racial distinctions in social practices, whether that was when marching, on buses, or within organizations. The initial integration of schools, employment, and public services literally threatened to create new descriptions of being with other persons that would dissolve the hold racial communities had on the lives of people. This threat was managed over time through the imposition of the institutions of formal racial equality.

THE PROBLEM OF SOCIETY

The study of race therefore allows us to ask the question of what "being-with" should require of the just society, what relationship our communities of practices have to the co-originarity of our human condition, and how to change the definition of "being-with" an Other in our everyday lives. I agree with Nancy that the with in "being-with," the coessentiality of Being, is "the heart of Being" (2000: 30). Nancy's argument is that Heidegger did not address, did not get past the investigation of Dasein as the definition of what it is to be human, to live in the world. Instead, according to Nancy, Heidegger left intact the traditional assumption, since Hegel, of the plural singularity of Being defined as implying rather than requiring an understanding of others (26). The point here is not to take up the legacy of Heideggerian thought, but to develop a critical approach to the description of racial politics as a normal requirement of democratic society. The instrumental definition of the relationship of Dasein to itself, as a self-referentiality without a gesture to the Other that is imperative, leads to a description of care that does not challenge existing conceptions of human difference. It is too appreciative of what is already available, ready to hand, in the subjection of the individual. Succinctly, Heidegger stops his description of *sorg*, care, at the moment that would require the study of how we use ontic categories of human differences, race, gender, disability, and so on ... to cover over the ontological assumptions that we use to define the conditions of humanity and its limitations.

This turning away from an accountability with politics, an abandonment of the Other even in the moment of describing them, defines an ontic account of race that exists without ontological mooring. It makes no sense in this construction, and therefore it is tempting to dismiss race as merely something epiphenomenal to something else, anxiety, boredom, or fear, for example, rather than remember that this detachment of ontic from ontological is a requirement of a metaphysical decision of difference and therefore a central ontological assumption of the human being rather than something trivial. That this theoretical abandonment of the Other took place in the shadow of the Holocaust is not coincidental.

Racial categories for Heidegger cannot be based in science or a decision without then requiring some idea of the human, which Heidegger is trying to avoid. As a result he cannot address the racial politics of National Socialism. It is in this moment that I believe the writings of Carl Schmitt concerning friend and enemy and the politics of the exception come into play as a way to address the implications of what could be termed an incapacity on the part of Heidegger's work.

How we understand Being is given by how we understand others. If we place this theoretical problem of "being-with" that Nancy identifies at the center of our exploration of the role of race in liberal democratic America, it becomes more apparent that there is an issue with the fact that contemporary politics describes race as a problem for individuals rather than as a collective conception of human differences.

Nancy argues for what he calls the copresence of being, the singular plural, which, similar to Wittgenstein's description of learning, emphasizes the need for a human being to always be defined in conjunction with another human being (2000: 39). How we cover over this fact or how the social relationships describe this fact determines our ability to address the problem of defining human typologies that distinguish a racial hierarchy of value (77). The focus on an Other to our Self in traditional approaches to the problem of race merely circles around the idea of a self that originates without a necessary connection to an Other, a self that does not already contain within its self-description a part of other human beings (Gilman 1985).

At the social level at which race occurs, race is a community of values by which to mark a mutual distinction, a Black human to a White human, not a Hegelian description of an individual self coming into being for itself (Nancy 2000: 81). If we speak of copresence instead as the original plurality of a self, race seems strange, obviously concretized from out of a desire to punish or control the description of an other person. This is what leads Nancy to speak of the stupidity of race. As he writes, "The individual is an intersection of singularities, the discrete exposition of their simultaneity, an exposition that is both discrete and transitory" (85). How can race then exist and persist? That it is a product of a logic of community does not explain its development, merely its intransigence in the face of liberal democratic institutions that privilege individual rights to protect the politics of representation. Race is more than a mere problem of a historical creation that must be corrected; it flourishes in the shadow of the discourse on individual rights and democratic law in the US. Nancy's idea of a racial singularity that intersects with other aspects of the individual does not explain how this occurs. It does not get at how we develop race to define the plurality we share with others.

Race is not a result of ignorance or a historical mistake that is perpetuated within societal institutions as an artifact. The idea here is that we conflate a community of social practices, ideas, and events with the description of human copresence; we create a subject that is constantly trying to erase the impact of this fact on our social world, and we call this race. Race is not then opposed to individualism or the possibility of a subjection defined as a discrete exposition of the individual. It is the decision to form a specific idea of community to describe our copresence with others. In this interpretation of Nancy, race is given as a response to the limit placed on freedom by itself.

As Nancy writes, wickedness, from which evil derives, is a result of freedom. It is the ability of freedom to undo itself, to be free from freedom, to form corruption, defilement, and depravity as an act of freedom, and not as its opposite (1993: 126). Race is not a coincidence of history, then, but a way to show ourselves as superior through the act of constraining an other; the idea that "we do it because we can" becomes a central characteristic of racism alongside that of the need to refuse the interrogation of the decision to erase copresence as a gesture of uniqueness. What we have is a plurality that also implies a hierarchy, but that depends on this decision of difference being defined as seemingly natural or real, not contrived, so that the specific community components are not available to suspicion.

Three aspects create the possibility of racism: a decision, the concealment of the social and ideational conditions for this decision, and the attack on being-with as co-originarity that is described by this definition of hierarchical human origination. These three elements are inseparable and codependent in response to the decision to create a typology above the plurality of the human presence in the world. Where do my body and experience begin and end? Who am I in contrast to an Other? What are the limits of freedom? These questions become the basis for the decision to create race. But it is a creation, not a natural fact of the human world, and this is what makes it a product of what Nancy calls wickedness (1993: 126).

If we return to the problem Ion faces in Foucault's exposition, of finding his birth mother to instantiate his ability to found and lead the society, it is possible to think of race as a way to avoid competition, to define oneself as unique and deserving of a status and attention above that of others. Defining the community of race as entered into at birth comes as close as possible to the copresencing otherwise available to each of us as a description of how we live through an other person. It substitutes natal family, genealogy, and the visual cues of phenotype for true diversity, providing instead a formal typology of "diversity" within which humans are placed. This typology allows for the expansion of the finitude of knowledge otherwise constraining the presence of the individual human being. The racial subject as a member of a community of values and practices defines a subset of human plurality as an acknowledgment of the fact of plurality. This is in contrast to developing communities from the contingency that would define the singularity of human beings living alongside other human beings.

The description of race is therefore inaccessible to the singular human being, since race does not derive from the description of original singularity but of an original differentiated plurality. It is a different way of defining the origin of the human. This gesture by definition is always hierarchical and inimical since it denies a common origin for all human beings.

I want to briefly mention here Derrida's critique of Nancy's use of birth as a reified conception, as the founding moment for a community. Nancy is using the possibility of birth as a way to approach the problem of community as a static, collective entity, as a critique of a status only available by birth. In the same way, Derrida describes the *voyou*, the outsider, as a way to delineate sovereignty, without taking into account the problem of how we arrive at the conception of difference; it is, as we see with Schmitt, already assumed (Derrida 2005: 68). The status of those outside is already given by Derrida in determining the citizen-subject, those who are able to determine the laws of the society. This is explicitly confirmed as Derrida's approach to the problem of the Arab, the immigrant, when he writes of the contradiction of a politics that assumes that one has to already be a part of something to have a critique of it, to understand it (29, 72). This is a part of the description of the autoimmunity of sovereignty that he defines

(109, 123). The secrecy that Derrida suggests rests within democracy, the secret society within a democratic polity, would also allow for undemocratic areas of politics, similar to the layers of authoritarianism that Arendt describes that form in the polity, but where the practice of race would, like an amoeba, a virus, or an autoimmune response, reach throughout sections of otherwise democratic processes and make them something else entirely (65). I am not convinced that Derrida does not share a similar implication with Nancy when he says, with respect to the event of the democracy to come, that "the newly arrived whose irruption should not and cannot be limited by any conditional hospitality on the borders of the policed nation-state" (87).

To return to Nancy, race requires defining the purity of events and actions that can resist mixing, that resist the pull of relationships, things, events, values that otherwise would find critical answers to the questions race defines for what is an other to my self (2000: 149). So, if this were the case how should we describe a way to overcome the effects of this constant gesture to establish a barrier between what we know as real diversity and what we believe as a result of racial communities? How do we address the fact that we live side by side first and in spite of the pull of these communities on persons? Nancy's argument for the inoperative community and the collapse of the myths that allow for coherence in response to this politics does not achieve this overcoming. The finitude of our singular plurality causes interruptions in the formation of a community. Persons are not reducible to their discrete subjections but always exceed the description of difference. This means that for Nancy, the politics that would describe racial communities as socially coherent is always threatened by the truth of the human plurality. At the same time, Nancy does not describe how we would go about addressing an attempt to constantly reproduce a description of community, of racial types as a social description as an operation against, as a response to the truth of the inoperable nature of racial community. Race is a politics that seeks to conceal the truth of human finitude. This brings the discussion to the problem of the imperative to seek the truth of racism, and the work of Foucault on the definition of an ethic of care.

COMMUNITY AS A RESULT OF THE ETHIC OF CARE

What is the appropriate description of community for this idea of race? This politics of community would have to do the work of socially differentiating between races and create racial subjects that could exist in spite of a constant challenge to their definition.

In the series of lectures collected in *Society Must Be Defended*, Foucault (2003) develops a description of race that depends on this possibility of exclusion as an exercise of biopower. As he says,

> The fact that the other dies does not mean simply that I live in the sense of his death guarantees my safety; the death of the other, the death of the bad race, of the inferior race (or the degenerate, or the abnormal) is something that will make life in general healthier: healthier and purer. (2003: 255)

Not only was race therefore a way to establish "a biological-type caesura within a population that appears to be a biological domain" (255); it also had a political function of establishing a community for which the exclusion of some was important for its health and well-being. As Foucault points out, in this perspective, "state sovereignty thus becomes the imperative to protect the race" (81; Esposito 2008). This description of racial politics supports the earlier discussion of Schmitt's definition of politics. The question is how we get at this definition of community in society, how do we criticize it?

Developing the idea described in his earlier lectures of the development of an ethic of care as a description of community (Foucault 2005: 117), in *The Courage of Truth*, Foucault (2008b) delineates a specific connection with an ethical care for the self and the political community. That Socrates asks Crito to sacrifice a cock to Asclepius in the *Crito*, Foucault offers as proof for an idea of a shared health as a part of membership in a polity, as something held in common with others that must be honored. What is shared could also be an illness of society, seen as something that must be guarded against through collective action (Foucault 2008b: 113). As Esposito points out, this was true of the Nazis: "In the autoimmunitarian paroxysm of the Nazi vision, generalized homicide is therefore understood as the instrument for regenerating the German people" (117). According to Foucault, Socrates instead describes a type of engagement as a prerequisite for membership in that larger political community, one that implies a concern both for other persons and for the direction of development in the society (272). But the tension, to paraphrase Esposito, is that between the two perspectives of a politics over life and of life (2008: 43).

This ethic of care could at first seem, as a limited political conception, to define a community of persons who hold the care of each other as important to the exclusion of those not in the community. What Foucault means by the ethic of care as an individual imperative in *The Courage of Truth* is not a problem of racial immunization and sovereignty but instead of using the care of oneself as a way to live an unconcealed life of individual sovereignty. The care of the self is therefore beneficial to others, as an example to others and also as a direct source of assistance and succor (2008b: 271). This is an argument for the importance of a community of persons who seek ways of caring for themselves that must persist in spite of the existence of other community ideals in the society. In this perspective we share an illness that is political because it defines communities of human types that we call race. This attempt to develop ways of caring for each other that heal race as a general condition of US society is a common solution offered to the problem of racial politics (DeMott 1996). The argument is that we find a new description of community, one of the human being that, while metaphysical in the same way, both particular and limned by a decision, is more inclusive than that of the specificity of race.

This is very different from a care that leads towards death, one that determines conditions on caring for others as a requirement for caring about oneself. By instead creating a critical solidarity with others through caring for oneself, the individual would resist the representations of race as communities of difference, the perception of race through this focus on oneself, one's own thoughts, and those of others (Foucault 2008b: 312). So why don't we develop this politics as an imperative? Because this idea of caring for oneself is only one of several social traditions that exist in the US, and the politics of race as a definition of sovereign authority overwhelms the individual requirements of care of the self; the idea of racial community works against the possibility of individual sovereignty as the basis of US democratic politics. The fact that this politics is described by Foucault as the work of individuals rather than the law or government does not address the basic problem that its ontological assumption already concedes the possibility of race, of concepts that importantly intercede in the everyday as descriptions of the human. We need some way to get at our racial subjection within these descriptions of social community.

TRUTH AS POLITICS

As was discussed earlier, Foucault argues for the importance of truth telling as a measure of the freedom in a society. To withhold the truth is to refuse to address the role of the wickedness that lies at the heart of freedom and that liberal democratic society also depends upon for its description of liberty. It is possible to justify slavery, segregation, and discrimination based on race so long as there is no reckoning between freedom and its product, the hatred of persons differentiated as also possible as a product of freedom (Nancy 1993: 128).

The problem is how to tell the truth. How do we change the use of race in society, this moving back and forth from the false ideal of absolute difference in types to the fictive real of the concrete differences these ideals describe for persons? This change would collapse the ideational construct that sustains our sense of community beyond the advent of copresence. Merely to say that something is a social construct in this event is worse than nothing. It suggests that the political, race, can only be self-referential and not arising from another view of human origination from that of copresence. In the *Apology*, Socrates reveals that death is also not the measure of this difference in politics (Nancy 1991: 15). Even the elimination of a person is possible if this is necessary to withhold the truth of the artificiality of, the decision to create, a specific community (Blanchot 1988; Foucault

2008b: 81). On the edges of racial difference we see that the violence and sacrifice necessary to maintain order is seen as justified, even necessary, to preserve the purity of types in separation from one another. Like Blanchot, for Nancy it is sacrifice that returns sense to the world, that on a practical level reaffirms the occlusion of the difference between copresence and the communities that deny its truth. As Nancy writes, "Freedom's own factuality will always be dissolved into that of necessity" (1993: 135).

The easy answer is to bring "being-with" into convergence with the idea of race and thereby to show persons their implication in the lives of others outside of the limitations race otherwise creates for them. This is easy because it is also not enough. It does not halt the renewal of the idea of racial difference, which can in fact live parallel to that of multiculturalism, for example, since the latter is itself a product of this idea of communities in competition with one another (Taylor 1994; Tully 1995; Kymlicka 1996). The problem of racial community definition is not resolved in the realization of our co-originality but in eliminating the ability to define specific pluralities from within the idea of plurality (Hooker 2009).

This can be observed by following the actions of Tiresias in *Oedipus Rex*, where he must use divine judgment to speak a possible truth to which Oedipus must answer. He does this by laying the ground for the return of the Shepherd, the truth teller, who is brought in under duress, only because of the challenge offered Oedipus by the potential collapse of his ideational construction of family, of community, and of his right and capacity to rule. The attempt to avoid certain consequences merely pushes around the conditions for eventuation. The truth resolves the existence of a wicked definition of authority, one that in this case creates in its operation the decay of the conditions for life. What motivates the critical approach to the truth is the existence of consequences that point to a problem of governance. This is the case today with race in the US.

Oedipus knows there is a problem, but locates it initially elsewhere, as a product of the ambitions of government, in the person of Creon, or in the ability of a Seer or even the Shepherd as a common citizen to speak in the society against government. The importance of *Oedipus Rex* here is in its story of how truth persists in its interrogation, in spite of a series of possible answers, each false, given as explanations for societal problems. What race has done is to warp the social relations in US society to an extent that liberal democracy is parasitic on the reproduction of racial communities. It therefore does not function well enough, nor is it the best that we can do. It does not work when you have a Republican candidate for president suggesting that a racial interrogative about the origins of another is appropriate material for political debate, that someone who is already president and about to finish his first term may not be eligible for the office. What would it do to the idea of US democratic governance or the polity to discover that Obama was in fact born elsewhere? What is the consequence of the duplicity that occurs on the part of Whites, for it is only for Whites that this is a problem, in the simultaneous political disavowal of a White racial community as something coincident with US governance and the simple, constant media message that Obama's birth certificate may not be valid? Race and the communities it defines are a major problem of democratic governance in the US.

The destruction of the false image occurs as truth unfolds and the way we approach the problem of race defines the solutions that we accept. Notice that with Oedipus, each truth eliminates the ground upon which the description of justice presently relies, until finally the entire edifice of values is refigured. There are different degrees of truth that address the specific descriptions of racism in US society. Each one depends on the common idea of race as the existence of several distinct communities. There is a logic to this truth about race, as it develops toward the interrogation of the way persons communicate with one another, approaching the possibility of the decision to race itself (Nancy 2000: 87).

In *The Courage of Truth*, Foucault offers the suggestion that rather than depend on a mode of community from a perception of illness or health, of a care of the self seen as a duty, as an antidote for the evils of race, for example, persons also develop through what is interesting to them (2008a: 118). A community then forms out of allowing for personal attachments, desires, and values to develop. These new practices could challenge the coherence of racial absolutism, by asking persons to want more than is given therein (Gilroy 2006).

At the same time, as Jan Patocka points out in *Plato and Europe*, when discussing the difference between Plato's and Aristotle's definition of care of the soul to connect the individual pursuit of the good with the needs of the community, the problem is in identifying the importance of a specific good against the general conception of the Good (2002: 180–213). Patocka reminds us that without a politics, "going after the good, we appear to others, and often to ourselves as those who strive for evil" (Schmitt 1996: 58). Some way must be found to measure the perspective of some against that of others within events, so as to challenge the formation of racial communities of difference. For Foucault this was the role of truth. As he puts it in *The Government of Self and Others*,

> And the problem in this agonistic game of the foremost in relation to the others, and of the foremost among themselves, is whether it is possible, legitimate, and desirable for there to be—as Pericles had been—just one who prevails over all the others. (2010: 226)

Enough about Whites: the discussion has gone from defining the decision as membership and its substance as prior to sociality, to defining a critique of the idea of race. Developing the critical description of racial politics by the Black subject provides one measure of US democracy (2010: 335). It is to this that we now turn our attention.

5 History and Politics

> A sense of inhabiting a moment of danger.
> —Santner, *On Creaturely Life*

> Dictatorship is not antithetical to democracy.
> —Schmitt, *The Crisis of Parliamentary Democracy*

President Obama serves as the focal point of a new racial politics. The Black community must develop a new political history of its place in the development of the nation. Doing so would change the current description of racial communities and their development, and allow for a critique of the paradigm of racial equality. It is remarkable how the history of African Americans is thought as a history of others, and not as the history of the US. Some Americans were slaves; some were treated with indifference and extreme racial prejudice; some were reviled and forced to remain separate from others because they were thought different, dirty, diseased, and dangerous. The stories of these people are not just an American story, but a part of the American story. To do this we need to, as Caruth argues, "begin to recognize the possibility of a history that is no longer straightforwardly referential ... permitting *history* to arise where *immediate understanding* may not" (1996: 11).

LIVING IN THE SHADOW OF RACE

How is the history of the community conceived of for African Americans? Blacks experienced a series of ruptures, events of violence and subordination that defined their status to Whites. But as Du Bois points out so famously, Black life was not defined solely by reference to the division between races (Du Bois 2012b). Life was encompassed by the racial distinction, but also lived in its shadow. For Whites this has meant that Black life outside of the exception, normal Black life within the description of racial difference, is opaque. In the context of the decision to race, Blacks are creaturely in ways that make them seem captive of their environment (Lupton 2000: 10; Santner 2006: 29). I am asserting that the decision of race acts as a form of what Agamben calls the anthropological machine writ large on the relationships between specific communities of persons. He writes that this machine "functions by excluding as not (yet) human an already human being from itself, that is, by animalizing the human, by isolating the nonhuman within the human" (Agamben 2004: 37). Since any activity outside the purview of the act of controlling for racial difference is invisible to Whites, the Black person seems to react to events and not create them. This moment of debasement and alienage, the signal of obedience and submission to the social description of the decision to race, cuts off Whites from Blacks even as all persons, both White and Black, experience the rest of life in a world where race does not completely mediate between persons and their ability to define themselves.

As Santner discusses in *On Creaturely Life*, symbolic forms that occur in response to events in human existence can persist beyond the end of the events in question (2006: 17). Unable to address this history of Black subjection where there is no resolution but that given by acceptable racial practices, the Black community becomes a repository of these unaddressed potential descriptions of a critical racial politics. Even though the practices have long disappeared, their impact continues within Black subjection from within the community even as it provides the possible location of a critique of existing racial politics. Since in each period the lack of political resolution and the continuation of race as a distinction occurred, the African American political subject today is not only a product of the evolutionary practices of nation-building in the ways that occur in standard textbooks on US history. This subject is also available to the layering of the accumulated history of race relations in the society as a collection of ciphers or problems that no longer are resolvable in themselves. To this haunting or spectral collection of experiences within the community is added the force of racial descriptions as a social politics, the subjection of Blacks by Whites (172). It is the decision that defines a Black and a White subject that creates the experience of loss of a community of persons without race. A critique of racial politics has to address the decision and the problem of White sovereignty, and therefore the problem of racial community as a collective identity, not merely Black subjection against the possibility of something alongside race that is unmourned. Otherwise, the political impact of what Santner terms "spectral materialism" is similar to that of Blanchot's unavowable community discussed above where racial subjects seek immediately personal solutions rather than consider ways to change racial politics in the society (52). I will return to this idea when discussing the novels *Iola Leroy* and *Plum Bun* in Chapters 6 and 7, respectively.

The question of how emancipation occurred remains relevant today as it points to the problem of the relationship between human and subhuman as a potential description of racial difference, as does the absence of reparations as a way to forgive Whites or be forgiven for enslaving different human beings. The type of White sovereignty that placed social control in the hands of individual Whites during Jim Crow described a social order where Whiteness meant absolute personal authority, and Blackness meant potential vulnerability and explicit subordination for an individual. How is this to be accommodated by the bifurcated Black subject of racial equality today?

The form of two-body subjection described by the distinction between the decision and the life beyond mirrors that of the difference between individual and the community. It becomes possible to describe oneself as an individual with only tenuous connections to a community that is defined as subordinate, if choices are available for the exceptional status of equality. On the other hand, it is impossible to bring this life into convergence with the racial divide, the veil or color line, the essence of the decision, for it is its antithesis. The political history of Blacks in America is therefore a split, aporetic narrative, where the two descriptions, of slavery and what happened under Jim Crow and now the exceptional requirements of racial equality existing alongside those experiences beyond the formal distinction of race even as it depends upon its effects, of giving birth, planting crops, building a business, having a family, being a child, falling in love, dying, and mourning the loss of loved ones. The melancholia of Black life, of realizing that we are only creatures of nature, is unimportant in an America where race creates another type of person whose life matters as a life worth living, for it is White life beyond race that must represent America (Agamben 2004: 68; Gilroy 2006). This should not matter, except that it is the inaccessibility of Black life caused by race that allows for the availability of Blacks to the violence that can exist today within the democratic political process (Agamben 2004: 40). To bring life back in, as it were, to the description of Black persons by Whites would be to destroy the salience of the decision of race. It is not possible to do this by asking Whites for recognition or merely producing Black culture that affirms the possibility of life beyond the decision. Trying to be friends as individuals across the racial divide only occurs in the shadow of race: people can hunt, pray, play, eat, and sleep together and it never threatens the fact of the racial decision.

We can see this problem for Whites of the split life of Blacks if we look at an example from a recent book, *The Help*, by Kathryn Stockett (2011). The text is written from the point of view of three different women, two of whom are African American. The narratives cover the perspectives of all three women and how they intersect, without delving into the lives of either Black woman except as it is relevant to the coming to terms with race as a division of humanity for the one White woman, Skeeter. In this way, the novel facilitates the development of the White community as a comprehensive description of the world, without daring to see, to challenge this idea of Whiteness in a description of how similar a Black life is beyond the decision of race. In fact, it is possible here to see how class differences are used by the author to stand in for and thereby conceal the decision to define racial types as absolute, as the narrative suggests that Skeeter has access to financial resources and employment possibilities that justify, in the last instance, an incapacity to connect with the social lives of the Black maids.

The reader is given only enough information to know that one of the Black women has issues at home with her husband, but not enough for this to allow for the reader or Skeeter to make common cause with her through the awkward sexism and misogyny experienced by Skeeter in her dealings with White men. This lack of character development demonstrates that the narrative does not want the reader to identify with either Black woman, but with Skeeter, whose struggle with the decision of race is facilitated by the narratives of both Black women as well as her own throughout the work. What the story does is bring the reader right up to the edge of Back life, entering their homes as a child, but only briefly, and interviewing the women at one home, but without any details of domesticity that would disturb the space created by race between Whites and Blacks.

This is similar to Schmitt limning the politics of race in his time through a description of friend and enemy. The awkwardness that Skeeter experiences in the novel when walking into the Black section of town echoes this idea of a proximity that does not and must not disturb. This is accomplished by not allowing the reader to lose sight of the decision. What you cannot do is visit just to do so, to live life with one another. The fact of race and what it requires of both social station and social role are always important for the description of Skeeter's interaction with every Black person in the story. It always matters that she is White and they are Black.

Any approach to Blacks by Whites across the racial divide results in the application of a definition of enemy. Living with Whites does nothing to change the status of Blacks. The young White Skeeter escapes the possibility of too much coordination for the reader with those Blacks that she interviews only by moving to New York. The author solves the problem of her potential erasure from importance to Whites by having her flee Blackness. This is done ostensibly in order to acquire professional success, but this movement away doubles as a means to sever ties with the approaching needs and similar ambitions of those Black people she has interviewed. Instead, she finds a way to use her temporary proximity to Blacks as an inspiration and source for her writing, but does not venture away from the fact of race itself, its place in her relationship to other persons. This is similar to classic approaches such as Conrad's *Heart of Darkness* or Naipaul's *A Passage to India* in the construction of how the decision of race can be approached by Whites in such a way as to profit from the difference itself. The White person laments the very fact of race in the very act of turning away from the possibility of no longer using it to define his or her world. This lamentation, this sorrow, is exciting in itself, both for the danger avoided, of collapsing or threatening the basis for the racial distinction, and for the proximity it allows to Blacks as creatures that are different from "us."

For African Americans three distinct historical caesura exist, Slavery, Jim Crow, and integration. These historical moments overlay each other today, creating the Black subject as property, rebel, menial laborer, and apprentice. Some of my ancestors were Blackfoot Indians on the border of Canada; my Black ancestors escaped north from Slavery, my adopted grandmother worked caring for Whites of her same age in a nursing home in San Francisco until shortly before her death, and my adopted grandfather was a handyman in his youth for Whites up the hill in Richmond, Virginia. I made sure to get good grades in high school in Albany, California, went to Swarthmore College, lived for years as an immigrant in Europe, and now work as an academic at the University of Alabama. There is no reconciling these histories, since in each case there is a disruption of the legal and social practices that define Black subjection.

I am unable to reach back across the political disruptions of racial history that have become necessary today to support the decision to race, to subordinate African Americans to Whites. For me, there is no continuous social practice defining an authority of community that is united with the American polity as a historical project of democracy. It has always been a White man's country for some, but this idea does not apply to my subjection as African American, a subject that continues to be described as a problem. So how does the Black subject cohere with the White description of the history and politics of the American democratic project?

Instead of the coincidence of democratic politics, as an African American I experience the political anxiety occasioned by the fact of slavery, that it occurred for members of my community as a part of US democratic history. Instead of being able to say it is resolved, scholars continue to argue over why the Civil War was fought, wrestle with the question of how to gauge the importance of slave revolts, and suggest that abolitionists and White sympathy led to emancipation. There is no single political narrative that connects the end of slavery with Black political activity; it is as though even in becoming free Blacks are not given the dignity of having achieved it themselves. The runaway slave fighting for his or her freedom is ignored since he or she cannot be placed in the context of a description of continuing White sovereignty and democratic politics without bringing the necessity of this connection into question. Of course, to facilitate the continued effects of race, this depiction of rebellion and conflict had to be subsumed in a vision of White pathos, self-recognition, and deliverance.

Reconciliation with the Master, his or her surrogates, and a state that allowed this to occur as an unfortunate business within a democracy is impossible. Because of this inability to close off the politics of race it is still possible today to hear Black people say that if they could, Whites would institute slavery again. The fact that persons are able to view others as capable of enslaving them is a problem. I suggest this as a way to show how unresolved this idea of Black slavery remains for our democratic polity. The openness, availability of the person as Black subject to this question of why we were originally enslaved and then emancipated, creates a history of pain, suffering, and political activity that cannot easily be realized or accommodated within a description of the American citizen-subject.

Bound up in this is the inability by both White and Black communities to define the freedom that has been achieved for Blacks in emancipation as similar to that moment celebrated with the end of the War of Independence, which in contrast allowed for the formal political founding of the nation. A similar reworking of the politics of race to allow for a single cohesive community of Whites and Blacks, a common democratic polity did not occur with the passage of the Thirteenth, Fourteenth, and Fifteenth Amendments to the Constitution. Nor did the terrible effects of the Civil War realize a rethinking of the problem of race on the part of Whites generally in the society. This was also true of the end of Jim Crow; there was no epiphany on the part of Whites or Blacks as communities of the need to set aside race. What I want to suggest is that this condition, of a political change in the description of Black status without a rupture in the depiction of race as a decision that must exist, its absolute and hierarchical definition, has left an effect on Black subjection that forces a constant return to the political problem of slavery and emancipation, Jim Crow, and now integration.

The problem of what to do with the political history of Black subjection in the US today is a dilemma that rests at the core of the American democratic project. This is because it also maps a politics onto the Black subject that reverberates as a series of disjunctures, of unresolved moments and events of racial description, that skew the ability to resolve the subsequent demand for racial equality in contemporary democratic processes.

A COMMUNITY IN TWO PARTS

To address this we need to explore with more emphasis the description of community that allows for racial politics and the subjection of individuals as Black and White. I think it is important to view race as defining two different political aspects or attributes of community. One attribute defines those practices that describe the absolute difference between races. This would be the activities that determine something as Black or White, and act to create the differentiation itself. For example, this could be rules for personal interaction between members of the two communities, violence or the threat of violence to define what is acceptable based on race, or patterns of resource distribution that are given by race. These are the direct application of the decision to create race. The other attribute defines those aspects of social practices that while impacted by race are not directly determined by this description of difference; they don't require its evocation as a limit condition. This could include, for example, what food a person buys, the clothes a person decides to wear, or what music a person listens to. What defines these attributes of the racial community is the way the hierarchy of value is confirmed.

This means, for example, that when Du Bois wrote of the color line in *The Souls of Black Folk* as being a veil behind which a person could live simultaneously with those practices conducted across the line, this was a response to the confirmation of racial hierarchy as allowing for specific interactions between Whites and Blacks (Du Bois 2012b). This confirmation of the decision and its indirect application to everyday life does not of itself determine friends and enemies in the sense Schmitt suggests is fundamental to politics. This fact identifies a problem with the idea that while the decision must remain the prerogative of the sovereign and in a democracy this is defined by popular sovereignty, the determination of the racial decision is the political relationship that defines sovereignty in the society. The decision of race depends on the definition of White community sovereign authority as the description of popular sovereignty in the US. To change the development of racial politics would then demand that we explore this idea of a White community such that it could be described differently and realize a different decision.

Of the two attributes of a racial community described above, the one that depends directly on the effects of the decision yields a politics that is readily described as racial. A description of racial politics has to include both attributes if any possibility exists of changing the description of racial community that has developed in the US. I want to spend some time discussing the implications of this idea.

BENITO CERENO

In his introduction to Schmitt's *Political Theology*, Tracy Strong (1996: x) suggests that the problem with Schmitt's conception of the political is just this inability to determine the perspective with which we view events. To develop this idea a bit more let's look more closely at the reference Strong makes to *Benito Cereno*. Written by Herman Melville in 1855, the novella discusses the relationship between Whites and Black slaves against the background of a revolt by slaves aboard a merchant vessel, the *San Dominick*. The story revolves around the interactions of its captain, Don Benito Cereno, and Captain Amasa Delano of another vessel, the *Bachelor's Delight*, which approaches to offer assistance. Concealing the fact of the successful revolt, a slave Babo accompanies Benito Cereno throughout his interactions with the other captain. While pondering the strange behavior of the Blacks and Whites that are aboard the vessel, which has clearly run out of water and supplies, Amasa Delano has no clue of the events that have unfolded prior to his arrival.

The idea that Blacks could conceal their rebellious activity in such a way is beyond Captain Delano's description of Blacks as subject to the decision of absolute difference. His creaturely description of Blacks is in contrast to the depiction of the other Whites aboard, including Captain Benito Cereno, as capable of deception, guile, justification, and self-reflection. Melville does a nice job of showing how this assumption of racial difference is so strong as to wash out the assessment of deceit and complicity by the Blacks that otherwise would occur to Captain Delano. During the exchange between the captains, Babo is reduced to his role as a manservant, not someone like himself, a person capable of making decisions. This is not merely the state of slavery, as Melville offers considerable evidence to show that it is the visiting Captain Delano who just cannot get past the idea of racial difference as prohibitive of Blacks thinking like Whites. Melville lets the reader know that the decision of racial difference is arbitrary and not definitive of a lack of political capacity on the part of those defined as Black. Since he cannot set aside this racial conception, Delano is unprepared for the events at the end of the novella when the other captain leaps into his boat and is fired upon by the Blacks aboard the captured ship.

What strikes the reader today is the sympathy with which we are made by Melville to view the plight of the White captain of the slave ship; after the mutiny he is reduced in character to such an extent that he eventually dies. It is as though Melville is suggesting that to lose the authority of the decision, his captaincy, is for Benito Cereno to lose the will to live. Even though he does see to the death of those Blacks that betrayed the trust placed in them by Whites, this is not enough to restore the sovereignty over others that Benito Cereno needs to captain a ship. This is the conditionality of the absolute difference of race.

The other captain is surprised when he first boards the ship that the Benito Cereno is not more forceful and decisive with his Black slaves, but explains this to himself as due to different approaches Whites have to the governing of Black slaves (Melville 1961:179). The essence of the decision of race for Amasa Delano was that Black slaves would know their place, be subordinate, and act with faith in the difference between themselves and their White master. As Melville writes, "In fact, like most men of a good, blithe heart, Captain Delano took to negroes not philanthropically, but genially, just as other men to Newfoundland dogs" (213). A form of trust was placed in Black slaves, that they would abide by this idea of their difference from Whites. This explains the fact that for Amasa Delano it was completely understandable that the few Whites on a ship such as this which had been at sea for long periods of time would be able to control the many more Black slaves without fear of rebellion or violence on the part of the Blacks.

That this trust was expected of slaves is described by Melville as a test of their barbarity and proof of their character as fit for slavery. For Amasa Delano only someone Black would not rebel against enslavement. The same thing is true today, as Whites say to themselves as a justification for the idea of racial difference that they would never put up with the treatment Blacks receive if they were "Black." This reveals another aspect of the absolute difference imputed by Whites to Blacks. That this idea of Blacks lacking a capacity for freedom is inconsistent with the situation described in the text does not obviate this idea of difference. Instead, Amasa Delano explains how the fact that Blacks resist slavery is then a measure of their specific type of deceit, their sly civility, and uniquely treacherous nature rather than a statement of their nobility, integrity, and desire for freedom from a creaturely life (Melville 1961: 258). The only consistency in this flipping of the imputation of incapacity is that of racial difference. The assignment of racial difference is comprehensive and absolute.

It is only upon the attack by a Black person on his person that Captain Amasa Delano concedes that the impossible has occurred, Blacks rising up out of their natural state of difference in that moment when they seized control of the ship and took sovereign authority away from the White master. Race was created as an absolute difference of the human but also at the same time as inhering in specific attributes. It was supposed to reflect human finitude, the limitations of our sensory and conceptual ability, and also to persist across our individual understanding as a description of community. As described earlier, it was both particular and universal, supposedly found in specific human traits but also supported by a gesture to fundamental human ontological claims as a form of metaphysics.

It is easy to see how at the time of Melville, for slaves to resist was perceived as against their own nature as Blacks, and yet expected without a strong hand over them. This perception will recall the definition of sovereign authority as self-referential earlier. Racial difference must be imposed as a description of communities in difference. Blacks were thought not even to know their own mind, to be mindless in ways that distinguish man from animals. As Arendt writes of the African, "They were, as it were, 'natural' human beings who lacked the specifically human character, the specifically human reality, so that when European men massacred them they somehow were not aware that they committed murder" (1985: 192). Melville gives us no way into the minds of the Blacks in the story, denying the main instigator of the rebellion a voice even as he goes to his death. What we do get is a history of failure, the inability, in spite of calculation and enterprise, to overcome the processes by which Whites secured the slave trade. Melville's ambiguity of description depends on accepting the absolute difference of White and Black, of friend and enemy, even as he points out the limitations on the description of human beings that occurs with the use of race.

The fact that, as Melville points out in 1855, for many Whites, their Black manservants, their house slaves, were thought closer in friendship to them than other Whites was possible so long as those who were Black knew their place, the absolute difference of type that defined their nature. For Schmitt, enemy can become friend, and friend enemy; mutual interests can trump antagonisms, so long as the decision, the sovereignty of the people, Whites in the US, is not put in question. The attack on the captain challenged this sovereignty, suggesting that perhaps the slave Babo and his compatriots could upset the decision that defined both the law and the privilege of determining exceptions to the rule. This difference in status is made clear by Melville in that the two captains are thought to exist throughout the story in a type of camaraderie, or friendship, an assumption of racial social bonding that stands in contrast to that between a White man and his Black manservant. This means that the difference between the relations between other Whites and that between Whites and Blacks is a political construction, and not social. The definition of a political community of race then frames the coming community with other subjects, those not of the same race.

The politics of integration today confuses the description of formal equality of opportunity with changing the political subjection of Blacks, as though these are equivalent. This is what makes it difficult to think through Melville's story where the absolute distinction between White and Black is made explicit rather than obscured as it is today by the idea of formal racial equality. For Melville, the Black slaves both betray themselves and reveal a deficit of character on the part of the White master when they are allowed to revolt successfully. The Black person was made out by the captain to be something he was not, something he cannot be and still be Black. Thus his Whiteness cannot in turn be supported and Benito Cereno dies.

Today, the reader of the novella is conflicted not by the narrative but by the knowledge that they are made to sympathize with someone denying other persons their freedom, since today racial difference conceals this fact behind the idea of equality. That this sympathetic individual is White is not incidental to this response, but has everything to do with it. Without the White person the story becomes uninteresting, without tension, and dull. Politics disappears once race is vacated. This is how race works today; it becomes as substantial as it needs to be to ensure the sovereignty of Whites as a community in the polity. But it can be as empty of content, as a pure politics of representation, as to suggest that someone Black can become president, so long as doing so does not threaten the politics of White sovereign authority.

Melville's answer to the impact of the decision on the lives of persons is given by how he ends the story. Echoing Tocqueville's warning about the role of Blacks in the new American democracy, Melville suggests that the very idea of "the negro" kills the former captain of the slave ship. That Captain Benito Cereno is Spanish and not American, as is Amasa Delano, is merely a device for Melville to conceal his true criticism, of slavery and its effect on the lives of everyone in the US. Schmitt had no such compunction, and this should warn us that we do not yet appreciate the nature of our culpability in the development of the politics of race.

A LIBERAL DIGRESSION

How does this idea of a racial community fit within liberal pluralist representative democratic institutions? This is also where the liberal theory of Rawls and others disappoint us with the inability to address the problem of race except as something that should not exist. Rawls suggests in his early work, *A Theory of Justice* (1972), that there is a distinction between a theory of justice and injustice, but this is inadequate because the idea of justice depends for its coherence on a comprehensive conception. If as in Rawls's later work (1993) we adopt a political liberalism, then justice must account for racism, not set its complex development aside as unfortunate. Rawls's model of reflective equilibrium is designed to accommodate the way people reason in politics, but in the US most people use race as though it exists as a social construction that differentiates importantly between persons. The problem of race in this context is that of how to remove a political description of Black subjectivity that you cannot accept, for which you have died symbolically, and been sacrificed so as to provide the community able to found popular sovereignty and democratic political practice.

This description of race persists past his or her death, the social and literal death of the Black person, and is assigned to his or her descendants in turn as a matter of community. How does he or she think through an idea that even death cannot erase in a liberal democratic polity, for which he or she is not even an individual but rather a plural singular, a type? How is he or she supposed to accommodate a struggle that is larger than one's own person? From within their community Whites would call this problem that of shame, a scar or disfigurement of the human that is justified by the inability to assert the needs of a Black community against that of their own; this is Schmitt's description of politics. Thus is the Black subject believed to be a product of a general human incapacity, a seeming projection of what Whites could have been, or were in the distant past, or can never become, and therefore something to be feared rather than embraced.

The matter of what is the human being, how we differ from one another, is understandably a central concern in the description of democracy and popular sovereignty. How do we change the adoption of race as a category of difference in the development of the modern democratic state? At a minimum race as a concept addresses the idea of what differences should make a difference, that which distinguishes politically acceptable from unacceptable plurality (Walzer 1984).

But the answer from within liberal theory seems to be that democratic politics must be able to accommodate over time even the description of friend and enemy that allows for race. Absent the social proclivities that make us who we are, how can we build anew our social world as a democratic society? What should our rules be for everything, even the exception to them? Those things that define a basic difference in the capacity of human beings should be affirmed as of first importance to resolve in a society and not left to the weight of the body politic on individual social development.

This is the wrong definition of the politics of race, one that hides its ontological assumptions behind formal concepts of difference. It is here that I also have difficulties with Agamben's (2011a: 60) use of the idea of the human being as nude, describing a state of being prior to politics. The nude Black, Brown, White, Yellow, and Red person of classical racial typology is visible only as a difference of phenotype, as a result of the supposedly objective Darwinian science of categories and evolutionary differentiation. Agamben describes the performance by Vanessa Beecroft on April 8, 2005, at Berlin's Neue Nationalgalerie, of one hundred naked women in this way: "Precisely in ample and well-illuminated space—where a hundred female bodies of various ages, races, and shapes were on display, which the gaze could examine with ease and detail" (Agamben 2011a: 55, 57). A difference observed must have importance, for otherwise why would it exist? If we then say that each of these categories addresses differences whose importance behind the skin is a matter of scientific curiosity, we have returned to the early work of race science and eugenics. To avoid this, Agamben's (1998: 125; 2011a: 65) idea of being nude, or being reduced to bare life, must therefore devolve further into a protohuman idea of individuality, not a physical body as such. Democratic society is populated by people, not mere bodies. Agamben (1998: 153) suggests that people become bodies; political institutions establish a body to match their need for a consumer, a patient, a criminal, and then reduce persons to this attribution of proper and improper difference (Campbell 2011: 75). This reduction is the attempt to contain the person within the confines of a multiplicity of attributions given by social practices, to finally make it impossible to recognize anything on the outside, any remainder that is not merely available yet again to a definition within the polity. This constant seething assignment of differences avoids the implications of its observations; it claims an innocence of purpose as the founding event of democratic politics when in fact it arises in the definition of sin and the improper (Agamben 2011a: 64).

As Foucault points out, it is in spite of the secrecy of Ion's birth that he is able to found the nation. It is only by opening himself up to the fact that his struggle for legitimacy is false; it was always false not because he was in fact born in Athens to parents who were Athenian, but that the necessity of origin was itself a false promise of community (Agamben 1998: 128). That is what Ion must learn as he is asked to struggle to claim his rightful place. In the context of racial politics today the problem is just this false necessity to define Whiteness to found the US polity. How else do you make the White person understand the false promise of race except by dressing him or her up as Black for a day or a lifetime? With the election of President Barack Obama, the US polity has a choice of directions: to make race unnecessary or continue with a decision of difference, where a difference must always be found to exclude some persons. Instead of resting the definition of popular sovereignty on inclusive politics, this describes a constant demand for discovering the enemy within and without.

When Agamben writes that "the desire to be recognized by others is inseparable from being human," he echoes Hegel (Agamben 2011a: 46). For Hegel, history gave the concepts for which persons sought and needed recognition, those things which meant you were a person. But the question is then what history provides the description of race such that it provides something for which persons desire recognition? What social conditions provide for someone to say, "Look, a Negro!" and why would someone struggle to be recognized as Black or White in this history? Why do we equate nudity and race such that race is viewed, revealed, and made available for inspection through forms of social control? Agamben writes, "The simple dwelling of appearance in the absence of secrets is its special trembling—it is the nudity that, like the choirboy's 'white' voice, signifies nothing and, precisely for this reason, manages to penetrate us" (90).

If Blackness is contingent on history it must also be available to erasure or redefinition. There must be counterdescriptions available historically. So why and how would one specific description of race exist such that we could coalesce our politics of friend and enemy around this definition? Especially, if we are Black in this version of history. It is with regard to this moment that Schmitt writes of the decision as the basis for sovereignty and the politics of the exception. Race becomes a central organizing moment in the society, not something that can be sublated or replaced by something more inclusive so that persons could engage in a politics of recognition. In this theoretical argument there is nothing on the outside of race, because just as with Ion's original quest to found the polity there is no political history in the US without race. The destruction and the revealing of truth by the decision etch a social-political memory of sorts, an onto-theological presence that defines the politics of recognition. So Whites speak of the politics of recognition and suggest Blacks just don't understand. And why not do so within this politics of race if you are White and desire to have this recognized by Blacks?

But if you are Black, instead of White, Agamben has it backwards. The solution to Hegel's phenomenological struggle merely leaves you in the situation of being defined as something neither dead nor human, and yet unable to change the description of race as that against which Whiteness may be defined. To accept the Nazi elucidation of the state of bare life in the camps, the Black as a natural servant and slave by Melville, is to demean the quality of the human being as something reducible to this state rather than always escaping this consolidation into a specific idea of the body (Agamben 1998: 125). The problem here lies in that moment in the *Phenomenology* when Hegel transforms quantity into a quality, when he decides on a concept to match the things available to his senses (Schmitt 1996: 59; Derrida 2005: 30). The concept then exists over and against the individual elements of this description, and we then become victims of the desire to be recognized instead of freed by this movement of ideas between persons. While Agamben addresses this in his description of the *anomie*, the space of indistinction he suggests must exist between law and language, between fact and norm; like Schmitt's definition of friends from the determination of his enemies, Agamben leaves us finally without a politics against race (2005: 59).

If we instead adopt Santner's description of Heidegger's distinction between human beings and animals, how we use race in the US would suggest that it is conceived as relevant as a determinant of *Dasein*, as a way to distinguish between those available to self-reflection on the being of Being, and those whose life is limited to mere existence, the opacity of being (Wolin 1990: 70; Gadamer 1994: 78–79, 129–130). The problem with racial typology today is more than merely saying each race is equal; it is a problem of the imputation of the absence of a quality whereby persons can access the process of thinking their own being. This is the heart of the race decision, and this fact does not change with the application of equality legislation from the 1960s in the US. At the same time, the ability of Blacks to think their situation through seems obvious, even for the master, and so something else must be at work to allow this definition of difference to persist.

Let us imagine a situation where two men wield hammers and seek to pummel each other into obedience. If this is Hegel's idea of the struggle for recognition it is easy to see the problem that race creates for the model. As they swing at one another, they force submission to then exact their will on each other, but what is their will such that they then race the other person; what is the relationship between race and hammer, the substance and form of desire? If race is the hammer, the concept is its own device. Then what is wielded by the Black man in resistance to being raced? If mere submission allows for any conceptual description of the Other, then where did race come from, and is not the theory of recognition equating all phenomenon by suggesting that race is like getting a child to eat his or her oatmeal, merely trying to make someone do what you want? Race is then not the end in itself; it is a means to an end, the violent subordination of a community of persons (Benjamin 1986a). What is race such that it can be used to force someone to submit to being the other, alien, and the enemy?

The desire to create a hierarchy of value for animals, for creatures where human beings are at the pinnacle of the arrangement, is applicable to human beings as well. In this perspective race science sought to apply criteria for animal species to the human, and prove thereby the importance of race for human beings. But this enterprise began after the decision to race. Race has a position of marking the open interpretation of meaning between human and animal; it is a readily available description, because it arises to define a hierarchy of value among humans, of the necessary uncertainty about our creaturely life in the everyday. To see another human being as an object of our desire is both required and disconcerting in what it says about our own person. To then postulate a second sense, an additional nature that is socially contrived, adds to the layer of doubt at our own ability to stand above the fray and experience the freedom of decision. It is this desperate longing for definition that according to Hegel allows us to conceive of the death of our enemy, of both the social world and the individual persons that attempt to define us against our will. This is a life of conflict, of violence hidden only by the vagaries required for the preservation of sovereign control over those spaces of definition available to persons.

For those working in the tradition of Schmitt, the only response to authority is to either capitulate or redefine the basis of sovereignty. Against absolute conviction the person who seeks to negotiate is viewed as being at a disadvantage. The solution for Schmitt is to make the ideas of strength, control, and subordination the basis for politics, and therefore to remove the potential for doubt on both sides of the conflict. The doubter has to both head off the application of the decision and nuance his or her answer such that the sovereign finds no target for exceptional politics. This was the main strategy of the Civil Rights Movement, to meet violence in the name of the distinction with both kindness and compassion for the perpetrator. To refuse to fight, and therefore to remove the premise upon which the sovereign White community acquired political authority.

The politics of the exception that identified Blacks as subject to direct subordination and social control by individual Whites during Jim Crow was useless if civil disobedience to legal segregation offered no resistance to violence. It literally became impossible to enforce the laws of segregation if the mechanisms used to enforce social order were ignored. If the possibility of pain and death are not a deterrent, the Hegelian relationship between subjects collapses, as the decision is made irrelevant to the experiences to which it attempts to be applied.

Herein lies the genius of the move by the US government to create a legal space for racial equality since the 1960s; instead of upsetting the decision itself, the response by the state was "merely" to remove the basis for the Black civil protest movement. Absent the laws of segregation there was no space for civil disobedience. The attempt by King and others within their organizations after the mid-1960s to shift the onus of racial sovereignty onto the injustice of the market, the executive power of the state in the form of the police, and the welfare state apparatus, failed to address the political decision of race because the reproduction of racial sovereignty no longer resided in these areas of the social order. The effectiveness of the movement did not diminish; it merely faded with the absence of targets.

This is evident if attention is given to how quickly today there is a political reaction by the state to traditional Jim Crow forms of individual White exceptional politics (McMillan 1989: 213). The use of hate-speech laws, the persecution of hate crimes, and the appearance of creating the conditions for racial equality in the law are necessary for the state to occupy its position as arbiter of racial politics. The strategy of civil disobedience against the laws of segregation lurks beneath the surface of the Black community's repertoire, if you will. This vigilance of the state is assisted by a White community eager to continue to support the mechanism by which the onus of race was transferred from their shoulders to those of Blacks. As Santner points out, "States of exception are the sites where, so to speak, the viciousness of the vicious circle at the core of the life of such institutions comes to the fore" (2011: 76).

The fact that African Americans must police their own behavior to take advantage of the idea of equality of opportunity and become exceptional Blacks, in spite of the continuing effects of race on their ability to accumulate resources to compete with Whites in the market, throws back upon this community the idea of passive resistance to the decision. The state and the White community, meaning any White person, can now use the idea of formal racial equality to challenge any attempt by Blacks to question the racial justice of procedures in place. It is very important that White individuals no longer police the idea of race socially as was necessary during Jim Crow. The "racist" as a subject position must always be threatened as inappropriate to the politics of racial equality. Instead, the White community can rely on informal mechanisms and the life supposedly lived as White beyond the decision to describe the consequences of race for individuals in the society. Inequalities are described as due instead to the desires of African Americans and their choices with the resources otherwise available to all equally. It is in their life beyond race, since the decision is concealed behind the two sutures and the politics of equality, where African Americans are in this moment reduced to criticizing the application of the law, not its form, and given the message of social progress to mitigate any attempt at protest. The only solution is to bring the two attributes of racial community into convergence, where the cultural products and protest against the decision are coincident. This requires that the Black community address the problem of formal racial equality as a politics.

On the surface this political idea of equality of opportunity describes the American dream of success, where if you are African American, several generations from now your descendants will be equal in wealth and political success to Whites. That time will heal the wound of race for Blacks, now that formal racial equality is mandated by law. At the same time, this narrative says nothing about the claims to community of Whites, how the idea of the difference of Whiteness continues to be developed alongside the description of political equality. What is the relationship between this idea of racial community and the democratic political process, private sector employment, educational attainment, and the ability to live and work anywhere in the country? This idea of success is a purposeful distorting of the dream elaborated in the speech by Martin Luther King Jr.

PERSONAL CHOICE AND THE MARKET: THE IMPORTANCE OF SOCIAL SEGREGATION

What is missing in this analysis is the problem of social segregation, that which persists across the different historical periods of racial politics in society. The market takes care of the problem of African American upward mobility and the police and poverty establish the structures of the hierarchical differences between White and Black as a matter of personal choice and circumstance in private life. The persistence of social segregation is the key to the entire apparatus of racial sovereignty in the US today. In addition to the market, personal choice became a key component of the new system of racial equality from the 1960s onward for continuing racial distinctions.

This means that the application of the structure of race was not inconsistent across the communities; it applied equally to both White and Black persons. Personal choice and social network became concepts central to the new social order. Whites should be allowed to choose whom they lived next to, played with, and married, as should Blacks. If these decisions were then mapped onto the differential resource distribution in the society, in housing, services, and employment, the idea of choice merely cemented the impact of already existing material and social differences due to race in the society. The two concepts for which the politics of exception is applied today, that of the racist and exceptional Black, rest atop a conception of the political normal which delineates that political efficacy, the control of economic resources, and the social description of the ideal American citizen-subject defined by the White community.

This model of racial equality depends on several problematic political assumptions. First, why should someone be able to decide whom they live next to, play with, or marry with respect to race? To suggest that someone can be said to choose to use drugs and engage in violent crime ignores the structural elements that determine the availability of these choices and emphasizes instead the subjective elements for persons. To ensure that White children play only with each other requires not only a hermetic neighborhood, but also keeping the children away from Blacks as much as possible. The White child does not "choose" to play with other Whites in this case, but is given in effect no choice of playmate racially. The social norms this creates are a substantial barrier to social interaction between White and Black, one that has been established from the first era of racial politics in the US.

This is an example of the idea of a political subjectivity for Blacks that contains within it the history of specific practices of the decision. These practices in turn continue to be conflated within the description of racial subjectivity such that their source is unavailable, their provenance uncertain, and yet the symbolic and social impact of their description is felt by the individual. This description becomes more problematic if we view the issue of race as one of established collectivities and not merely individuals without race.

USING THE INDIVIDUAL TO ESTABLISH THE COMMUNITY

This brings us to the next problem with the current description of racial equality: the reduction of the political effects of race to a belief or feeling. To the extent that everyone can avoid having these beliefs, he or she is defined as an individual and not a racial subject. I think of this as a political claim that if you simply say that you do not see race this will somehow be the case. It is easy to see how such a claim could then be used against a counterclaim to the truth that race is a problem in a particular event or context. To avoid the stigma of being a racist if White, or being defined as someone unexceptional if Black, there is therefore considerable social pressure to avoid referencing the fact of racial communities as a creator of values and social expectations for individuals. This practice of avoidance is an attempt to reduce the influence each racial community has for the person to the fact of the decision, which is described using the language of equality; the community that develops beyond the distinction remains diffuse and amorphous. As a result it is possible to avoid accounting for how race as a community of social practices impacts activity in the society. If this reduction is considered complete and the continuing impact of racial social segregation is ignored as being innocuous since it is not racial in the same way as the politics of the exception, it becomes possible to argue that race is no longer a problem for the society. The racist and Black exception and the formal instruments of equality are paraded as political truths to conceal the importance of the second attribute of a racial community, that which is determined by the racial decision but develops indirectly. That this social description of racial community remains continuous throughout US political history is not merely a warning that existing arguments for the success of the politics of racial equality of opportunity are suspect, but also points to the fact that there may be very little political efficacy for the idea of racial equality beyond its use as a means to control Black political mobilization.

The third issue with the current politics of racial equality arises because the outcomes must be seen as fair, as just, given the resources individual persons bring to the marketplace for goods and services in the society. If we ignore the fact of a difference in resources historically between the racial groups, then the problem for creating more racial equality is one of how resources are distributed after the initial situation. Is it necessary to put in place mechanisms to provide a more equal situation, given that Blacks began with few resources? What about the social-scale problem created if members of one community dominate a professional environment and therefore the social community they belong to unfairly determines values and expectations for employment and success? The market is also not without distortions such as inertia and lack of information, which could make it difficult for persons with fewer resources to compete.

What should the state do if someone says there are no Black persons qualified for the job but these persons exist outside of their search process, for example? What are the criteria by which hiring and promotion are accomplished, and should these be changed to reflect the ability of persons to do the job, or based solely on the accumulation of specific merits and credentials? Since a claim of racism is limited, it is not effective to argue that contained within this standardization problem race lurks somehow and is implicit. It is possible to exclude most Blacks based on the process of market sorting, and then to discourage those who do have credentials by invoking the idea of social isolation and possible stigma. The problem of race is therefore outside the sorting environment, and usually described as something the employer can do little about. This is how this two-level game works, from the decision to the social, from the metaphysical decision of race to the description of difference based on anything but a claim of absolute racial difference so as to justify the hierarchy of communities in conflict.

This set of contemporary racial issues provides an opportunity to return to the problem of how persons respond to others, defining those they are willing to associate with and how, and those they choose not to engage with. The assumption is that persons seek to define themselves with, or acquire recognition from, others. In addition to the problem mentioned above of the historical construction of concepts that are used to define persons as similar or different from each other, the idea that persons always seek to engage others is too simplistic. What about the definition of self through the turning away from something, the purposeful no, the description of negation of the relationship to the other? The ability to be indifferent to the Black person, beyond the hermetic definition of a White community, is a central element in the decision of race.

Instead of requiring an always outward, aggressive policing of the boundaries of race, it is possible to signal the availability of the Black community to exceptional politics by shutting them out and by ignoring them. This turning away is a major component of a traditional politics of race in the US, and defines how race was used socially in contrast to politically. To suggest that a Black subject should appeal or be a supplicant to Whites for a reconsideration of the decision misunderstands the political dilemma of race. How is the closing of the borders of community, the refusal of entrance, expressed in the relationship between two persons? As Nancy suggests, everyone is always open to everyone else (Nancy 1991: 61). Unless something is constructed conceptually that intercedes to halt the engagement among persons about who they are collectively, and therefore who they are to one another (28).

To address this *no* would require that there exist another level of politics from that existing between persons, one that could access the politics of the decision and the definition of White sovereignty. To respond to the political claims of a group only when they express a need or demand explicitly within established democratic processes suggests that the group designation is not a part of the description of popular sovereignty and that the distinction that defines the group is not a basis for politics. The decision of race can be described as both one of avoidance and aggression, of Whites refusing to accept that they care, because doing so leaves Blacks alone and creates and reproduces a gap between Whites and others that acts to discourage redefinition of the relationship, acting to define Black subordination to the desires of Whites.

This way of describing racial politics provides another explanation for the importance I have placed on equating racial politics in the US today with that of Schmitt's designation of friend and enemy. This aversion brings into question the assumption that persons exist as stable autonomous entities such that there is a distinction between them beyond that of their singular plurality, their ipseity, a description of something held in common, a community that is also important to preserve as a politics (Nancy 2000: 95). If persons share practices, then the decision of race is an act of violence to the interdependence of the individuals with each other and to their mutual occupation of a space. It creates a separation that exists outside of any one practice, but also defines those coordinated practices that occur between persons. This problem comes from defining friendship as liking someone, sharing something, living together, in contrast to disliking someone, avoiding interaction, and living apart. This is similar to the difference of emphasis as a politics on the birth or death of a community, what allows entrance and what prohibits membership such as was described earlier with regard to the *Ion*. The choice of emphasis matters for the theoretical discussion. For race, the problem lies in its use, which is to control the population and differentiate between collectivities and the resources they can expect. In Schmitt, sovereignty occurs not through debate but acclamation, which is exactly how Whiteness manifests itself (Kalyvas 2008: 124).

So we need to resist the temptation to see Schmitt's identification of friend and enemy as a symptom of individual personal practices, and see it instead as a problem of the collective assignment of social difference. It is not a matter of choosing one's friends and enemies, but of having these descriptions given to you as an individual in the society within the specific description of sovereignty that creates law. The definition of popular sovereignty is the opposite of a politics that accommodates the collective assignment of race to persons.

How is it that persons called Blacks can exist in US society? This question brings up what can be called the thanatopolitical aspect of race; why do Blacks still exist, and is this merely because Whites in the US have always needed them for economic development? Why is it important that some persons are always Black and why it is still important to be White? It must be important to the idea and definition of sovereignty that race as an idea assists in the political order.

Sovereign authority is efficient, so the use of race for several centuries in the US, since before its founding as a political entity, must serve a purpose. To race is not natural, but also not arbitrarily constructed out of the desires of individual human beings as autonomous persons. It can not be trivial to the political description of the social order if it has been one of the major sources for differentiating fair outcomes for resource distribution, employment, education, housing, and social mobility in the society. It must also be a part of sovereignty in the society, not incidental to its function. Whether Schmitt is believed to be describing a conception of popular sovereignty or that of the individual leader operating in a constitutional framework, he leaves unanswered and ambiguous the means by which the sovereign arrives at a description of politics.

The substance of politics is available for whatever the sovereign desires; the conflicts are chosen outside of the idea of sovereignty itself, as something just there and immanent. This politics demonstrates a remarkable dishonesty in its seeming objectivity, an inappropriate abstraction from the very reasons Schmitt seeks to theorize about constitutional democracy. It is inappropriate because his writing is an attempt to address the substantial problems that democratic societies faced in the 1920s and 30s, and today. This is social conservatism writ large upon the idea of the need for social order and the force of law, where the social possibilities of collective assignments of difference are seen as both necessary and where their justification simultaneously must remain unaddressed (Zizek 1999: 30). Nancy instead describes democracy as guaranteeing the sharing between persons of that which exceeds politics, described through "art or love, friendship or thought, knowledge or emotion" (Nancy 2010: 17). What democracy cannot do is describe a specific politics; as Nancy writes, "It is not up to it to give itself a figure" (27).

RACE AND COMMUNITY

While it is useful to work through Schmitt's description of politics as defining friend and enemy as a way to think of how race is used in the US, the fact is that race is not synonymous with friendship or communities of friends and enemies (Derrida 1997: 181). This becomes obvious if we consider how race defines who can be friends. We say, "I have Black friends," or "Some of my friends are White." We say, "I can't be friends with you because you are Black/White" or that "It is hard being friends because he/she is Black/White." This type of assertion frames friendship in terms of race, as a description of norms, interests, and behaviors that are learned as part of being of a particular race. To the extent that friendship as *philos* is believed to be a central component of a political theory of democratic society, this determination of friendship by race is a serious problem; it should signal to us that our society has broken down along racial lines, that in spite of arguments to the contrary, the US is still very much a racial polity. The persistent need to justify, explain, or otherwise defend friendships across racial boundaries in the US, even if it is only by declaiming "He/she is my Black/White friend," allows us to see in a straightforward way how friendships follow race if possible; that is what race is designed to do. Race is supposed to determine how we interact with each other, and so is something more than a mere designation of difference. This means that while Schmitt's description of absolute sovereignty and the definition of the political is useful, it does not get at the extent to which race determines political development in the US.

The state of racial politics in the US is often expressed by the statement "You can't legislate equality." If we accept the argument above that the change to formal racial equality was designed to preserve the hierarchies and resources of Whites as a community in the face of civil unrest by Blacks over Jim Crow politics, then the inability to legislate or otherwise alter the description of the racial social communities signals the lack of sovereign authority on the part of the government. The US government can be viewed as complicit with a group of persons who sought successfully to ensure that certain claims of equality were not made by the government. But what I mean by group here is not simply specific persons, but persons who collectively have a specific interest, a desire for absolute difference and its hierarchical social realization based on race.

In our contemporary politics only the exceptional White person, the prohibited racist, could agree with this stated desire, and so the claim of specificity, of interests in common, and even the idea that there is race, is refuted by both government and Whites as a community of persons. Only Blacks continue to argue for the importance of race, or so it seems. The "White liberal" states loudly, repeatedly, that he or she does not even see race, as he or she relies on the government to police the limits established on the types of equality claims that can be made on behalf of the Black community. If you ask who is White or Black in a room, what is it that is being referred to? If you speak of diversity, culture, or difference, are you not often speaking about race? Aren't you using the idea of race as the unifying term for "the hierarchical articulation of a series of functional faculties and oppositions" (Agamben 2004: 14)? The conversation about race is attenuated in public so as to guard against its leading to questions about the place of Whiteness in society today.

There is nothing inherently wrong with a subset of the citizenry in a democracy capturing the political priorities of government. As Schmitt points out, a democratic government based on the will of a minority is still a democracy, so long as "the essence of democracy is preserved, namely, the assertion of an identity between law and the people's will" (1988: 26). In the US today the legitimacy of the government depends on its ability to safeguard the political interests of the White community. It is not the interests of individual citizens that determine the scope of popular sovereignty; the highest politically efficacious unit in US society is the White community of citizens. To challenge the extent to which equality of opportunity has changed the condition of racial practices in the society is to bring this political efficacy into question, not that of the political positions of individual persons.

As Esposito suggests, ruled by fear a society literally tries to control its occurrence at the expense of the sociality of the human being (2010: 24). He writes,

> Here lies the double layer that is least visible in the Hobbesian text. Differently from what is generally held, the political-civil state is not born against or after the natural one but through its reversed inclusion in terms of an emptiness rather than a fullness. (25)

But fear is not all that humans experience, nor can we live democratically as a polis if this idea overwhelms others also important to the human being. The creation of a concept that impartially organizes the population into phenotypes merely begs the question of how we will come together in its shadow and what impact this idea will have on our future. The negation of political community in the creation of the community of opposites must be conjoined with a way to live alongside race. The decision itself is insufficient to create society and to tell people how to govern.

I believe that race has been able to persist because it organizes the lives of persons such that the antagonism of the decision, its violence, is always limited by the need for social order. This is what distinguishes the politics of race from that of Schmitt's abstract description of friend and enemy (Esposito 2010: 51). Race preserves the distinction of communities while affirming the need for both, or several, communities. It offers a sacrifice of the person to an idea that mitigates the vulnerability that otherwise exists for individuals in the continual transfer of authority to popular government (55). In this way, people give themselves over to something other than themselves, a community, even as they, or perhaps as a way to, retain their subjection, as individuals against the comprehensive description of popular sovereignty as law in a democratic polity. Race becomes not only a way to make sense of other persons but of resolving the internal political tensions of the society (75). As such, in the segregation of races there is a retreat from the scope of popular sovereignty in the offer of the possible security of person, a description of history and tradition, and a model for social order that cannot be rescinded or given up by the individual for the indeterminacy of the polity as such. It is as though you asked someone to give up, to abandon, the idea of attachment to his or her mother or father for something that threatens the very concept of family.

The history of the United States is very much one of failing to distinguish the law from the racial community, of making the law of the racial communities, of the superiority of White community interests coincident with that of the polity (Esposito 2010: 84). An expanded conception of popular sovereignty is a threat to race in this regard (Derrida 2005: 157–58). It asks persons to give up a specific description of themselves. What type of solace does a truly popular sovereignty offer for individuals against the demands of the majority and the requirements of citizenship such that we would be willing to give up the idea of race each of us holds onto?

The social description of race does not need to directly challenge the political salience of the distinction itself, so long as each racial community exists alongside but not coincident with the other. This is a form of separate but equal where the solution to Jim Crow politics was to expand the space for interracial competition and leave intact the pretensions towards the distinction of race that have existed in the US since the 1600s. No other avenue for political and economic success for African Americans is possible except that which supports the development of race as a social community, the persistence of social segregation. In this way African Americans are invested in the political apparatus that is the current description of racial equality by their very desire to escape confinement in specific practices of racial subordination.

There are then real limits to the claims African Americans can make against their status no matter where they are in society. This is why Obama as president is noticeably unable to engage the larger problems created by racial difference, and why those of us African Americans in the academy and professional life find it impossible to be more than examples of how racism does not exist any longer in those forms available under Jim Crow. Exceptional African American individuals are used to cover over the use of race by government to engage in what used to be described during Jim Crow as the exceptional politics of incarceration, impoverishment, and marginalization of other African Americans. Now these discursive practices are described as the normal condition for African Americans. Exceptional African Americans are always told, and always indirectly, that they should be grateful for the difference between themselves and their purported brother and sisters in the Black community. For therein lies their success, their recognition, their security from the more obvious deleterious effects of race. A form of virtual sacrifice is enacted in the moment of their acquiescence, of the Black community as socially cohesive and therefore a potential source of protest against the current politics of race, and of the ability of Whites to prohibit all African Americans from specific achievements.

Under integration any Black person can potentially acquire any professional position in society, but only on the condition of his or her being the exception. It just cannot become normal that African Americans succeed at school, work, and politics. It is within this political narrative that Whites protest that they no longer are able to achieve the same positions as before in society, that any Black person in a position they might want represents a loss of status, a product of unfair anticommunity practices. It then becomes possible to argue that this new regime for race is unfair to Whites since all descriptions of race are now private. The caesura of the shift in regimes between Jim Crow and integration is glossed over in the political settlement that race no longer matters. With the collapse of public support for addressing racial politics, the idea of racial community as conflict disappears, and following the reasoning of Esposito when discussing the importance of community in the work of Kant and Rousseau, without a formal racial community there is no thinking of race in public (Esposito 2010: 62). Race disappears from politics, even though it persists as a form of exception waiting to return to public view in the maintenance of a private racial life. The instruments used to determine exceptional African Americans have to remain private, not public, but at the same time this undermines the political basis for the continued shift from formal racial desegregation to integration.

The public conversation about race becomes defined by statements such as "Why promote Blacks if racism is a thing of the past?" "They are already successful enough," "They are privileged over Whites," and "Since it does not matter if someone is Black or White, why keep statistics?" It is in this moment that the continued dependence of the US government on support by Whites for its legitimacy, as a description of the coincidence of both community conceptions, becomes clear. In spite of its nonsense, its impossibility, in fact because it finally is without meaning, race is still able to unify persons across the singular plurality of existence (Nancy 2000: 153). Race is the ideal concept for a politics that must always conceal the vagaries of life in the interest of social order, in the subordination of persons to a sovereignty that exists for itself first, an idea that can be used to cover the absence of other ideas in the polity that define the human collective at large. Race posits a difference that depends not on the existence of the other, but on the ability to define a collectivity beyond and against the subject, something that Schmitt, for example, placed at the core of his conception of politics.

We must remove from our discussion of race and politics the idea that someone or specific persons created race, or used it to establish a community. Instead, race arose as a useful concept from within a wide variety of social practices that were critical to forming the nation-state of the US from the 1600s. That it existed prior to this is obvious, as it is a form of particularly nefarious social shorthand for a decision of difference. This does not mean that individuals in turn make the decision to race. It is already there for its subjects; it exists prior to the advent of any specific racial subjection in the space available for the description of the law and social community in the society (Esposito 2010: 97).

The preexistence of race suggests that what is missing in this analysis is the heterogeneity that describes the community of persons absent this type of distinction or decision of difference. Absent the imposition of race, persons live in a relationship to one another that reflects the "impropriety" of this living alongside one another. Without the decision, the concept of community is defined following Esposito as like the sea. A human sea turbulent and constantly changing, with tides washing over shoals, beach, and valleys only to recede due to forces outside of itself (2010: 107). As Esposito writes, "The sea's withdrawal leaves the land to be. Isn't this the very same figure of community, its originary munus, by which I mean what gives us a 'common name' only through the lack of 'our own name' " (109). The necessary gives way to the inexplicable; the substance of political theory becomes how to describe this without returning to a desire for origins such as expressed in *Ion*, or to accept that the ideas that we develop foster the basis for the concealment of a divided, terrifying society for some to the benefit of others. We have to change our perspective from that of trying to privilege lives, the experiences of specific persons as a necessary, regrettable limit on the scope of government to instead one that develops the quality of a life, of each person's life in a democratic society.

Part III
Black Politics

6 Slavery and Its Aftermath

> I sometimes catch myself again making a scene before her, in order to catch up with her, and I smile at this sign of life, of life in which I am no doubt still obscurely trying to keep her, that is, keep her alive. To "conjure death," as she says in her last text—implies both to conjure it up and conjure it away, to summon ghosts and chase away, and thus pursue the other as the other dead.
>
> —Derrida, *The Work of Mourning*

> But for the revolution, this extraordinary man and his band of gifted associates would have lived their lives as slaves, serving the commonplace creatures who owned them, standing barefoot and in rags to watch inflated little governors and mediocre officials from Europe pass by.
>
> —James, *The Black Jacobins*

Beyond the decision to race is a Black community that is fractured by the cumulative effects of the experience with racism. This community is unable to coalesce so as to act against the description of absolute racial difference in terms of formal equality of opportunity. As a result the Black subject finds itself made available to the new politics of the exception as the only reprieve from the deleterious material and social consequences that reflect the continuing authority of the White community in society.

To generate the social resources necessary to challenge this description, in contrast to using the avenues for success given by the politics of formal racial equality, the Black subject must gather together the history of the community's response to racism into itself. This cannot be a reproduction of the decision to form racial communities against their factual incoherence, their inoperative definition of absolute difference, and so when I speak of community here it is something political that contains persons of all races even as it addresses the problem of the Black subject. But what is this politics that is being addressed? The Black subject has to remake itself from the remainders of its community experience beyond the decision. This is the undoing of the effects of White sovereignty on Black subjection over time, the redefinition of the Black community through changing the decision of race. To suggest that this is a project of truth telling is to reduce the social practices critical of race to the actions of individuals without a politics that addresses the problem of the definition of race as communities of difference. While truth and care are important as placeholders for a politics critical of the use of race, from within the apparatus and the problem of the racial bifurcation of discrete social communities this politics is comprised of several components. Simply put, the social practices critical of race must address the different applications of the decision across society. Up to now the discussion has focused on uncovering how race continues to exploit a desire for authoritarian practices within the democratic polity. This has been important to show the types of political problems that race creates for US society. The work to counter these requires the development of strategies that define new descriptions of Black subjection and the racial communities from which these arise. To do this we need to explore the political resources available from within racial practices and the description of the community beyond the effects of the racial decision.

It is with this in mind that I turn in these next chapters to the study of African American fiction. Each selected text offers a specific framing of the problem of Black subjectivity that I will argue is a discursive element in a critical racial politics today. This argument is different from what has come before since it no longer seeks to describe how race works. Instead, it describes what has been occluded, covered over, or eliminated from the potential actions of the Black subject in response to the evolving racial apparatus. For example, the return by us to the problem of the collective idea of race, of a unified Black community historically in a text such as *The Marrow of Tradition* written by Charles Chesnutt in the decades after the Civil War, relates directly to the prohibitions we place on Black community political solidarity today (1993: 26–27). These texts each allow us to address the historical effects of normal, in contrast to exceptional, racial politics on the description of Black subjectivity as well as the caesura brought on by the events that led to emancipation, the demise of Jim Crow, and the approaching end of integration. In this way I want to develop our awareness of the political strategies available to address the current political description of racial politics. In this chapter I describe some of the political solutions developed within the Black community by individuals in the decades following the Civil War by studying Frances Harper's *Iola Leroy* and Charles Chesnutt's *The Marrow of Tradition*. To discuss the politics available to the Black subject during Jim Crow in Chapter 7, I consider, respectively, the texts *Plum Bun* by Jessie Fauset and *Uncle Tom's Children* by Richard Wright. To address the strategies used to define a resistant Black subjectivity in the current period of racial equality in Chapter 8, I examine the texts *Silver Sparrow* by Tayari Jones and *Brothers and Keepers* by John Wideman.

ASSEMBLAGE

How do we reassemble ourselves after events of such magnitude that they bring about wide-scale societal trauma? One way is to erase our commitment to what came before, to give up the practices that determined how we framed our desires, who we wanted to be, and the ambition we had for society. This was attempted in the 1960s by the use of the political sutures of the White racist and exceptional Black to create a new normal wherein racial equality could be described. The problem was that social practices that established racial communities were unaffected by this political construction. Things would have been very different if the state had determined that it could in fact begin the dissolution of racial social segregation, and had created instruments to do so.

This would have meant, for example, much more far-reaching efforts at affirmative action, financial reparations, and a restructuring of the asset base to create relative equality across the general population (Massey and Denton 1993; Conley 1999; Oliver and Shapiro 2006). This would have meant not consolidating the definition of the Black normal subject around the practices of criminalization, the War on Drugs, and incarceration mills (Davis 2003; Brown et al. 2005: 147; Clear 2009; King and Smith 2011: 228–33; Alexander 2012). Unable to leave the decision of race behind, the US polity in the 1960s established a partial solution, as it had after the Civil War. Today we face a crisis of direction and will at this moment in US racial politics, one that threatens to strengthen authoritarian structures at the expense of racial progress.

Husserl writes in the introduction to *Experience and Judgment* that "We would not be able to understand this definite historical origin of productions of sense in historical subjects if we did not re-accomplish them ourselves, if we did not re-experience this origination of the operations of idealization from original life-experience" (1973: 49). Similarly, Hannah Arendt speaks to the problem that the Black community experiences in the US of breaks in history that cannot be overcome except by reexamining the narratives themselves, when in *Men in Dark Times* she writes of the awkwardness that Germans experience when asked about the events that occurred during the Nazi regime (1968: 19–21; Sebald 2003: 10–13). For Arendt, it is in the process of exteriorizing the subjectivization that occurred during the time, which is otherwise hidden from view by the impact of events on individuals, that it becomes possible to address the horror of the politics during the period (1985: 465). As Benjamin writes, "Only that historian will have the gift of fanning the spark of hope in the past who is firmly convinced that *even the dead* will not be safe from the enemy if he wins" (1969b: 255). Renarration allows us to address its description within contemporary subjection. This is what makes the discussion of the Massacre of 1898 in *The Marrow of Tradition* by Chesnutt so appealing. Chesnutt provides, as Frances Harper does with *Iola Leroy*, access both to the way that Jim Crow began as a system of political instruments and to how race was described then in ways that find expression in Black subjection today. By identifying specific social strategies developed historically in the politics of racial subjection today we can return to a particular moment of political resolution, not directly as immediate experience, but as a narrative to be reconsidered and redefined.

The view that we have of racial events in history really matters. It determines the solutions we have available to us (Brown 2001: 156). For the Black subject this is a matter of coming to terms with both the scale and quality of events in the past; the sequence of unmitigated violent acts, slavery and the trade in humans, the migration to escape Jim Crow practices and convict leasing, tenant farming and urban poverty, political isolation and helplessness, the daily practices of subordination to Whites and their community (Wilkerson 2011). To return in this way to the question of the political construction of the Black community takes for granted that doing so does not threaten the survival of the persons who are Black. Something will still define Black life even if we try to change the description of racial politics. It will just not be in response to a decision of racial difference or the description of authenticity that is one of its indirect effects (Shelby 2005). We will not lose the ability to be human.

ALL OF THE TIME IN THE WORLD

To speak of history is to speak of time. This reconstruction of the Black subject assumes that life is a matter of normal and exceptional activity, that there are by turn periods of stability and rapid change. That time changes, it slows down and speeds up, that we return to something only to leap ahead to something new, we lose track of time (Sebald 1997). Finding ourselves unsure of whether we are in the past or present, along with the democratic polity, we are unable to progress past these effects of the racial decision.

What kind of people are we in America? The Americans of the occupying forces in Germany during World War Two are described by Sebald's character in this way,

> The womenfolk went about in trousers and dropped their lip-stained cigarette butts in the street, the men put their feet up on the table, the children left their bikes out in the garden overnight, as for the negroes, no one knew what to make of them. (1997: 70)

What should we make of ourselves; how should we be described? An event so traumatic that it threatens life causes the collapse of time; its effects remain within the community and its subjection of individuals long past its expiration date. What do we do when these events are continuous over generations, with new iterations to be addressed by each generation? How should we address the effects of racial subordination and social control that were not life threatening as a description of political development in the society?

To be Black or White is therefore to potentially define oneself against all of the history of race in the US and the effects of this as a description of community. This is impossible and paralyzing, and so something else must be offered as a solution. It is not enough to claim that the steady perturbation of race on social life has made experience inaccessible (Agamben 2007: 27). The opacity that Whites have learned historically to see in Blacks as a part of the racial decision, the creaturely aspect of Black subjectivity that was discussed in Chapter 5, is not apparent for a Black subject that is considering the possibilities for political action at odds with the description of him or herself by Whites. Rather, the constant social attrition of racial description is conceived by the Black subject as the definition of what race is, and so the act of reflection on these experiences is an important political moment for the subject. For the Black individual the ambition would be to bring together the elements of the fractured community to begin to progress, to return in some way to the scene of the horrific events against oneself and all other Blacks.

This is in part what Saidiya Hartman (2007) attempts to do in *Lose Your Mother*, returning to the physical spaces and geographical location of the slave-trading posts of West Africa. What Hartman discovers is that, unlike the character Austerlitz in Sebald's novel of the same name, who returns to the events of his youth, personal memory is not passed down over generations (Sebald 2001). Sebald in *Austerlitz* has his main character work through the effects of being sent as a four-year-old child on *Kindertransport* to England at the start of the Second World War and losing his parents in the process. In contrast, the slave forts remain as alien to Hartman as if she were a stranger to the land in Africa that she visits.

It is not a personal memory we are looking for but a change in the description of who we are through a reconsideration of the past as a collective enterprise. In order to do this we need to explore the fictions we use to make sense of events in the past. What follows are several chapters that work through some of the political descriptions available to the Black community that I think important to bring back into contention with the current politics of race. I challenge our difficult relationship to ourselves and our community as Black exceptions to a rule of racial subordination that we wish to change (Shelby 2005). How do we find ourselves willing to pay a price for success that allows for a majority of the community to remain in its traditional role at the bottom of society? It is only by redefining the politics of the exception that we can move forward as exceptional and normal Black subjects.

Along with this idea of trauma as a problem of history for victims of racism it is important to understand the problem for a democratic polity that arises for those communities of persons that perpetrate these injustices. These are the persons whose subjection within a racial community as a decision requires the definition and subordination of others. The responsibility for a traumatic or violent event against persons has to be accounted for and addressed by those who engaged in it as well as the victims. What I am pointing out here is not first the problem of justification, but of trying to erase the political effects on the polity of the occurrence of collective injustice so as to recover or discover democratic politics.

In a society that is constantly developing politically, the mechanisms by which the society reorganizes the public interpretation and the institutional response to events are very important. In *Iola Leroy,* the idea of political progress that describes the freeing of the slaves and their struggle to become a part of the larger polity as citizens describes a political optimism and the promise of social possibilities that led instead to Jim Crow. A similar type of political closure or rupture occurs with the end of established Jim Crow legal policies supposedly to allow for a new politics, that of racial equality, to develop. Instead of seeing this as necessary to the positive political development of the society, I see this problem of a necessary blindness or inability to address other interpretations of politics beyond the scope of the idea of racial progress as a real dilemma. Similarly, we will see in the discussion of *The Marrow of Tradition* that in the wake of the devastation of the South in the Civil War the political progress of Blacks did not match the reality of how Blacks were integrated into the society once free (Du Bois 1962; Woodward 1966; Foner 1970; Sterling 1984; Cohen 1991; Hale 1999; White 1999). The US is not a society in which rights trump social reality with regard to race.

As I have described above, a similar disconnect between political rhetoric and social reality was accomplished by portraying the events of the 1960s as allowing for a new era of politics. Rather than emphasize the similarity of racial practices with those that had come before, the new focus was on defining a space for racial equality through government action. Only by using the new fiction of conditional and exceptional racial equality as a barrier to critical racial politics is it possible to meet the needs of a revisionist politics to describe the past as something that can be forgotten, since now race is unimportant in the US. To this willful forgetting as a way to refute criticism of the new model of racial equality there is added a concern by those Whites born after the 1950s of their own culpability in the politics of Jim Crow as this has gone forward into the present. It becomes very important for these individuals to refute or reject counterarguments that things have not changed or are merely different but that race persists as a problem in society. The alternative to this rejection is to accept that White community life today is similarly blind to the problem of race as were their parents and grandparents during Jim Crow. We may rediscover the hanging tree in our midst, the location that is forgotten but plainly visible if we care to find it in towns across the nation.

The idea that racist events happened in the past, and so therefore they somehow should stay there as an example of how much society has progressed, is a powerful argument for most Whites to leave behind the relationship of their own families to Jim Crow events in the past. However, as Habermas points out with respect to the arguments of young Germans who are grandchildren of those involved in World War Two, the young generation "grew up within a form of life in which *that* was still possible" (1989: 232). This is true for White Americans today as well.

Unlike in the case of the National Socialists in Germany in World War Two, the White community in the US did not lose the political struggle in the events of the 1960s so much as change how they were able to support the importance of the racial hierarchy in the society. Similar to the politics of mourning, guilt, and critical reflection that Germany is still addressing with great difficulty, the need to reconcile the democratic state and its citizens with the events that occurred under Nazi government authority, in the US it was important to argue that not only was racial equality now within reach, but that the majority of Whites and the description of the White social community beyond the decision was the main force behind the social progress that was taking place. Certainly what Michel-Rolph Trouillot suggests in *Silencing the Past: Power and the Production of History* is true: there are structural similarities in the erasure and banalization of the effects of race in the US and the Holocaust in Germany (1995: 96). At the same time, the accounting for the effects of Jim Crow on US society is very late in coming, and perhaps this, as in Germany, is a testament to the difficulty of assimilating the events of the period to the censured and new world described so as to allow the repetition of racial practices (Browning 1993; Goldhagen 1997).

The Civil Rights Movement was accorded a place in history as having made the community of Whites aware of the horrors of racism, even as the social description of race continued unabated in society. The lionization of Martin Luther King Jr., similar to the election of Barack Obama as president, served as an important reference point in the new politics of racial equality. Once reviled, King is now lauded as having brought through his suffering and death an immediate knowledge of the plight of Blacks to those millions of Whites who otherwise were not aware of the effects of race in the society during the eight decades of Jim Crow politics. From this perspective, that both men received the Nobel Prize for Peace is confirmation of the continued operation of the apparatus of racial equality.

It was necessary to conceal the continuation of the social segregation of the races after the 1960s by raising the question of the responsibility younger Whites had for the events in the past. Unlike in Germany in the 1980s, when the Historian's debate took place, it is only now at the turn of the twenty-first century, with the increasing realization on the part of academics in the US, that racial politics has not been resolved through the political structures that support formal racial equality, as well as the aging of the generation that were adults during the 1950s, that allows for an increasing interest in a critical historical perspective of the Jim Crow and slavery eras (LaCapra 1998: 43–72). Another factor may be paradoxically that with a sense of racial innocence by Whites comes also a false sense of impunity or personal distance from the events that took place prior to the 1960s; Whites have accepted the political idea of their difference from the racist as a subject of ridicule and disdain, and that allows for a position of being innocent of blame and therefore able to confront whatever history they find as something they are not implicated within. This innocence is just not true nor is it possible without something more substantial politically than the definition of the exceptional status of the racist (King and Smith 2011: 113).

Unlike in South Africa, a truth and reconciliation commission in the US is impossible (Tutu 1999). I don't believe that the problem is that of an apology for slavery, which would serve merely to act as a caesura for the present politics of racial injustice and the apparatus. There has been no acknowledgment of the events of Jim Crow as a personal charge or responsibility by Whites as individuals and there has been no collective White apology to Blacks for the past. There has been no way for Whites to admit to themselves what it is that racial politics does in the US today. Instead, the White community has framed the new politics of equality as not requiring forgiveness on their part, since there is no acknowledgment of continued culpability. This also causes particular problems for the uncovering of the practices that continue to determine Black life, both that directly resulting from the distinction of race and that which develops in the daily definition of personal choices within the political apparatus of racial equality. We need to find a way to "comprehend without exonerating, without making oneself an accomplice to flight and denial" (Ricoeur 2004: 327).

In these next three chapters I develop an argument for a politics of the Black community in the midst of the development of racial equality in the US. Of each pair of texts, one text addresses problems of Black community development in the space created by race and the other text focuses on racial politics in the period. These are not sentimental pieces where race is resolved as a problem for White Americans but are instead works that portray the difficulty Blacks encounter in each period of US history (Sebald 2006: 101). I believe that the Black subject is formed from the unresolved continuous practices of racial difference over time. These practices can be defined from within the formal distinctions of racial political change, slavery, Jim Crow, and integration, without privileging too much the uniqueness of a specific period. I think there is a continuity of racial practices that can be described separately from the narrative that there has been racial progress; I also don't think we know how to characterize this idea of racial progress separately from the economic and political development of the US generally.

In this way I want to develop an argument that reorients Black community political concerns to that of racial politics. As Santner writes of the relation in Sebald's *Austerlitz* between memory and our relationship to other persons,

> This is, then, not so much a substitution of memory-work for politics as it is the imaginative construction of the kind of sites where such

encounters might take place; it is furthermore an ambitious and exemplary performance of the specific sorts of *labor*—of *study*—involved in sustaining fidelity to such encounters. (2006: 141)

This is true of the fiction texts discussed below.

Fiction offers a description of the values and ideas available at the time a text was written. In the case of African American life, with a number of exceptional cases, few Blacks were able to work within academic professional circles until the 1960s so as to do the type of research on race that members of the White community could (Du Bois 1962; Cooper 1988; Hurston 2008). This means that fiction is an important window into the world of a particular period for Blacks in US history. If racial politics describes rules for the normal and exceptional actions of government, if it provides a definition of what race is as a social concept such that it can be the object of politics, then fiction writing identifies the normal perception of popular conceptions of race, Blackness, and the problems of subjection that race creates. I think that African American fiction writing is an important source for our understanding of the Black community of the past and the future.

IOLA LEROY: INTRODUCTION

Published in 1893, *Iola Leroy, Or, Shadows Uplifted*, by Frances Harper, describes the challenges experienced by a young African American woman, Iola Leroy, at the end of the Civil War. The book was a best seller when it was published, and is the first novel by an African American woman to be widely read in the period immediately after the Civil War. The novel describes some of the concerns that the newly freed Blacks had in trying to define a place for themselves in the society, and the energy with which they sought to be included in the efforts of rebuilding society after the war. The book provides a series of discussions on the perception of race and community by Blacks as well as a description of the type of choices available to members of the Black community in the immediate postwar period. It is an important novel for what it tells us about the urgency with which former slaves tried to improve the resources of the community after emancipation.

A light-skinned Black woman, Iola grew up without being aware of her racial history, only to be enslaved when her father died and the truth was revealed. Prior to her enslavement Iola's education and deportment were those of plantation White society. With the coming of the Civil War, Iola fled to Union lines and stayed with the army instead of fleeing north to her brother. She wanted to try to find her mother, who was sold separately from her, but while waiting for some word she provided assistance as a medical nurse to the wounded. During her time as a nurse, the White doctor Gresham falls in love with Iola. She is the classic American tragic figure of someone who looks White but is Black, as though somehow this fact of possibly being White makes race more difficult to accept or justify than for someone who is darker skinned (Bogle 2001). Harper describes Iola as someone who reflects on race and slavery, and in doing so Harper describes a political subject able to understand the problems that newly freed Blacks experienced, with few resources, little or no education, and uncertain prospects. That Iola has a superb education, has had considerable social resources at her disposal for much of her life, and also has been a slave at the mercy of the master means she can serve as a foil in the novel to discuss the types of choices educated Blacks had in response to the needs of their community, as well as address the desires of Whites to integrate the newly freed Blacks into the society.

The two political narratives about the development of racial politics in the coming Jim Crow period are also present in the novel. These were the idea that White Northerners freed Blacks, and therefore the definition of race as facilitating White community cohesion remained an important justification for Black subordination after slavery, and that the Civil War was a conflict between parts of the White community, a fraternal conflict, and never really about Blacks or engaging their racial subjectivity at all (Woodward 1966; Blight 2002; Goodheart 2011: 182). From this it is easy to imagine support for the political argument that the hierarchy found in the plantation economy between Whites and Blacks must be maintained no matter what for the surety of the social order.

FRIENDSHIP AND AFFECTION

The story *Iola Leroy* addresses what has been a central theme in racial politics in the US, the idea of interracial relationships and what they mean for persons on both sides of the distinction of race (Harper 2010: 53). The narrative begins with a description of the lives of Iola's parents. Her father is a wealthy White plantation owner, Eugene Leroy, who falls in love with a Black slave woman, Marie. Eugene pays for her education in the North, providing her with the intellectual training otherwise unavailable to someone of her status. Eugene explicitly provides the means for Marie not only to be free but also well-educated so as to be able to have a partner who is his social equal. He can't marry a slave legally, and so Eugene frees Marie (Hodes 1999: 28).

Upon mentioning that he will engage in this prospect to his best friend, the friend scorns him without surcease. The love Eugene expresses for Marie and the reasons he finds her a person of integrity and sincerity are nothing to the friend when he discovers in the course of the conversation that she is Black. The suggestion by the friend is instead that Eugene merely keep Marie as a mistress, or indulge his desires with her as a someone without other recourse. Deborah Gray White writes about this problem of the woman slave having few choices to avoid this type of relationship. She writes, "Although not all white male-black female relationships were exploitive, most began that way, and most continued that way" (1999: 34). The friend questions the morals of the woman, and when she is described as looking White, questions the moral character of "quadroon" women generally. The framing of the larger narrative of the book with this initial conversation between White friends about race and relationships is important. Not only is race perceived as a division between social worlds that is formidable but this is discussed without great weight being paid to the problem of slavery itself. What matters is that the racial status of the persons involved and the social hierarchy must be preserved. The implication is that Blackness allows for slavery, that it and other debased human conditions are morally justified by this fact, that it is a quality of the person that defines all aspects of the human and not merely a superficial assignment of difference. A social difference is a moral difference, and this fact means everything with respect to the type of racial equality that we accept.

Eugene explains that he is able to see Marie as an equal, thereby erasing the stigma of race, because she spent time by his side healing him from the effects of a dissipated life. His physical and spiritual recovery from a life of debauchery and immoral activity were facilitated by her presence in his life. The parallel with Socrates and Diotima in the *Symposium* is not unimportant here. Eugene was able to see Marie as something more than a mere instrument of redemption. Her devotion to his well-being, her own integrity, and moral presence allowed him to find a way past the presence of the Other to something in himself as well: a common space for both of them of intimacy and companionship beyond race. The author does not have Eugene pontificate about the evils of racism and slavery; instead, his friend and the readers are clearly expected to find this description of an understanding that can exist outside of race credible.

They both understand that race depends on refusing the life together that otherwise occurs between persons. For the friend, this type of budding relationship is what has to be avoided to preserve the races and the idea of race. That he reviles and scorns Eugene's willingness to upset the conditions of racial status for Marie serves to prove for the reader the veracity of the claim that certain types of social circumstances erase the distinctions of race. Anger and fear would not be the reaction to something impossible but is the response to something threatening. The author clearly sees the racial distinction between two persons as more complicated than that of physical proximity and social contact. This is apparent later in the narrative when their daughter Iola Leroy refuses to marry the white Dr. Gresham even though they both have feelings for one another. This perspective brings to mind the description of community by Nancy, where race would impose itself as a concept between the sociality that otherwise occurs between humans.

GOING IT ALONE: WITHOUT COMMUNITY

For the argument I am making here the main theme of the story is the description of the political limitations of personal activity to address the larger problem of the creation of racial communities. While important as a first step, White personal transformation with someone Black is insufficient; instead, the individual has to confront race as a description of social communities. Once Eugene and Marie are married they spend years in social exile, with no White woman of substance willing to be entertained by a Black hostess; the implication is also that his male friends keep their distance. As a result, there are not enough social elements in common with the racial construction of the White community to maintain a social presence; the couple literally ceases to exist. The problem that the author establishes for Eugene is that while he is unhappy with the situation, and ensures that his oldest children attend schools up North during the regular school year, he does not take seriously the prospect of a calamity forcing his wife and children into slavery.

He does not take the precariousness of their situation seriously enough. He does not recognize that the characterization by the White community of their relationship is not merely one of indifference, but is inimical to their existence. This remains true today. Race is a political decision that requires a cohesive White community. His stance towards race is that of finding someone he loves and building a life with her ostensibly apart from the fact of race (Harper 2010: 92). He does not free the other slaves on his plantation, even though he does treat them well, for slaves, and this is a further example of not applying his own experience of the importance of resisting the social description of a difference of race between him and Marie, and his children, to include the social politics that fosters a definition of the larger White community.

No mention is made to their children of Marie's former status as slave or her being Black. Marie's race becomes concealed through the device of the children they have, which is justified, according to Eugene and Marie, by the idea that the children should be spared the onus of addressing the racial conflict that persists around them. They are raised not knowing they are Black and instead learn to be White. This is a necessary function of the erasure of Marie's Blackness as a status; this tension between her new status as "free" and what defines Blackness is evident today for those Blacks who are today defined as the exception to racial subordination.

The author does not suggest that the children should know they are Black because there is a quality about themselves that is not otherwise being addressed socially. She does not have a naturalistic view of race, but instead expects her readers to agree that race exists as a decision, not a natural condition of the human. The author even has the young Iola defend the institution of slavery to her peers while in school in the North, all the while unaware that she is also Black by social tradition. Anyone can argue for the decision. The tragedy that moves the story forward is therefore two-fold. Eugene dies and his wife and two girls are enslaved by his cousin, while Eugene's son remains up North and free. But they all now know they are Black. As Du Bois writes in *Dusk of Dawn*, "I felt myself African by 'race' and by that token was African and an integral member of the group of dark Americans who were called Negroes." (Du Bois 2012a: 115). With this device the author returns them to the community of Blacks struggling to define what freedom from slavery meant after the Civil War. At the same time, the author signals by the impact of Eugene's death the problem for Whites who seek merely to live alongside or beyond the decision of race. It is not enough.

The resolution of race through letting beings be, of providing a social space where a community without race can exist, does not eliminate the coincidence of the relationship with other social practices that define race in the society. History must be undone. The work of clearing is otherwise too great, and can never be comprehensive enough to halt the capacity for the racial politics that demands social investigation and confirmation of the distinction, the answer to the question of "What (race) are you?" More needs to be accomplished than to identify how race works, whether this is simply stated through the politics of friend and enemy or more complex constructions of difference. That Eugene and Marie have their children pass as White as a way to conceal the possible impact of the decision ends up merely confirming the importance of race for them. The author clearly accepts that passing is not a viable option because each of the light-skinned children is explicitly asked why he or she does not pass for White only to reject this explicitly as an acceptance of the politics of race that he or she refuses to condone. To pass is to accept race in the way that Eugene and Marie do, to leave the politics alone, not to deny the hold it has on oneself and others in society. The discourses around the "problem" of miscegenation and passing facilitate rather than challenge the basis for the decision of race in society. Both conditions are effects of race and not the substance of its reproduction.

This also reveals something interesting about "the color problem" or politics of complexion amongst Blacks in the US at the time. If the impossibility of passing as an effective politics is accepted, then there is no difference between someone light- or dark-skinned who is Black within the racial decision itself. The availability of anyone Black to the politics of race is separate from an idealization of Whiteness in society which creates a hierarchy based on these characteristics for both communities. In this case those who "don't look Black" but are Black are perceived as a threat to the distinction in that they can potentially move into White society without discovery. The author avoids addressing this issue since none of her characters try to pass as adults. Instead, the light-skinned characters are made to challenge socially the problem of racial "visibility" and the way phenotypical differences are used in social discourse to conceal the true basis of the decision of race.

BEYOND PERSONAL POLITICS

It is left to Iola, the daughter of Eugene and Marie, to work out the problem of seeing around the Other to reconstitute a Black community that can address the politics of race. She has to get out of her own way to develop an effective critical race politics. Slavery had defined a Blackness and a social community that needed to be addressed with emancipation. Iola decides that she should dedicate her own life to learning and teaching the Black community the social practices that freedom demanded. She applies this idea to those Whites in her life as a way to teach them to develop a politics beyond the personal practiced by her, Eugene, and Marie.

In a repeat of the way Eugene fell in love with Marie, the White Dr. Gresham observes Iola tending to the sick and dying in the army camp towards the end of the war. He is informed of her race, and while initially this creates a barrier to his affections, he moves beyond his misgivings because of the social engagement they have with one another. For Harper, love and affection cross the distinctions of race. This was different from the affection and loyalty described and accepted as important between slaves and masters, but was a common theme in the society as relationships between Blacks and Whites occurred in the shadow of slavery (Hodes 1999; Rothman 2007).

Dr. Gresham approaches Iola with the fact of their developing affection for one another, and suggests that they marry. Her response is the key political moment in the novel. Knowing that Gresham's family would require her to pass, Iola says that she cannot live as White in his community while race continues to oppress her people. The problem is not color but the decision itself. Iola is specifically concerned with her mother in her conversation with Dr. Gresham, as her mother's fate is unknown. It is obvious when she eventually becomes a teacher in the South to newly freed Black children that Iola's commitment to herself now includes erasing the effects of race on society. Even after finding her mother and moving to the North, Iola's response to Gresham remains the same. Even though she is deeply attached to him, Dr. Gresham unfortunately does not see his role in relation to race differently than Iola's father Eugene. The isolation from the politics of race that Gresham requires for racial equality is insufficient and is already well-rehearsed on the life of Iola. The reader is made aware of this directly as well in a series of discussions about race between Gresham and others.

The problem with Gresham lies not in his physical person or the ability of Iola to fall in love with him, but in his inability to see himself as other than White in ways that her White father, Eugene, also felt allowed for a separation of race from the concerns of everyday life. The fact of Whiteness conceals its own complicity in a description of absolute authority that then gives the illusion of being able to master even the fact of the decision of race. In other words, Dr. Gresham and Eugene Leroy both think that since they are White they can even overcome their own subjection, the fact of what race has created and creates for them and others, without the constant critical work on race this requires.

None of the Black characters in the story have this perspective; they remain terrified of the possibility of the effects of the politics of race. It is only the White subject in the narrative who says not to worry and that race does not matter. Only someone created to think that he or she has individual control over the basis for the decision of race would argue that it does not apply to a specific case. Those who are described as victims of the hierarchical distinction are not in a position to assume any authority over its application. The tragedy, of course, which Harper the author makes plain through the enslavement of Iola upon her father's death, is that this assumption of clearing or of individual White sovereignty is an illusion that further assists in obscuring the decision as a definition of racial community. The White person is not able to create a space by him- or herself where race does not matter.

This is merely to retreat into a space that does not exist, something outside of the decision to race, or to be too convinced that the authority of an individual White person can trump the desires of the White community. There is a hint of this argument in Gresham's pretension to marry Iola and tell no one of her Blackness, to let his Whiteness define Iola's race as well, much as Iola's Whiteness as a child defined Marie's status as "free." The possibility for Iola of living as a White person while married to Gresham does not exempt her from the constant work of the decision on his or her social life. It does not remove the effects of race; it merely shifts the onus onto the White community of which the person is now a part.

Gresham is an important character because he nonetheless accepts that something has to be done to challenge the viability of the community of practices that defines Whiteness. Like Eugene, Gresham sees the problem as one of "public opinion," but not as something that has to be addressed or it overwhelms the possibility of living with Iola (Harper 2010: 179). Gresham concedes to Iola that she can work on the other side of the color line, on the problems of race for Blacks, but Gresham is unwilling to similarly change the character of the political decision of his family for Whiteness. He does not force his mother to accept Iola as his Black wife, or a possible life with Iola within the Black community, which he should do according to Iola, but rather asks Iola to become White so as to marry.

The political solution that Harper offers is therefore the relatively straightforward but difficult idea of allowing for love across the color line, of recognizing this fact and of engaging the idea of race as a challenge to love successfully for everyone. The critical assessment of race by this fact of love becomes a way to create human beings that can love. The implication is that absent this challenge, persons both Black and White suffer from relationships truncated by race. Harper approaches the idea of love through the idea of giving care to someone. Rather than leave the question of ontology unaddressed, this is a love that eliminates the importance of race for those persons involved. Both Marie, Iola's mother, and Iola form relationships with White men through the act of caring for them. In Marie's case, she actually cares for and nurses Eugene, the person she falls in love with, while Dr. Gresham sees Iola in the act of caring for other persons and finds himself smitten. In both cases the care is given without recompense or expectation of reciprocity. They both sacrifice themselves for another person, and for Harper this idea of sacrifice is enough to overcome the impact of the decision of race on their immediate environment. Iola then dedicates her life to teaching in the Black community, without arguing that the community should similarly offer itself to Whites as a collective gesture of love. The politics of care remains local and individual in ways that ultimately do not protect the couple or family from the effects of race around them.

Unlike her father Eugene, Dr. Gresham refuses to allow love to create even the immediate family; he wants Iola to pass as White, and does not want to accept the contempt and the hostility for Iola that would occur from those Whites in his family. He is therefore rejected as someone that Iola can love. As Iola says regarding the choice of her brother not to pass as White, "It were better that he should walk the ruggedest paths of life a true man than tread the softest carpets a moral cripple" (2010: 206). For Harper this statement of Blackness seems political; it concerns not only the plight of the newly freed Black slaves but the choice of how the country will address the future politics of race. In 1893 Harper wrote that "the problem of the nation . . . is not what men will do with the negro, but what they do with the reckless, lawless white men who murder, lynch, and burn their fellow-citizens" (169). The societal problem is therefore more complex than that of Black individuals working on Whites to develop ways to care through sacrifice, and letting them be, in an act of selflessness. The solution to race for Harper is located instead in the cluster of practices that challenge the statement that "this is a white man's government, and a white man's country" (174).

WHITE POLITICS

The popular belief that the Civil War began as a conflict over trade and ended as a conflict over the role of race is explicitly stated in the novel (Du Bois 1962). Since slaves were property, the relative absence initially of race as an issue in public debates during the war between the North and South makes sense. Harper points out that it was only when the North was willing to realize the status of the Black person as more than a slave was it possible for them to win the war, and that the argument over trade was in fact an argument over whether Blacks could be described as property (2010: 108). The political and economic development of the US was dependent on changing how racial difference was described.

The novel begins with the discussion by slaves about the possibility of going over to the Northern lines several miles away and therefore becoming free. The author has the characters describe what this would mean for their relationships to other Blacks and to their White masters. The terms of the discussion are striking because the initial issue is the choice of staying or leaving slavery, not the granting of emancipation by Lincoln. Harper's point is that the decision that led to slavery did not create abject subjects, merely degraded subjects (96).

For Harper and her readers it was taken for granted that the politics of race required that persons be willing to place their lives at risk, and enjoin the possibility of absolute sacrifice. Only then will it be possible to dissolve the decision that creates the friend and enemy distinction so important to Schmitt's description of politics. The problem for the collective description of race is that it is possible to degrade someone's life to an extent where the promise of a life enslaved is better than the probability of unknown terror and of uncertain suffering. It is possible to preclude the moment of sacrifice as a choice, and thereby eliminate the possibility of love between persons.

Harper is explicit about this possibility when she describes the difficulty slaves faced when attempting to win freedom, and how Whites educated slaves in the terrible things that would occur to them if they disobeyed or escaped (2010: 110). The importance of terror, fear, and intimidation to limit the social ambitions of Blacks is a constant theme of White racial politics. It remains a central element in the use of crime and policing to describe the Black community today. The problem is that changing racial politics for Harper was clearly linked to a willingness for Whites to do more than acquiesce to "public opinion" and instead to force those in their community to change their social behavior towards Blacks. In both the case of Eugene and Dr. Gresham it is the corresponding fear of what might happen to them and their relationship to the community that causes them to turn away from social change. In a way similar to the terror created to keep Blacks in their place, Whites also, as Harper makes clear, were made to feel that the social distinctions of race were absolute and inviolate, on pain of violence and ostracism. How else could Harper's readers accept that a cousin of Eugene's who met Marie as his wife for years prior to his death immediately works to sell her and Eugene's children into slavery when this becomes possible? What do events like this teach Whites about the price of violating racial social distinctions? It is very important to understand that both Blacks and Whites live under threat by race, and that the application is thought to justify every depredation.

Rather than read *Iola Leroy* as a traditional tragedy, I see this text as providing an important early political statement about the limits of personal affection and relationships to address the politics of race. It describes how Whites attempt to meet and overcome racial politics but fail because they are unwilling to ask other Whites to change, and explains through the actions of Iola and others why some Blacks make a choice to address the development of the Black community when their own personal politics fails to elicit social equality.

A LIFE MEASURED

What strikes the reader today about *Iola Leroy* is how contemporary it seems. In the story the fact of slavery is secondary to the problem of race as it manifests between persons. The distinction of race is viewed by the author as the cause of slavery. In fact the story begins towards the end of the Civil War, with the imminent demise of the Peculiar Institution. The reader experiences a sense of disorientation from the fact that the social practices that describe racial differences have not changed significantly from when the book was published in 1893. This can be confusing, as our idea of racial social progress today depends on the success of both White and Black members of the polity. It is important not to confuse this idea of progress with the possibility that racial difference remains central to social order. While the language we use has changed, few today would not understand the continuing force of the idea expressed by one of the White characters in *Iola Leroy* when he states, "only sustain business relations with the negroes . . . not commit the folly of equalizing yourself with them" (2010: 184). This was the message that underscored the institutional developments that led to Jim Crow segregation and, in spite of rhetoric to the contrary, persists in the social segregation advocated between races today.

At the same time the idea of race as a structure is too simplistic in a situation where the description of its effects is constantly shifting to support a qualitative distinction between human beings as a collective identity or object. We can now see that race is clearly a distinction that takes the form of a decision outside of the realm of politics in order to insulate it from criticism. The collectivities established find importance everywhere because the decision is outside of social practices; it just is for the individual. To the extent that it is possible to obscure this fact, a discourse becomes available that suggests that race is instead something held as a belief system for particular individuals. The story of *Iola Leroy* describes the typical racial politics of the period after the Civil War, and reveals how the desire to live with race, even as some are asked to sacrifice themselves to the fact, against the fact of the decision itself, defined a Black subjectivity beyond any peculiar institutional description of social difference between Whites and Blacks. Iola and other Blacks in the novel seem immediately familiar to an African American reader today, since this subjectivity is identical to that defined in a community living beyond what makes us different from Whites. The choice of living with race and struggling against it remains a central element in how African American social life is measured.

FREEDOM

Frances Harper describes the political dilemma that the fact of slavery presented for Blacks and how slaves often turned to the ideal of America, as a description of freedom from oppression, to justify their rebellion from their status as property (2010: 16). They did this without embracing the conception of themselves as the internal enemy of the nation only by 1) suggesting that this definition did not apply to them, since they had been working for the nation their entire lives, or 2) seeking to shift the focus of the ideal from that of a struggle to the death to that of the nature of the demand for liberty. The aspirational ideal of America as "the land of the free" was thereby well-rehearsed within the Black community in the period leading up to the end of slavery. The message also communicated to readers was that the problem with the social definition of race was not merely that it was arbitrary but that it was impossible to successfully police interracial relationships (Hodes 1999; Rothman 2007). This policing became a function of social codes and norms developed in the White community that defined what distinctions were important to make between members of both racial communities.

Why would the promise of political participation at the time hold such weight for Blacks? Why would slaves and free Blacks believe that there was something to be gained by embracing the political ideals of the society? This is not the simple question of their familiarity with the society and the inability to find a similar promise in the idea of emigration to an Africa most had never seen. Instead, the Black community had been present throughout the period of the Revolutionary War, and had been a part of the struggle for freedom from colonial rule, and had as well been an important source of labor during the economic development of the first half of the 1800s. Rather than being ignorant of the larger political conditions occurring in the world around them, by virtue of the continuing diaspora of Blacks to the New World and their important role in the local economy, the Black community was a part of the solution in the struggle for US independence and the subsequent development of the nation.

The opening for slaves to accept the ideal of liberty within the description of US popular sovereignty lay in the possibility of escaping to the North, the idea that there was freedom elsewhere in the country, and the belief that it was also possible to be freed. This is one reason for the political importance of laws such as *Dred Scott v. Sandford* forcing the return of the runaway slave. To allow former slaves to remain free was to delimit the description for Blacks that their race required slavery. This also meant that some fluidity of racial status was available and the promise of freedom within the racial definition of difference was therefore substantiated even if only as the exception. The normal subjection of Blackness by the decision was always at the point of deciding between freedom and death, was always concerned with death and violence, and not with the development of a life as a slave. There was no refuge from the decision for the individual in that case, even though slavery was believed by Whites to allow access to all aspects of the life of a Black person.

To be a slave was to be free only to the extent that Whites were not given access to one's thoughts, cultural products, and other activities. A point made clear when a young White man in the novel says about the description of the runaway slave as the contraband of war, "I think ... it is the best kind of good. It means if two armies are fighting and the horses run away, the other has the right to take them" (2010: 22). What was the result for Blacks of the desire for freedom was for Whites reduced to a description of property rights. This gap between Whites and Blacks in their perception about the politics of race haunts the society today. Whites still struggle with the idea of Black equality, what that should mean for them, while Blacks are concerned with improving their economic, political, and social position. The division of race makes it impossible to communicate this difference of perspective.

Black slaves were popularly described by Whites as incapable of independent thought and action, and the argument was that freedom would result in former slaves having little industry and initiative; Whites were required to form goals and spur Blacks to act on their own behalf. Carried to its logical conclusion, this perspective supported the assumption by Whites that even slaves felt they would rather have slavery than freedom. The ideal slave was someone who was grateful for this specific subordination, and expressed this in his or her service to the master (Melville 1961; Harper 2010: 48). The problem with this view is that what the White community was describing as a sign of industry and ambition was whether Blacks would do what was expected by Whites, not what Blacks desired to do on their own. Independent volition by Blacks was defined as suspect and a potential challenge to the description of racial hierarchy. Against this idea in the story *Iola Leroy*, the slaves discuss the fact that they take care of Whites and so therefore can also be expected to successfully fend for themselves once free as well. But the fact that the author Harper includes this discussion in the story reveals the sensitivity with which Black freedom and White authority was viewed when the book was published more than thirty years after the war. This idea of being both capable and docile is the hallmark of Black subjection today.

What is important is how the Black slaves made sense of their connections to White persons, specifically those whom they must serve directly. The author Harper has the slaves reveal both a sense of duty and obligation and a need to take advantage of freedom when it was possible and to abandon those relationships that had defined them for so long with others. The bitterness at their lot in life, the social roles that slavery had occasioned is obvious, and yet for Harper the idea of being a slave was more important for Blacks to address in terms of leaving and a rejection of the role than as an opportunity for a reprisal for harms done.

What is the slave after slavery? In the absence of other obligations that trump this condition, the slave would rather take his or her chances to run away than continue as a slave. As Harper points out, for the slave the idea of emancipation, of a change in status towards others, was weighed in the balance with the concrete set of relationships between White master and Black slave that allowed for lives together in the shadow of the decision (2010: 33).

Slavery allowed for no limits to the actions of mastery but those given by circumstance, social custom, and the desire to preserve the value of property. But it is the human excess, that social remainder that was not encompassed by slavery, that demanded a Black community separate from that of Whites. As with Socrates and his relationship with Diotima in the *Symposium*, to nurture that beyond the decision of difference requires other persons who desire to share; they each need something else that can also define their lives (Plato 2003). The social distinction of race would otherwise reduce the interactions of persons across the racial divide to that of mere instrumental subordination, whether slave or free. As Harper's character Robert says at one point, "I think that some of these Northern soldiers do two things—hate slavery and hate niggers" (Harper 2010: 46). Today we praise the importance of racial equality as a solution to US political and economic development, while believing in the importance of the preservation of supposed racial social differences. The issues of friendship and affection are therefore central to a change in racial politics.

RACIAL UPLIFT

It is in texts such as *Iola Leroy* that the first public announcement of a coherent postslavery community of Blacks is identified. No longer split by the status of free or slave, Blacks could in the aftermath of the Civil War begin to speak, to write, of the connection those who had been free, slave, and passing could now have with one another. This took two explicit forms.

The first was a desire to uplift the race, to recover the lessons of learning and social development necessary to become a stable society. Was this project measured by the desire to be included alongside Whites as equals, or in itself, as a way to recognize a common plight regardless of education and former status? If the latter, this was a way to continue to bring into question the description of a society without race, in spite of its effects, and as a consequence of its impact on human lives. This was a project that sought a common theme for everyone regardless of race, a new society without this distinction. The importance of this political idea is obvious in the use Harper the author makes of Whites as also sympathetic figures throughout the story, as desiring to create an attachment to Iola that would exist in spite of race. Harper suggests this is not possible without a confrontation of Whiteness by Whites, of the idea of a White community authority in the polity that is malleable and even dissolvable.

If instead the recovery of Black education and social development after slavery was a desire for living in a specific relationship with Whites such that they would deem Blacks their social equal, this was a measure of the ongoing politics of race in the society. How could Blacks individually survive with White hostility and contempt in place after the war? How was it possible to overcome two centuries and more of differential development such that Whites would be able to see Blacks as equal as human beings? It is easy to see the theoretical problem with using any measure derived from within the practices of community given by Whites as the basis for equality. This description of authority to determine equality would itself further establish the basis of the distinction between Black and White. Harper clearly felt that love was not enough to define a space outside of race, and so the choices for Blacks came down to trying to find a description of community that would define social progress while in the shadow of race. The description of community for Blacks that defines a measure of progress against the pull of racial difference continues to be developed today.

The second form of politics available to Blacks described in *Iola Leroy* in the period after the Civil War was that given by the perception of a shared experience of the distinction of race. This was variable in one respect, the impact race played in an individual's life as a description of specific experiences, but was the same in the condition of a difference that was both devastating and immutable; once Black there was never the possibility of going back to a Whiteness that was a quality of being and not merely a composition of specific elements. Only Blackness was defined by quantity: how many White ancestors did it take to erase the Black, how many parts make a whole, what does it take to no longer be Black? With the end of slavery all Blacks suddenly became measured not as potential property, as a commodity for transactions between citizens, but according to a perceived difference from Whites as human beings. The price of this difference on individuals was tremendous, literally passing from an unperson, a thing, an always available object of White desire, to that of a person, the progenitor of desires, a political participant who must remain always free. This was a central theme in *Iola Leroy*, as Iola was described as having that fragility of spirit, that sensitivity of purpose that comes from having suffered a great harm, a great loss of status. Her having discovered both her Blackness and slavery in an act that was forever after ongoing defined a commonality with those Blacks who had always been made aware of their status.

It is this loss of status for Iola in *Iola Leroy*, as she moves from being White to being Black, that describes the fragility of the democratic impulse in the US polity. To have as an element of the institution of popular sovereignty the possibility of the individual losing one's status as an author of the society, its source for political norms, is terrifying for the individual but devastating for democratic politics. To make individual political authority conditional on racial status subsumes popular sovereignty to racial descriptions of community. Tocqueville's early description of the Negro problem as being at the center of US political development misrepresents the importance of race (de Tocqueville 2003). The fact that there are Blacks and Whites and that these communities must persist for us to believe this is still America denies the idea of a democratic America to come, any future without race.

THE PROBLEM WITH AN ETHIC OF CARE

It is in the discursive practices of this move from slave to free that a Black subject begins to describe a tension between individual freedom and the political constraints of racial community. The inability to challenge the effects of race while a slave was carried over into freedom. It was in the moment of the redemption, or emancipation, of slaves that the centrality of the decision of race was reaffirmed at the core of the US democratic experience. The split in the White community brought on by the war should have allowed a reassessment of the role of race and the possibility of the erasure of race as a community status that makes the difference between otherwise free men and women. In part this moment is contained in the discussion around land appropriation and reparations, but that is only part of the equation (Du Bois 1962; Woodward 1966; Litwack 1980).

What was most important was the inability to leave behind what was described earlier with regard to *Benito Cereno* as the inability of Whites to overcome their description of Blacks as creaturely and opaque to normal perception. The democratic impulse was clearly not strong enough amongst the White citizens of the period, and reveals a description of political development that is based on coercion and forced acquiescence and not a reflection of considered conversation and mutual respect between equal citizens. That in both examples in *Iola Leroy* of Whites seeking relationships with Blacks the idea of "public opinion" is enough to dissuade a stronger effort to alter the conditions set upon the relationship reveals how the idea of

Whiteness was important to preserve even in the face of both interpersonal affection, love and principle, as a politics. Instead we need to look at how the Black subject is described in both examples of relationships, and not merely repeat the recentering of the White experience as the description of events and as the truth of race.

In both the relationship between Eugene and Marie, Iola's parents, and in the case of Gresham and Iola, the care that the Black women take with the other person allows for love to develop for the White men. This description of an ethic of care defeats the prejudices of both Whites across the generations and should then be considered a powerful antidote to racism; except for the fact that traditionally Blacks are supposed to care for Whites, this is one of the most important social roles described by subordination. To make oneself valuable, an asset to the well-being of the White person, indispensable to the proper deportment and social standing of Whites, which is how both White captains describe the role of the loyal Black manservant in *Benito Cereno*, does not challenge the hierarchy of race but affirms it (Melville 1986: 212). The mammy was likewise expected to devote her working life to ensuring the well-being of her White charges through caring for them (Fleming 1998: 123; Bogle 2001). This remains a central discursive element in racial practices today.

The question we need to ask is whether Marie and Iola in their roles are able to find a way to engage in an ethics of care in spite of the description of race. Socrates and Diotima each learn through caring for the other, and this generates the philosophical experience as a politics of origination. Can we think of Marie, who is initially a slave whose master falls in love with her, as able to choose to care for another person? Isn't the description of the slave that of devotion but not love because of the nature of their relationship to the object of their affections? Isn't it only the White person that is capable of love, of engaging in a relationship of thinking and learning with another, in the description of race in the US? What I mean is, can a White person see a Black person as loving another, or does the distinction of race prohibit the ability for Whites to create a polis with Blacks?

Both Marie and Iola are free when they acknowledge their relationships with Eugene and Gresham, but I don't think that alters the problem of the substance of the ethic of care we would ascribe to them with regard to Whites. In both relationships race is not erased but something to be constantly negotiated as important to the survival of each relationship. The problem is the idea of "public opinion" that each White man is unable to set aside. This is a description of the collective decision to race, a description of communities of difference, which would resist its dissolution through the individual care for another. It requires a collective response where none is possible.

As Derrida reminds us, "Sovereignty is incompatible with universality even though it is called for by ... democratic law" (2005: 101). This means the racial subject must access the functions of government in spite of the racial apparatus, as a problem of, as Foucault puts it, the *de facto* limitations of government (2008a: 10). Foucault defines this not as a measure of the legitimacy but rather of the effectiveness of government. The community politics of race is a direct challenge to the relationship between persons and government in *Iola Leroy*, in the scope of freedom for Black citizens that must be protected by the government. The freedom that Marie experiences is unsupported by law, as she finds out once Eugene dies and the cousin is able to get the marriage annulled. Sold back into slavery, Marie's care for Eugene is revealed in that moment to have not changed the politics of race. It is not enough for her to appeal to the government for succor from the situation because of the truth. The limitations of the *parrhesiast* as the truth teller to provide for democracy are evident in this case.

SCHMITT AGAIN

The moment when the federal government abandoned the cause of the freedmen shortly after the war to accommodate the needs of Southern White elites signaled the privilege of racial community over democracy, but also placed very real limits on the extent to which an ethic of care between individuals could in the future alter the racial political landscape in the US (Du Bois 1962; Woodward 1966; Litwack 1980). Iola turns away from Gresham's love because it is insufficient to change the racial politics that comes between them, and she has no recourse in the law, in a government that has granted a citizenship and freedom that must remain empty of promise while White sovereign authority determines government practice. Iola is unable to care for others unless some other description than that of captive and opaque Black subjectivity is available to her. This has to be provided by government, and the failure to address the consolidation of political control in the hands of Whites in this period was a missed opportunity for US democracy.

As Schmitt points out when discussing the secularization of theological concepts in the construction of modern state sovereignty, the state "intervenes everywhere" in society (2005: 38). In the context of an argument by Schmitt for the importance of the decision from within the political relativism and human critical understanding that informed popular sovereignty in a democracy, the failure to expand the description of popular sovereignty, in spite of extending the vote to Black men, to attenuate the political importance of White community interests was a serious problem. In spite of a change in status, the description of Blacks as a community, and therefore Black individuals, as subject to the politics of the exception, was exempt from the political, economic, and social protections extended to citizens of a democracy by virtue of popular sovereignty. That the US can be described as a polity where "the people hover over the entire political life of the state" (49), and where "it has long been known that the idea of the liberal rights of man stemmed from the North American States" (62), but this same idea of the people is unable to address the use of race to define a community politics reveals the exception made for Blacks within US democratic politics.

It was only through the use of the exception as a rule for the description of Blacks as community in the polity that it was possible to describe the US as democratic. In Schmittian terms the politics of White community economic interests would otherwise reveal the processes at work in the society as at best partial democratic objects, with areas of politics stubbornly dedicated to ensuring that possible Black economic interests remain unaddressed and subordinated to White sovereign control. It is this political description that Iola Leroy must negotiate in her personal life and in the life of a community of Black free people that is forming in the wake of the Civil War. The tension between the moral decision and political legitimacy that Schmitt argues is the essence of sovereignty in the modern state can be resolved only by raising the question of the dependence of the US government on the particular decision of race (2005: 65). Why not dissolve the constraint placed by the idea of racial communities on democratic development in the society? This is the question that the text *Iola Leroy* cannot answer because of its focus on the definition of freedom for individuals, the reduction of politics to the care of individual persons, and the ability to live in spite of the decision of race. Instead, the Black subject needs another way to address the politics of White sovereignty in the society.

THE MARROW OF TRADITION

In contrast to *Iola Leroy*, which is a study on how individuals define their personal relationships against the backdrop of the racial communities of which they are a part, *The Marrow of Tradition* by Charles Chesnutt provides a description of the structure of Black subordination that Whites developed in the period after the Civil War. The following discussion will focus on three elements in the novel: the description of community and race politics, the possibility of mobilizing the White community to define the hierarchy of race, and the response of the critical Black subject to the developing apparatus of racial social control.

Charles Chesnutt wrote *The Marrow of Tradition* as a historical account of the events that led to the Wilmington, North Carolina, race riot of 1898. What motivated Chesnutt to write about this particular race riot was the particular egregiousness of the crimes committed against Blacks during the riot, and the indifference of the state and federal government to the plight of Blacks in the town (Woodward 1966: 86–87; Sundquist 1993: vi). On the other hand, this particular White riot was by no means an aberration, and the use of organized terror and violence to "maintain political, economic, and social domination" of Blacks was common in the period after the Civil War throughout the South (Shapiro 1988: 13; Brophy 2002). In the novel the White elites in Wilmington develop a discourse amongst themselves of the threat posed by the perceived social and economic progress of Blacks in the town. One of the themes in this discourse is the former social practices of Black subordination during slavery that were no longer available to Whites in 1898 (Litwack 1980). It was difficult to reconcile this perception of the normal place of Blacks relative to Whites as requiring slavery and the steady accumulation of wealth and commensurate social status that was occurring as Blacks began acquiring education and providing goods and services to their own community (Du Bois 1962).

At the time of the story, the city of Wilmington had a majority Black population, and many city officials, including a coroner, policeman, judge, and school board member, were Black. Two of the five fire stations were Black, as were all the members of the board of health, and three of the town aldermen (Sundquist 1993: viii). Whites in Wilmington were able to meet Blacks on the street and in their professional lives who were better off than themselves and whose source of economic wealth was not directly connected with White community interests. Not only did this challenge the perception of White superiority but also represented a potential independent political force in the society. Above all other concerns such a situation was a threat to White sovereignty and social control.

RACIAL INHERITANCE

The story begins with Major Carteret arriving home only to find his pregnant wife Olivia, both of whom are White, ill in bed from the shock of having seen her Black half-sister Janet Miller and her child while out riding. This is explained by the particular racial history that the family has. Shortly after the death of her mother, Olivia went to live with her aunt Polly, while her father lived with his Black housekeeper Julia, and they eventually had a child, Janet. This was during the period of Reconstruction and so Whites and Blacks could marry. Unbeknownst to the White community in Wilmington, the two did marry and so Janet is a legitimate heir, as is Olivia (Chesnutt 1993: 258). The father's will is hidden by Polly upon his death and so instead of receiving an inheritance and social legitimacy the two Blacks, the wife Julia, and her daughter Janet are removed from the house and forced to live on the largess of the Black community. At the time of the story many years have passed, Janet has recently married a wealthy Black doctor named Miller, and they have bought the Carteret family estate in town. Due to the war, the Carterets had been unable to keep their former financial status and eventually had to sell their estate. That Olivia marries Major Carteret and lives in reduced circumstances in her father's house while her half-sister Janet has been able to buy the former Carteret family estate sets the stage for the racial tensions of the novel. The coincidence of White sovereignty and political development in the society is the central theme from the very first pages of the novel.

Janet has a small child even as Olivia is expecting her first. Rather than embrace her sister Janet, whom Chesnutt describes as identical to her in appearance, Olivia Carteret is mortified by the fact that her father had a child with a Black person and that Janet has the temerity to act as a social equal rather than as someone subordinated by the shame of her situation. The relationship between Olivia and Janet thus described by the author matches an important element in the history of racial politics in the US: the idea that White transgressions of social segregation must be kept from impacting the politics and social description that determines legitimate membership in the polity. The persistence of the birther politics that seeks to challenge the legitimacy of President Obama is in part a response to this idea of erasing or concealing the fact that White individuals also persistently challenge the idea of racial difference. Whites also require social control to ensure their adherence to the racial values of the White community. In this perspective it is President Obama's mixed-race status that demands a constant return to the politics of illegitimacy, not only the fact that he is Black. That this type of challenge to the status of someone as important to the polity as the president of the United States is considered for even a second as worthy of public debate is a serious problem for a politics that would argue that race is unimportant today in the US.

At the time of the setting of the novel, Blacks were making a claim to political equality in local towns and cities throughout the South after the Civil War and this was a potential problem for Whites and their ability to control local institutions. The Black vote was a new variable in any town where the male Black population was a significant portion of the electorate, but it was what the vote represented that was the main problem for Whites. Pushed to its logical conclusion, political equality would require a dramatic change in the economic and social relationships between Whites and Blacks. The novel describes the process by which local White elites developed techniques to mobilize Whites as a community against this possibility of Black political equality. In doing so this also developed the social description of the racial hierarchy in postemancipation society.

That Olivia Carteret's father had a Black daughter was a problem for Olivia because Janet used this fact of birth to demand equal social status with Whites. For the Carterets the legal structure of Reconstruction had to be changed rather than continue to erode the sovereign status of the White community (Du Bois 1962; Woodward 1966). Her Black half-sister Janet was out in public, explicitly social and engaging in the public discourse with Whites who knew Olivia; this was unacceptable to the tradition of racial hierarchy that the Carteret's represented (1993: 256). The fact that Janet could greet Olivia on the street rather than hide in shame at her supposed station was a direct challenge to the prevailing idea of racial social inequality. These circumstances prompt Olivia to her sick bed, only to give birth to the child Theodore shortly thereafter, the symbolic birth of the White community to come inspired by the continuing conflict over the meaning of racial equality (10).

WHITE MOBILIZATION

From this opening the novel goes on to describe the machinations of the White elite to stir up anti-Black sentiment. Using their control of the popular press, Carteret and several others, including General Belmont and Captain McBane, develop a plot to fight for political control of the city against Blacks and their White supporters. The problem as they see it is expressed by Captain McBane,

> Things are in an awful condition! A negro justice of the peace has opened an office on Market Street, and only yesterday summoned a white man to appear before him. Negro lawyers get most of the business in the criminal court. Last evening a group of young white ladies, going quietly along the street arm-in-arm, were forced off the sidewalk by a crowd of negro girls. Coming down the street just now, I saw a spectacle of social equality and negro domination that made my blood boil with indignation,—a white and a black convict, chained together, crossing the city in charge of a negro officer! (Chesnutt 1993: 33)

Over the course of the novel these White men periodically meet to strategize, but also to provide Chesnutt with the opportunity to portray the popular assumptions about race of the local White community. While preparing to launch their political campaign, events in the city provide an opportunity to address the issue directly when the lady who raised Olivia Carteret, Polly Ochiltree, is brutally murdered. The White man responsible, Tom Delamere, makes a hobby of dressing up and performing in blackface for his compatriots and so he uses this as a disguise to conceal his true identity as the murderer. The fact that he is also wearing a borrowed servant's dinner jacket wrongly implicates the Black man whose outfit it is. The police arrest Sandy, the servant of Tom's uncle, and there is a furor as the Whites in the city gather to lynch him. The ease with which Whites in town mobilize to see justice done outside the law reveals the existence of a coherent racial social community to which members feel solidarity. The framing of a Black man for the murder serves the purpose of consolidating White community interests at a time when the town's elites were trying to galvanize Whites to resist the growing economic and political resources of Blacks.

That the White culprit Tom Delamere uses blackface to engage in stealing and murdering someone, and then attempts to pin this on a Black person as a result, is an interesting bit of creative license on the part of the author. Since the novel depicts the beginning of Jim Crow politics it is appropriate that this is represented by someone in blackface, since "Jim Crow" was the name of a traditional stage figure of the blackface minstrelsy theater who was a passive and happy Black fool. That this figure came over time to symbolize the entire racial apparatus of the period is an important statement of the political requirements it established for Blacks.

Before anything can happen, the Black man is found innocent but in the interest of not casting blame on the White community by indicting one of their own, the real culprit is merely ostracized socially by other Whites and not charged with the crime (228–34). In fact, in spite of the murder, Tom soon inherits from his uncle, who dies shortly after the event due to grief over the truth of his nephew's guilt (235). In fact, Tom's perfidy is rewarded because the importance of the cohesion of White sovereignty overwhelms even a concern for violence to one another amongst Whites. Even the murder of an elderly White woman is permitted in order to preserve the desired politics of race in the polity.

Denied the opportunity to capitalize on the guilt of a Black man for such a crime, the plotters next begin a political campaign in earnest. Major Carteret tours the state giving speeches on White supremacy, suggesting that "The provisions of the Federal Constitution . . . must yield to the 'higher law,' and if the Constitution could neither be altered or bent to this end, means must be found to circumvent it" (241). This is a good example of the conflict between the decisionist politics of race and democratic legitimacy. Carteret is appealing to the same higher law that Chesnutt writes "imperiously demanded that the purity and prestige of the white race be preserved as any cost" (259). A state constitutional convention is called and the laws are amended to reflect the desire to disenfranchise Blacks in North Carolina. In spite of this victory, frustrated with the slow pace of events the three plotters republish an article published earlier in a Black newspaper, the content of which is described as evidence of the contempt Blacks hold for Whites.

The problem is the absence of a government authority that could intervene to ameliorate this growing conflict of interest between Whites and Blacks. The ability to get the state government to disenfranchise Blacks reveals how White community political interests coincide with sovereign authority in the society. What the plotters have to accommodate is the fact that Blacks are free and can therefore mobilize against any encroachment of their rights. We can think of this as the lowest level of democratic political equality, where social congregation and political mobilization are permitted. The strategies to constrain the political ambitions of Blacks had to occur so that they could not effectively resist as free citizens.

The publishing of the article enflames the White community in the city and a riot ensues in which the majority of Blacks and their White political sympathizers are driven into hiding or out of town, Janet's child is killed as well as two other Blacks, Mammy Jane and Jerry, who act throughout the novel as loyal servants of the White elite. The feelings of the plotters are straightforward, as Captain McBane says, "This is a white man's country, and a white man's city, and no nigger has any business here when a white man wants him gone!" (253). With this act the political aspirations of the Black community are destroyed (King and Smith 2011: 60).

Early in the narrative, Mr. Delamere expresses the belief common to the White community in the inferiority of Blacks. As he puts it,

> You are mistaken, sir, in imagining me hostile to the negro. . . . On the contrary, I am friendly to his best interests. I give him employment; I pay taxes for schools to educate him, and for court-houses and jails to keep him in order. I merely object to being governed by an inferior and servile race. (1993: 25)

What this brings to mind is the difference between being a customer and a merchant, providing a service for others and needing a service provided, being a person who pays and someone who has a product that people will pay for. The traditional politics of race describes the difference between Whites and Blacks as one of human type and not a question of whether Blacks can own property. As Olivia Carteret puts it, "While the negro, by the traditions of her people, was barred from the world of sentiment, his rights of property were recognized" (271). It was therefore possible to separate Black financial success from the social description of racial difference, so long as White community political control was not abrogated as a result of this success. This no doubt sounds familiar to us since it reflects the same racial politics that we experience today.

The problem for Whites in the period after the Civil War but before the Jim Crow racial apparatus was in place was just this idea of the potential scope of Black political equality. The conflict between Whites that allowed for there to be a change in political status for Blacks, a conflict which Blacks slaves were in a position to take advantage of and use as leverage to acquire freedom, was quickly resolved at the national level. Once this occurred the White community was slowly able to coalesce again as a cohesive political force and establish new social conditions of racial hierarchy in the society.

THE GOOD, THE BAD, AND THE SMART

The measure of political control was in the description of the good Black person. Throughout the novel Chesnutt has the Whites differentiate between Blacks who do as they are told and those who do not. This may seem a crude way to put the collective desires of a community of persons for the control of a single individual, but I think this perception of "doing as you are told" accurately represents the way individual Black actions are described between Whites as a community. The challenge is one of the Black subject against this discursive political mobilization of the White community, not merely against the individual White subject. As the Black lawyer Watson, who is leaving town as a result of the riot, says to the Black Dr. Miller, "I don't imagine they mean you any harm, personally, because you tread on nobody's toes" (279). Major Carteret makes a point of asking his compatriots that the riot spare Dr. Miller for the same reason: "He's a very good sort of a negro, doesn't meddle with politics, nor tread on anyone else's toes. His father was a good citizen, which counts in his favor. He's spending money in the community too, and contributes to its prosperity" (252).

That this was prescient is shown later when Dr. Miller is asked at the end of the novel to tend to the Carteret's child Theodore, who will otherwise die. Major Carteret was responsible for the riot that cost Dr. Miller his son. This final reconciliation between White sovereignty and Black labor is the major political statement by Chesnutt in the novel, and brings to mind Stuart Hall's description of race as the modality in which class is realized (Hall 1980). However, the description of the benefit of the labor comes after the designation of racial difference, after Dr. Miller is earlier reminded explicitly that he rightfully serves in his occupation only those who are Black. Some measure of racial economic and professional equality is important to enable Whites to use the skills that Blacks bring to the society in ways that are not predictable. Chesnutt suggests that some freedom of educational success and professional development for some Blacks is important for the health of the White community. A Black doctor is still a doctor when only he or she can cure your child (1993: 329). What is made plain in the novel is the fear Whites have of allowing too much success for Blacks such that they begin to resist incorporation into the roles defined by the racial hierarchy. The quantitative is subsumed within the qualitative designation of racial difference.

Already in 1901, Chesnutt was able to write about the explicit strategy of ensuring that Black exceptional individuals are tolerated so long as they do not apply their conditional social and economic freedom to demand equality with Whites or engage in uplifting other Blacks such that this threatens White community interests. This type of conditional success for specific individuals could even then be called "racial equality" without unduly challenging the political control of the White community of the society. As General Belmont says, "One swallow does not make a summer . . . when we get things arranged, there'll be no trouble. A stream cannot rise higher than its fountain, and a smart nigger without a constituency will no longer be an object of fear" (252).

It is in the figure of Jerry Letlow, who is Black, that Chesnutt develops this idea of what Whites desired Blacks to do to reflect the new racial social order after the Civil War. Jerry is a loyal servant of the White community and an open supporter of the distinction of race. It is important for racial politics in the novel that Whites not fully give equal social status to Blacks, whether this is to shake their hands as an equal or acknowledge them in the same way as they do Whites (29). As the Black lawyer Watson points out during the riot, the fact that someone White engages in the social form of recognition does not mean he or she will break ranks with other Whites and defend you against the effects of race.

In describing this role of the good Black, Chesnutt focuses on how some Blacks desire recognition for their service to White interests and how they perceive the social stigma of inferiority, even as they accept these actions that mark them as inferior. For Chesnutt the good Black is someone who views the pleasure he or she affords Whites as more important than his or her own community. Paying close attention to the sovereign status of Whiteness, these Black individuals do not desire to test these social provisions but instead try to reinforce the hierarchy of race as a way to advance their own personal success. This is the politics of recognition.

When Mammy Jane is seated with the Carterets and White guests for the baptism of Theodore early in the novel, this is taken by her nephew Jerry Letlow as proof, which he points out with approval to the other Blacks who must sit in the gallery, that she has the trust of those Whites in attendance (12). With recognition comes trust. Jerry, who works at the paper owned by Major Carteret, finds out about the racial plotting taking place but he does not warn members of his Black community, but instead looks to his own selfish interests. He continues to work at the paper, and in doing so attaches himself to the outside of the White community like a barnacle, on occasion serving as a comic example for the White elites in their conversations about race. Jerry is discovered by the Whites to have tried to lighten his skin because, as Chesnutt puts it, "he had realized that it was a distinct advantage to be white,—an advantage which white people had utilized to secure all the best things in the world, and he entertained the vague hope that by changing his complexion he might share this prerogative" (245). From within the politics of recognition, which accepts the social concepts of racial difference, a distinction can be made between light- and dark-skinned Blacks as a quantitative difference. It is only in this politics that someone can also be "fair-skinned." Jerry is then told by Major Carteret not to vote and agrees to this so as to keep his position at the paper. Jerry believes that to do otherwise is foolish, for what more can he ask of Whites then a right to earn a living alongside them (247).

Jerry Letlow is the Black person who believes that his world is completely encompassed by race, and therefore has a tendency to watch for when an exception to racial segregation occurs, as though a breaking of the rules is always possible for them, uniquely, and they desire this first and foremost. The assumption in this case is that for the inferior, a temporary suspension of the rules of status is a reward and that the inferior desires to be seen first as an equal. This assumption depends on the acceptance of the status of inferiority by the person and the ability of the superior to define the relationship between them. This misunderstands the difference that race describes. As Major Carteret expresses in his contempt for Jerry, "Even if he could, by some strange alchemy, bleach his skin and straighten his hair, there would still remain, underneath it all, only the unbleached darky,—the ass in the lion's skin" (245). It should also be recalled here that the Black half-sister Janet is described as being identical to Olivia, and therefore looks White. In the story the politics of Whiteness is not located in phenotypical appearance but in a politics of lineage and ancestry that can exclude evidence of racial impropriety.

In contrast to Jerry's desire for a politics of recognition, and Dr. Miller's independence and potential for instituting social change, Chesnutt describes the character Josh Green as a Black man with the resoluteness to challenge the force and violence used to keep Blacks in their place. What he lacks as an uneducated individual with courage is a sense of what to do with his desire to fight against the pressure applied to the community. Gathering a group of men during the riot, Green meets both the lawyer Watson and Dr. Miller, and asks each in turn if they will give them guidance in their physical confrontation with the Whites gathering throughout town. Watson suggests that nothing can be gained by resistance except death (282).

Unlike the lawyer Watson, Dr. Miller argues for the importance of a long-term strategy of resistance, not the heroic stand, flight, or subservience. As he puts it, "In this riot we are placed as we should be in a war: we have no territory, no base of supplies, no organization, no outside sympathy,—we stand in the position of a race, in a case like this, without money and without friends" (283). Dr. Miller is acknowledging in this way that the effective politics of race is that of friend and enemy. What he admits is that no amount of force will overcome the desire for Whites to come together as a community to ensure Black subordination, that instead the Black community has to develop a different politics from that which accords it few resources. Josh Green dies fighting heroically and succeeds in exacting revenge on his nemesis, the former contractor of convict labor Captain McNabe, one of the three original instigators of the campaign that has led to the riot (309). Josh Green is admired by both White and Black for his courage, while the complicit Jerry Letlow dies an unsung member of the Black community he sought to leave. Watson flees to secure his family elsewhere and therefore concedes the political space to Whites.

Only Dr. Miller avoids his easy elimination from the field and is determined to fight another day. He does this by not directly challenging the social segregation in place but providing the care the White community needs to survive. This echoes the politics of personal care in *Iola Leroy* but expands it to include an interrogation of the description of the White community. By the relationships that coincide between Olivia Carteret and her half-sister Janet, Chesnutt suggests that the nobility of sacrifice involved in Janet and Dr. Miller helping the child of the enemy who is responsible for the death of their child will change the future obligations Olivia has towards her sister. Chesnutt ends the novel before we know the outcome of the assistance Dr. Miller gives to Theodore. This leaves the outcome of this politics in the hands of the Whites. What will their reaction be to this realization of the need for Blacks, one that is personal? The problem with this depiction is just in this failure to describe how Black individual interrogation changes the politics of the White community. Do the actions of Dr. Miller, in spite of the impact of the riot on his life, serve as a limit to future conspiracies by Whites to define Black political aspirations? No, because in this case acts of Black assistance occur in spite of race, not because of it.

FAILING TO WORK TOGETHER

From the story it becomes clear that White sovereignty allowed for exceptions to the treatment and condition of Blacks both during and after slavery. The slippage between the rule of law and actual social control was dependent in each case upon the perception of collective White racial interest. Relationships of intimacy and mutual dependence were possible as long as these were not seen as threatening the social prerogatives of White superiority, the distinction of social difference, and necessary inequality. This meant that Blacks were always required to assess the reactions of Whites to ensure that White superior status was confirmed. To not acknowledge this status socially was to challenge the distinction. This stance of the Black person to the White subject remains important today. The necessity of indeterminacy with respect to the confirmation of status allows Whites to retain the authority of the decision; they reserve the right to assign values to actions based solely on their perception of events. This is the central theme of events that Chesnutt describes as leading to the Massacre of 1898.

This authority extended to deciding that exceptional cases for success were permitted; certain Blacks could excel without having to be put back in their place, removed from office, fired, or punished in some fashion to eliminate the threat to sovereign White status. This was the corollary for the suspension of the law in dark times, the need for exceptions to the law to maintain the racial social order. As Chesnutt has a judge say in response to a request to halt the impending lynching of Sandy for supposedly murdering Ms. Ochiltree,

> He admitted that lynching was, as a rule, unjustifiable, but maintained that there were exceptions to all rules, that laws were made, after all, to express the will of the people in regard to the ordinary administration of justice, but that in an emergency the sovereign people might assert itself and take the law into its own hands—the creature was not greater than the creator. (193)

The judge succinctly lays out the problem of the Jim Crow period with regard to the Schmittian political enterprise. That the description of race is foremost a collective description is obvious, and yet at the same time individual Whites reserve the right to determine exceptions to the social order as it applies on the ground, as it were. This means that the White subject controls both the relationship he or she personally has to individual Blacks and determines the collective description against a Black collective definition of difference. This twofold definition of race, of popular sovereignty and its subjection of the White citizen that we see already developed in the text by Chesnutt, allowed for the transition to the period of integration decades later where the White citizen could renounce personal authority for popular sovereignty and yet retain the political investment in the collective description of racial difference. In the interests of preserving White sovereignty in the US it became necessary to cede the ability to act individually to maintain the racial social order.

At the beginning of the Jim Crow period, when the definition of "White Supremacy" was deemed necessary to ensure that the connection was made for individual Whites to the needs of the sovereign collective, Chesnutt is able to describe one of the instigators as believing "in the divine right of white men and gentlemen, as his ancestors had believed in and died for the divine right of kings" (34). This displacement of the body of the king and his divine standing onto the body politic and the rights of citizens in a democracy, and then in turn as a description of the US polity, onto the preservation of the status and specific privileges of Whites is an important political development in the polity (Kantorowicz 1997).

According to Chesnutt, the problem of White social control was in part due to the fact that Blacks were no longer subject to the same set of social constraints as before. The former slave was property, and had protections therefore as well as definite social limitations. The freedman was able to vote, and was thus available for another form of violence, that reserved for one's fellow citizens (Chesnutt 1993: 212). As the threatened lynching and the riot in the story make clear, the protections of law were only as strong as the racial social order required.

Today this is still true. The new status of Blacks as African Americans allows for professional equality even as it makes the individual vulnerable to private censure and social exposure to reinforce political concerns of peace and security. The forms of policing and social control today reinforce the idea of exceptional African Americans at the expense of the collective description of Black inferiority. This is possible because, as with the transition from slavery to Jim Crow, the shift from Jim Crow to integration requires the erasure of the history of what has come before it. As Chesnutt writes regarding the perception of Whites after the end of slavery, this was "a new generation, who knew little of the fierce passions which had played around the negro in the past epoch, and derived their opinions of him from the 'coon song' and the police reports" (238). That this is also true today is all the more tragic, but is consistent with the argument that race is a decision that is inadequately addressed within the US.

In *The Marrow of Tradition* the indeterminacy of exceptional application by individual Whites, and when a White person might invoke the absolute claim of supremacy, ensured a degree of social control beyond the application of the law. The open interpretive quality of the assignment of difference, of how to apply the privileges of racial status, made it possible to control the actions of Black subjects based merely on the potential for discipline and retributive practices. Blacks in this sense had to police their own actions, to control themselves as inferior subjects to Whites. As *Iola Leroy* reveals, it is this that is the most pernicious aspect of race, the internalization of the social controls necessary to avoid disobedience to the sovereign. That this sovereignty was described as popular and democratic did not obfuscate the real definition for Blacks of this politics as one that allowed for White sovereignty. Chesnutt writes, "The negroes were taught that this is a white man's country, and that the sooner they made up their minds to this fact, the better for all concerned" (241).

Terror and violence were held out as the consequence of disobedience to the racial hierarchy. Today the fear of prison and the expectation of arrest and violence at the hands of the police are matched by the use of internal controls by African Americans in the community to ensure that no one African American achieves more than is allowed by the requirements of equal racial status. Only the designated exceptional Black, such as the need for the Black doctor Miller in the story by Chesnutt, is permitted to exceed the limitations set by both communities.

The admonition to "Not think something of yourself, to rise above your station" is an explicit statement of the conditions defining the racial order for the Black individual in the US. To police this limit was a requirement of Blacks in the period of Jim Crow, given the type of events described by the Massacre of 1898. This self-constraint is an understandable collective response when the reaction by Whites to a threat is similar to what one of the White elite conspirators says in the novel when they have caught the Black person who is accused of murdering Ms. Ochiltree,

> Burn the nigger. . . . We seem to have the right nigger, but whether we have or not, burn a nigger. . . . The example would be all the more powerful if we got the wrong one. It would serve notice on the niggers that we shall hold the whole race responsible for the misdeeds of each individual. (182)

The indeterminacy and arbitrariness of response by Whites during Jim Crow allowed for a degree of social control well beyond any possibility in the law. The importance of White racial riots, lynching, and arbitrary violence in curtailing the attempt to seek redress in the law or through political mobilization should not be underestimated.

Today this social control by fear is manifested in the imprisonment of so many of the Black community, the indeterminacy of arrest and police surveillance, the actions of the social worker, and other institutional mechanisms. Formal legal segregation has been replaced by a structure of institutional controls that in their activity pose a significant threat to the Black individual and their choices in life. This idea of threat and intimidation is different from the description of a politics of friend and enemy by Schmitt, as it reveals a requirement for affirmation and violence beneath the identification of status. But fear is not the only thing that allows for race to persist as a decision. Fear arises after the ability to determine the status of an individual and the collective. In this way race is perceived by individuals initially as a positive conception; it allows for community against the larger undifferentiated mass of persons, and then defines a requirement of protection and security against those outside the community (Esposito 2008). This is one of the things that makes it so hard to eliminate race as an idea of importance.

For Harper, as she expressed in *Iola Leroy*, the solution was to try to " . . . consider a wrong done to the weakest of them a wrong to the whole community" (2010: 178). Blacks thereby would be afforded the protections of the popular sovereign instead of White sovereignty. This is similar to the basis for the difference principle for Rawls in *A Theory of Justice*, and it depends on the ability to get all to agree that this is a basic idea of sovereignty in the society (Rawls 1972). That something exists as a community outside of those persons we interact with in family, the neighborhood, the bowling team, school, and church. To fulfill the promise of America for Harper and Chesnutt is to enact a political community, a polity that eclipses the work that race does to establish always exclusive communities of persons. If this polity is developed through a politics of friend and enemy, the only ready solution by which to subsume racial social descriptions is with the presence of a threat that forces unity. This is what Chesnutt describes at the end of the novel with the threat to the Carteret child. Another possibility is to erode the basis for the decision itself in social activity such as that which defined Eugene and Marie, and Olivia Carteret's father and the mother Julia, of Janet.

OF ETHICS AND INEQUALITY

This brings us to the main theoretical claim I wish to make with the novel. Both Whites and Blacks face the politics of race as a test of democracy and sovereignty, but also of the ethics that the society should affirm. As the White elite in the novel try to mold public opinion so that Whites in the city do not abandon the cohesiveness of the social community for an expansive description of Black political equality, Blacks are trying to form a social community that can sustain resistance to this claim of inequality. Major Carteret and Olivia Carteret personally experience racial politics as having lost status and authority relative to some Blacks, while also experiencing a diminished capacity to limit the competition for resources and goods in the society. The loss of Blacks as property challenges Whites to arrive at some form of economic relationship with them, and changes how Blacks are viewed socially and politically. Whites face an ethical test as a result (Foucault 2005: 448). In the same sense, Blacks must describe their new relationship to Whites: to what extent does citizenship and the right of Black men to vote, the support of the Freedmen Bureau, and the new mobility that freedom allows attenuate the description of racial hierarchy? The strategies that the Carterets choose to resolve racial politics fail, in that they fail a moral test, since they allow the decision of race to stand without understanding the consequences. The political assumption that they express is that the subordination and authority over Blacks that they seek to implement in the society does not irreparably threaten the ability to improve their own social standing; Whites can survive just fine without ceding authority to Blacks. They misunderstand the problem of race as one of friend and enemy, of community sovereignty and decision, and so jeopardize their son to the racism necessary to sustain this political perspective.

Coming to the realization that they need Dr. Miller, the Carterets attempt to sustain this perspective of partial inclusion, of support for special cases or exceptional Blacks who can assist Whites without threatening the authority they have as Whites. The inability even in this moment to accede to the desires of Blacks for the political equality to allow their community to develop without fear and social constraints is a failure for Whites in the novel. While the Whites manage to drive out the nascent ambitions of local Blacks through the riot, they also fail at providing an ethical element that proves important to their own care and self-development. Dr. Miller and Janet fail to change the conditions of the decision, even as they are challenged morally by the claims to help the child. As with the novel *Iola Leroy*, even though the realization is that they must proceed together socially, that they need each other, both Whites and Blacks fail to alter the conditions of the decision of race. Even though race is insufficient as a source for self-knowledge, of personal development of an ethical life, Whites are unable to accept the form of community available that denies race, in the novel evident in the person of the half-sister Janet and her willingness to set aside a politics of revenge and allow Dr. Miller to heal the White child of her announced enemy. So how do we achieve the type of politics in the US necessary to allow Whites to let go of their political authority? Clearly a mutual dependence in the context of political, economic, and social development is not enough of an incentive. Even the acknowledgment that Blacks are necessary to caring for oneself is not enough for Whites to set aside the idea of racial difference (Foucault 2005: 496). The idea of an ethical test for individuals fails to elicit a change in racial politics. Even the threat of death is not enough, and so some other form of politics must be established to achieve this result.

7 Jim Crow

> "What you say there, nigger?" And it came through the flames in his nigger voice: "Will one a you gentlemen please cut my throat?" he said. "Will somebody please cut my throat like a Christian?" And Jed hollered back, "Sorry, but ain't no Christians around tonight. Ain't no Jew-boys neither. We're just one hundred percent Americans."
> —Ellison, "A Party Down at the Square"

> Disciplinary normalization consists first of all in positing a model, an optimal model that is constructed in terms of a certain result, and the operation of disciplinary normalization consists in trying to get people, movements, and actions to conform to this model, the normal being precisely that which can conform to this norm, and the abnormal that which is incapable of conforming to the norm.
> —Foucault, *Security, Territory, Population*

By the 1920s, Jim Crow was fully entrenched as a system of racial hierarchy in the US. It established legal rules for the social delineation of racial difference, upward mobility, and political participation and allowed the individual White subject to police the racial social order. There was no difference between government and White sovereign interests, and the perception of threat to the racial hierarchy was enough to mobilize both local White citizens and the government. The individual White person was deemed sufficient to facilitate social control, and was expected to do this by constantly referencing the criteria defined by the collective description of racial superiority. The requirement was that no Black person should exceed the status of a White person except under specific unique conditions. From within this comprehensive structure of social practices Blacks could only aspire to live within the material limits of their collective description, or pass into Whiteness if possible.

There was no social description for Black individuals who could exceed these limits, since there was no legal space for racial equality in the society. Instead, Blacks were able to accumulate wealth and status within their segregated community so long as this did not threaten the racial hierarchy. The only Blacks who were able to violate the requirement of segregation were those who represented Black community interests to Whites, for example, the writers and artists who were asked to portray Black life to an interested White audience (Lewis 1981; Locke 1999). Black elites who were asked to control their local communities were nonetheless still Black, and could not be seen by any White person to challenge their status of inferiority. With

White patronage, the assignment of representative status by a significant number of the White community, it was possible for Jessie Fauset, Langston Hughes, Zora Neal Hurston, and Richard Wright to become something more than mere Blacks working behind the veil (Locke 1999). They were given access to White readers because they facilitated the development of White community knowledge. Their success confirmed the adage of different and unequal, rather than challenged the distinction of race.

It was in this period that Blacks sought to define the relationship between material success and the distinctions of race. With the benefit of a full generation of schooling, employment, and migration behind them, by the early 1900s Blacks could now view the problem of race absent the obscuring mechanism of slavery and its extremes of deprivation (Cooper 1988; Wilkerson 2011). The question could now be asked, Why can I not aspire to equality of position with Whites? Why does racial status define success, when all other personal attributes remain equal? This is the period when the social definition of White racial superiority was increasingly challenged by Blacks. The response from the White community was increased oppression and the development of scientific theories of racial difference. The idea of racial exoticism and cultural difference was important to this politics as well. Black Face, minstrelsy, the invention of Harlem were as important to the idea of racial difference for Whites as explicit social control. The writers of the Harlem Renaissance struggled against the role of providing a venue for Black exoticism and difference, allowing their White readers to revel in the depiction of the effects of racism on Black life, even as they sought to find an answer to the dilemma of success, of having aspirations beyond merely being a Black writer, but a writer of the American experience (Lewis 1981; Wintz 1988; Locke 1999). This was an explicit concern for Jessie Fauset in *Plum Bun*.

THE ROMANCE OF RACE

A bildungsroman in the mold of Goethe's *The Sorrows of Young Werther*, the novel *Plum Bun* begins with a young Black girl, Angela, who, in contrast to her younger sister, aspires to a life not alongside but within Whiteness (Goethe 1959; Fauset 1990). She and her sister Virginia grow up in Black Philadelphia, with hardworking parents (Du Bois 1996). The mother is very light-skinned and can pass when she desires for White. Angela has inherited this complexion while Virginia is darker like her father. The mother regularly enjoys going to the restaurants and shops pretending to be White for a time, partaking in the things offered to Whites but not available to Blacks, but otherwise lives comfortably in the Black community. She regularly takes Angela on these little pilgrimages, while Virginia spends time doing things with their father. As a young child Angela tries to make sense of the presence of two worlds, one Black and defined by her neighborhood, the jobs her parents are limited to, and the circumscribed social choices the family has, and the other the types of shops, restaurants, and services available to Whites.

On one occasion when Angela and her mother are out and passing as White they run into the father and Virginia on the street. The two pairs walk by each other while pretending to not know each other. Later that evening the mother apologizes to the father, saying that she should have acknowledged him even though she would no longer be passing, and that it was important not to let her ability to pass determine her relationship with him. This event serves as an important moment in developing Angela's perspective on racial politics. Angela is not privy to this conversation and because of this thinks that this is an appropriate way to behave. That it is necessary to sacrifice relationships to the decision. For Angela, passing becomes possible in that moment; she feels that it is acceptable to disavow the Black community and its social connections. After her parents die, Angela decides to go to New York with the inheritance she receives, and Virginia stays in Philadelphia. Angela explicitly decides to live as a White woman and leave behind Black community life. She rents an apartment in New York and begins a social existence as a young White woman artist, taking art classes and engaging in an active social life in the city. Eventually Virginia also moves to New York but they live in completely different social communities, one White and one Black.

The juxtaposition between Angela and her sister Virginia is that between the two attributes of the Black community identified earlier: social practices within the collective and against the decision. Angela is able to pass for White and, unlike Iola in *Iola Leroy* and several of the characters in *The Marrow of Tradition*, she attempts to cross over into the White community. Fauset uses this device of passing to describe the problem facing Blacks with regard to the social and material limitations of race in the period. In contrast to the political discussions of race found in *Iola Leroy* and *The Marrow of Tradition,* where there is a sense of political possibility for the Black subject, in *Plum Bun* the idea of challenging the consequences of race as an individual are notably absent. Instead, Angela and Virginia work within the existing descriptions of racial communities and the social politics these define. This exploration of the effects of race is done at the level of the individual. This is because by the period of the novel there is no longer a question in the polity about the way to define the racial hierarchy and the limits of White sovereign authority. The social control of race is no longer a problem of law and larger political debate amongst Whites; instead, by the 1920s in the US the place of Blacks was considered settled in the society. This anticipates the politics of the period of integration and racial equality of opportunity, in that no formal law regarding race is necessary once equilibrium is found between the different political aspirations of the racial communities and the institutional structure in the society. Race becomes by definition something to be considered only at the level of the individual subject rather than a larger social and political problem. Thus the description of her journey, from Blackness, to Whiteness, and back.

In the North in the 1920s the degree of social control was exercised individually with a comprehensive sense of White collective identity. This mandated fewer legal protections of the rights of Whites, since the aspiration of Blacks were explicitly contained socially. In fact, in this way Whites in the South can be thought to have had less of a compact and comprehensive White collective identity. This difference was in part due to the variation in political and economic development but also a consequence of the greater proportion of Blacks in the South. These facts necessitated legal structures to ensure the racial social order. In the North for two centuries a description of Whiteness had developed that, in its inclusion of new European immigrants as White by choice, was cohesive and ordered (Roediger 2006, 2007; Ignatiev 2008). The White Northerner who spoke of the treatment of Blacks in the South under Jim Crow was at the same time unequivocal with regard to his or her relationship to the definition of racial difference, its duties and obligations as a White person. The effects of race were invisible only for those taught to ignore its impact and to live within the confines of its description of difference. Angela was unable to do so.

Since the personal description of race, in contrast to addressing the politics of the decision, is the only political activity available during this period for someone in the North, Fauset has Angela contemplate race as a child after an experience of being called out socially as "Coloured" in school. Exposure to the services and products that were only available to Whites, and the treatment she received by Whites when they discovered she was not one of them, gave Angela a sense that, more than material wealth, Whiteness was better and necessary to gain access to specific types of living conditions.

As Fauset points out, there were Blacks with material wealth; what they lacked was a certain quality that gave them access to the best goods and services in the city. Walking with her mother downtown and in the shops, Angela discovers that in spite of her middle-class status within the Black community, she is unable to access specific services and material goods unless she passes. Virginia is darker skinned and prefers social practices within the Black community, such as the church and singing the spirituals, in ways that Angela does not.

Unlike her mother, who enjoys passing for several hours to partake of certain shopping or services in the city, but feels this is a statement of the ridiculousness of race, not a description of herself and her allegiance to Blackness, Angela resents the barriers that race creates. She does this both with respect to the limitations she sees within the aspirations of Blacks around her and with regard to the easy availability of resources and social promotion for Whites with her personal talents and abilities. She is literally, in the constant back and forth of being perceived as White by Whites only to be uncovered as an impostor by those Whites who know her racial status, made to feel that her family and racial status is a constraint on the social mobility otherwise available to her. Instead of choosing to pass, she is always passing unless she announces her race, introduces it into a conversation that otherwise expects her to be White. This provocation, or insertion of her status, the need and expectation by society that she engage in this, makes her responsible for the presence of racial difference in the midst of Whites. She is the person who is expected to utter the words to exclude herself and to accept a racial difference that she does not want. This expectation of outing herself for the benefit of Whites, so that the hierarchy can be preserved even when they are not able to identify her, becomes a source of resentment. It is important to consider this position in light of the constraints placed on the exceptional Black subject today.

In other words, Angela begins to ask why she should have to tell people her race, why she must take on the decision instead of those who have a problem with Blacks in their midst. As she states in a version of that typical first early childhood encounter that often defines the problem of race for most Blacks in America, "Tell you that I was coloured! Why of course I never told you that I was coloured! Why should I?" (Fauset 1990: 44). This requirement of announcing, of taking on the decision of race herself and her status in public so as not to be an impostor is repeated for Angela (73). As Angela states, "This was a curious business, this colour. It was the one god apparently to whom you could sacrifice everything" (44). The author Fauset in this way addresses the problem of how persons are supposed to take on the idea of race, the impact of the decision on individuals under the social requirements of Jim Crow. For Jim Crow to work, to successfully socially segregate the races and thereby maintain an absolute distinction between races, it was necessary for Blacks to accept the conditions of difference. If Blacks did not police the boundaries of their social constraints and acquiesce to their condition, racial segregation would be impossible to maintain. This is true as well today.

This is not to say that the Black community was somehow perceived as responsible for their status as different in this period; such a view would be established as normal only later under integration. Instead, this was the period in US society where Jim Crow had to be justified to avoid social unrest. What basis could social and legal segregation by race have in the US after slavery, except for the possibility of identifiable qualitative differences of type? In *Plum Bun* Fauset tests the extent to which Blacks as well as Whites will internalize the ideas of race and inhabit their subjectivity as defined by the decision, rather than the life developed alongside race. Virginia experiences racism, but does not aspire to the goods and services, the social status, reserved for Whites by the institutions of the polity. What Virginia has to do, as the darker sister, is to reject the practices that separate her from Angela, the belief that to be Black is greater than other social practices in her life. Angela does aspire and tries to refuse the subjectivity given by race through transgression and imposture. While she does not give in and take race on as a personal assignment, a public admission of culpability to the decision, by the end of the novel she is forced to realize that Whiteness is itself fraught with a politics. To live as White and rich was not a solution to social ills but rather a retreat from the possibility of a larger community, from a popular sovereignty in truth.

This position is revealed in the way Angela returns to her family at the end of the book, not as someone who agrees with the decision of difference, but as someone who realizes that denying her family and those ideas that she developed within the Black community while affirming Whiteness merely shifts the problem of race onto Blacks again. Why are they different? Why can they not acquire certain resources and live a certain type of life in America? Why are they a problem? (Du Bois 2012b). These questions were directed at the Black community by Whites as a justification for the impact of the decision on the law and social life during the period of Jim Crow. This definition of the desire for social equality by Blacks as trying to be like Whites, as striving to be White, reinforced the description of the latter's superiority.

Instead of desiring to be White or like Whites such as Jerry Letlow in *The Marrow of Tradition*, Angela initially wants what Whiteness is supposed to allow in the society, only to realize that being White merely shifts the perspective without removing or addressing the problem of existing in a description of a social community that truncates her desires. Angela wants to be appreciated for her art, as someone who can do art, not to be liked or be able to be social (1990: 344). The assumption is that a combination of superior culture and material wealth describe Whiteness, or at least its idealization. Angela then rightly expects her artistic merit to overcome any lingering doubt as to the truth of race, since of course as someone Black who is passing her success proves the equal cultural capacity of both Blacks and Whites. A similar approach is taken by Du Bois when in the *Dusk of Dawn* he describes how the assumption of superior culture gives way to the acquisition of wealth as the true distinction of racial difference (Du Bois 2012a: 189). But the striving for wealth as a marker of equality does not address the impact of the decision in dividing the community of persons from one another. The sacrifice of a common politics for individual success does not negate the importance of racial difference. In spite of Du Bois's suggestion to use economic power to reform racial politics in the US, the individualism necessary to acquire sufficient wealth has come at a price that prohibits, even discourages, a description of Black community politics (Du Bois 2012a: 208).

Fauset nicely turns this problem of seeking affirmation around by having Angela act from her position as a White person, in her final confrontation with Anthony Cross, who admits he is Black, as a barrier to having a life with her. Angela does not reveal her status, accepting instead that being White requires the responsibility of the destructive qualities of the decision. In that moment she realizes what she has asked of herself and her community, to be subordinated to something that constrains relationships and limits the choices someone makes in life to no purpose but its own definition. Even as she is deceiving others, she has taken on the deceit that is at the heart of the acceptance of Whiteness.

This definition is a destruction of popular sovereignty, democracy, and those social relationships that depend on something other than a necessary conflict and divisiveness. In this moment, Angela is fully White, no longer passing, as the last requirements of family are severed in the interest of giving her sister Virginia the love she deserves. Angela admits her own implication in the suffering of Blacks due to race and its strictures. Even though, like her mother before her, who also passes on occasion, she refuses to accept the fact of race, its description of a qualitative difference between persons throughout the story. This is not a traditional novel of passing or of social protest. To be White is not to be equal, to be just, or right. Instead, Fauset has tried to show the inadequacy of race to solve the problems of society. Whiteness, for all its glitter and promise, allows for sexism, classism, and the denigration of an entire population in its name. It is to show this that much of the text describes Angela's struggle to define a role for herself, not as a White impostor, but as a woman and someone who is relatively impoverished, someone who needs to work and is unable to live well without the material and social dependence on others, even though she is now White. This provides an important lesson in how Whiteness does not provide the promised panacea for social ills in the society.

Angela sees that Whiteness provides only the benefit of the decision itself, a hierarchy without substance, and therefore is unable to resolve other social considerations. Its hierarchical form pollutes all the social practices with which it comes into contact. Unlike when she was younger, as an adult living in New York Angela understands that Whiteness is not enough, being merely a way to substitute a decision for a description of the human. It is here, in this way, that it is possible to see the problem with Schmitt's account of politics. The decision is made to substitute for the lack of content of sovereignty; it conceals the deficiencies of the description of the sovereign that would otherwise necessitate a constant justification of the creation of laws. The decision to race conceals the inability to legitimate sovereignty except through violence, even if this is the subtle violence of the border, of the exclusion of those who are defined as different, the noncitizen. This is not the description of a democratic polity.

Once she is passing, Angela is always cognizant of the effects of this dual awareness on her relationships, of the inability to cross back from Whiteness fully, "There will be lots of times when in spite of myself I'll be 'passing' " (1990: 373), and the concomitant inadequacy of race to resolve anything beyond itself. She and her sister Virginia, who remains Black, view one another "from the two sides of an abyss, narrow but deep, deep" (315).

GENDER POLITICS

In addition to the description of race, the novel provides a description of gender politics. As in *Iola Leroy*, in a narrative that sees Iola as defining the impact of race very much in relationship to men, *Plum Bun* defines Angela's racial political development in similar terms. Fauset's Angela is unable to marry without the resolution of the politics of race. Instead, Angela develops a community with women who are self-consciously aware of the problematic gender politics of their day. If the move to become White is empty of content beyond the decision to exclude some persons, so too is the idea of gender. The arbitrariness and violence of the decision is concealed in the constant gesture of return to the distinction; it just is this way, it is natural, it is the law, I am a man, etc.

For Angela the injustice of gender politics is revealed in the way she wrestles with her ability to be financially independent and the attempt by society to describe this in terms of the ability of men to provide financial security. She is uncomfortable with the way her professional ambitions are supposed to be described by society with respect to the men in her life. For example, at the end of their relationship, the author Fauset has Angela's lover Roger say, "You knew perfectly well what you were letting yourself in for. Any woman would know it." In response, Fauset writes, "The phrase had the quality of a cosmic echo; perhaps men had been saying it to women since the beginning of time. Doubtless their biblical equivalent were the last words uttered by Abraham to Hagar before she fared forth into the wilderness" (1990: 231).

The author's solution to the viciousness with which the decision of racial difference is justified, to cover over its being empty of content, its unreality, is for Blacks to endure, to be a people that endures (313). As Fauset writes, "They had to persist, had to survive because they did not know how to die" (309). This need to endure is evident in the descriptions of Black life in the transition from slavery to Jim Crow in *Iola Leroy* and *The Marrow of Tradition*. So too is the fact of survival, even when the conditions are terrible. The politics of the exception is unable to fulfill its promise of total social control because its actions are based on the decision, which will disappear once the Other is expunged. It is this which, unless something is done, dooms the Black person as a subordinate, to continued existence.

The inability to ensure closure and finality without destroying the premise of its sovereignty is what forces the concealment and creates the terror required by the decision of race. The bare life created according to Agamben that results from its full operation is merely the symptom not the source of the problem of the decision, and so is inadequate to the expression of the political condition of Black subjectivity. At its heart lies the idea of friend and enemy, of the need for an enemy to define friends, assign those we want close to us, and define a society of Americans. The novel *Plum Bun* was published in 1929, and is contemporaneous with the developing importance of the work of both Schmitt and Heidegger, and yet how different its perspective is on the problem of political authority and governance. As in the novel *Iola Leroy*, Fauset, in *Plum Bun*, puts the onus of race on the work of racial convention, on White public opinion. When Angela does finally reveal her racial status in public to support a fellow artist, the response in the press is an invocation of both the need for racial purity and the inherent danger she represents in her passing to the cause of Whiteness (352).

Instead of defending the reservation of authority to the sovereign, the depiction of the character of Angela invokes the Wittgensteinian (1992) idea of norms as learned, as conventions that can be changed, and of a popular sovereignty that is as unfeigned as it is unruled by the need to fix those inside and outside. Fauset's solution to the politics of race is laughter. Clearly this is also not enough to challenge existing descriptions of racial difference in the society, even though it does form a social politics that rejects the importance of Whiteness (Santner 2011: 109).

Laughter is Angela's response to having taken the problem of passing so seriously, of accepting the criteria of a Whiteness that could allow for no Black part of herself. In fact, the several White friends of Angela's do not abandon her once they find out she is Black, preferring their friendship with her to the supposed racial purity of their social environment. In doing so, they also evince laughter, and a lack of attention to the social costs of their allegiance to something more than race. As Henri Bergson writes, "Our laughter is always the laughter of the group" (2008: 11). As one of her White friends says, before knowing she is Black, "There're hardly any of unmixed blood in the United States . . . if I met a coloured woman of my own nationality, well-bred, beautiful, sympathetic I wouldn't let the fact of her mixed blood stand in my way, I can tell you" (1990: 325). Laughter allows for the conditions for love and for politics to be set aside as the main focus. Instead, the inability to determine events and subjection in one moment, within an event, is relegated to a partial description rather than a comprehensive representation of the person.

The tragicomic gesture is possible because individuals always retain the potential to work against the confines of a specific subjection, a social description of themselves. Fauset overtly attempts to work through the idea of the tragic as defined by race. As Angela puts it, "Well, she was sick of tragedy, she belonged to a tragic race" (143). This practice of the comedic can result in merely an "empty gesture," but as is shown in the case of the relationship to the Black Anthony Cross and the "White" Angela, the release from acknowledgment given by laughter enables something destabilizing; it creates an uncertainty that threatens sovereign authority because it is critical of existing conditions. Anthony Cross, realizing he has fallen in love with Angela Murray, says that he is unable to pursue his affections because he is Black and she is not. Unaware at the time that she is passing, Anthony argues against the value of his own affections since, as he puts it, " . . . there is no future, none, none, Angela, for you and me. Don't deceive yourself,—nor me" (292). Angela herself has the potential to alter the tragedy of this moment, of changing his life.

It is in respect to the tragic that one of the most important ideas occurs in the novel. In the critical scene where Angela reveals that she is Black to the White public, one of the reporters says, "Back of most of the efforts which you people make to get into schools and clubs and restaurants and so on, isn't there really this desire for social equality?" (344). What the person means is that Blacks merely desire social acceptance, recognition by Whites. In a description of absolute difference such a position concedes the status of each individual within the collective distinction. The Black person looks to the White person, as the measure of Whiteness, for approval and equality, some sign of acceptance and affirmation of worth as a Black person defined as absolutely inferior. The standard of Whiteness is not disturbed in this description of politics, of recognition of one by one. What needs to occur instead, of course, is to demand the upsetting of the values of the distinction such that there is no White to judge Black aspirations, that there is no Black from which to be described tragically.

The comedic element in this is liberating, and in that moment for Angela it becomes clear she needs to act to correct the politics of recognition of Blacks by Whites. She does this by announcing that her acceptance by Whites as a member of the community was by her choice, that in fact it is at this point, when the tragedy of race is described as merely one of recognition, that she refuses to accept this form of politics. That the moment is explicitly linked by Fauset in the novel to the violence of the Klan, of which the lynching campaign was in full swing at the time, and the description of Whiteness as synonymous to America is not a coincidence.

Angela laughs in the moment, when one of the reporters asks her to take her admission of race back, to become White again in the refusal to speak (1990: 347). How would she take it back, an admission of having passed? Perhaps by laughing and saying that in turn this new description of Black does not encompass her? This she does not do; instead, Angela uses her laughter to cover over the gesture of admission of her disavowal, in turn, of Whiteness. She laughs at the reporter for being so caught in the decision to race that he cannot accept her statement, asking her to return to an account of the politics that upsets the decision and its impact on her. In her admission, Angela, in one perspective, that of the White reporters, falls suddenly behind the veil of Blackness and so disappears from view as someone intelligent, available socially, and equal. Without a description of admission, of entrance and constitution, this is an example of how we would be left with a community defined solely by social and literal death (Blanchot 1988).

Unless the description of absolute difference that describes a qualitative distinction between Black and White is challenged by the actions of individuals, a different politics than that offered by Schmitt, this distinction is merely affirmed. Without a disenchantment or distance from the comprehensive depiction of race, our actions repeat the recognition given by the idea of the veil and communities on each side. Fauset is clear about the desires of Blacks politically, for a life led without the effects of the distinction, not its positive reification as an example of minority politics or the expression of Black culture. This is also the limit to what can be done with laughter. Laughter allows for a person to go on, to continue living within the conditions set by race, but it does not itself render meaningless the decision to which it is a reaction.

The challenge of a politics of social equality is that it suggests that Blacks are attempting to mitigate the effects of the distinction of race, but doing so without challenging the conventions of race. It suggests that Blacks are unaware of the absolute description of difference in their subjection. Hegel's use of history to define the concepts in the phenomenological apprehension of the Other presupposes the introduction of absolute concepts of difference that are originally derived from social desires. Within the politics of the event these are given as true and therefore no longer matters of convention. Harper in *Iola Leroy*, Chesnutt in *The Marrow of Tradition*, and Fauset in *Plum Bun* each reference the problem of a "public opinion" or social convention as the political location of the decision to race because it is inaccessible. Angela's laughter is a concession to the way race determines her world and those of the Whites around her, but in the novel the majority of White friends do not abandon her, but rather suggest that it deepens the importance of their friendship since there is no duplicity involved in their interaction. But like Iola in the novel *Iola Leroy*, now that she is Black again, Angela turns away from an intimate relationship with another friend who is White to begin a relationship with Anthony Cross. In her return to Blackness, under conditions very different than Iola, who was enslaved, Angela finds what Blanchot calls an "elective community" in contrast to the traditional community of race (Blanchot 1988: 46). This is comprised of both Blacks, such as Anthony Cross and her sister, but also Whites that she befriended in New York. Becoming Black, but with the aspiration to be social with Whites, around Angela there forms a community of those without a community, a negative community that cannot have a name but does exist (Blanchot 1988: 25, 50).

This type of community marks itself for Angela by the fear she experiences that she will lose her close White friends immediately after her announcement. This was not a traditional relationship within the bounds of racial difference, of course, because Angela, even though she was passing at the time, found herself caring about them and they for her. Race had nothing to do with these friendships inside Whiteness and so when she was no longer White they followed her in a sense into a space outside of race. The difference between the social space created by Eugene and Marie that was insufficient to protect Marie or her children and that around Angela is not the difference between slavery and Jim Crow but that Angela found Whites able to confront racial "public opinion" just as she does in that moment when Angela no longer passes as White to the reporters. Eugene and Dr. Gresham in *The Marrow of Tradition* were unwilling to do this. What we lose in this politics is the ability to change existing racial community politics, and instead opt for a smaller social community of persons that cannot speak against race. Instead, its members must remain silent and therefore hidden from the perceptions of Jim Crow politics. Both Blacks and Whites form this negative community as a solution to the implacability of racial distinctions, just as friendships occur all the time today across the boundaries of racial communities. Fauset's solution is important but unsatisfying as a description of a politics that can change the description of racial communities. In part this is because this type of negative community cannot be avowed by either Blacks or Whites against the description of either racial community (Drake and Clayton 1962: 118).

I now want to turn to another text from the Jim Crow period, one that suggests a different response to this dilemma than laughter, the unavowed community beyond race. *Uncle Tom's Children*, by Richard Wright, provides a clear description of another aspect of African American subjection during Jim Crow.

ON MENDACITY

Uncle Tom's Children is a collection of short stories by Richard Wright. It was first published in 1938 and is comprised of six short stories, two of which, a story that depicts the harrowing pursuit by Whites of Black Communist Party members in the countryside in "Bright and Morning Star" and an autobiographical sketch of the young Richard's early years in the Jim Crow South in "The Ethics of Living Jim Crow," were not included as a part of the collection until the second printing in 1940. The collection describes how Blacks struggled to live under a politics of social control that was both ambiguous and allowed for individual White interpretation and social control of Black activity. The need for social adherence to the description of racial hierarchy that it depicts is comprehensive and absolute. In "The Ethics of Living Jim Crow," Wright describes how he first began learning the conditions defining his Blackness during Jim Crow. As a child he got involved in a stone-throwing fight between a group of Black friends and some White kids from across the tracks. Instead of throwing cinder block stones, the Whites threw broken bottles (Wright 2008: 1). After he is hurt in the brawl, his mother comes home and beats him while insisting that he was "never, never, under any conditions, to fight *white* folks again" (2).

This was the beginning of Wright's education in a distinction that identified the wealth of "White houses surrounded by trees, lawns, and hedges" with Whites and the poverty of cinder blocks and the railway tracks with Blacks (3). The story describes a series of events that demonstrate the social mechanics of having to "stay in your place" to allow for safe contact with Whites. The argument I want to make is that this dynamic remains true today, even if the costs of disobedience to White social desires are not measured in terms of personal violence but rather in losing one's job, being treated with contempt, and similar actions to signal social disapproval. When Wright thinks to complain to the boss of poor treatment by his White coworkers, he states the problem succinctly: " . . . the boss was a white man, too. What was the use?" (5). Threatened for being ambitious and acting as though he could ask for training, Wright learns that the use of violence by individual Whites to ensure proper respect and subordination exists right under the surface of the rigid social rules of race (7). The beating of a Black woman by shopkeepers where he worked, while a policeman watches passively only to drag her off to jail afterwards, is matched by the implicit threat afterwards when the store owner explains, "Boy, that's what we do to niggers when they don't want to pay their bills," as the store owner's son grins and offers Wright a cigarette (8). This is not the breakdown of law and social order, but the description of race as allowing and requiring exceptional action on behalf of a sovereign definition of Whiteness.

That it is a description of sovereignty is apparent from another example Wright gives later in the story. Wright receives a ride on the back of a truck full of young White men. When asked if he wants a drink, Wright responds by laughing and saying, "oh no!" He is immediately hit in the head by an empty whiskey bottle and falls out of the moving truck onto the ground. As the truck stops, the White men pile out, stand over him and say, "Nigger, ain't yuh learned no better sense'n tha' yet? . . . Ain' you learned t' say *sir* t' a white man yet?" As they drive off they say, "Nigger, yuh sho better be damn glad it wuz us yuh talked t' tha' way. Yuh're a lucky bastard, 'cause if yuh'd said tha' t' somebody else, yuh might've been a dead nigger now" (9–10). This is a display of absolute sovereign authority held by individual Whites who have the right to demand that a Black person speaks or acts in a certain way or violence is allowed to enforce whatever desires Whites have. There is absolutely no option of self-defense or legal recourse from this type of violence. The violence is immediately racial and explicitly a way to define White superiority. According to Wright, the requirement to demonstrate Black subordination was to say "Sir" or "Ma'am" when addressing a White person, to never be in a White neighborhood after dark, and to be invisible in situations where your presence was not required for a service or to assist Whites, "for you were not regarded as human" (11).

In spite of the treatment of Blacks, things ran smoothly under Jim Crow; social life was ordered around the issue of Black subordination without open conflict or protest. Even the slightest deviation from the norms of social behavior for Blacks towards Whites was always supposed to be met with an immediate reprimand and the threat of violence. The law did not create the social pressure on Whites to adopt these practices; instead, this came from the community itself and could be considered a form of social duty required of Whites. Learning to lie, to cheat, and to steal, since

Blacks had no property or rights that had to be respected except by the limits of social custom, was the price of Whiteness. A degree of secrecy and private conversations about Blacks with Whites, a shared discourse about Blacks, was important to ensure racial social control. Whites also had to act with authority, engage in violence, and report or respond to any infraction against the racial social order. The law then was created to assist in this subordination.

The ability to have this conversation about Blacks is the moment when the White community coalesces into more than something social. To speak of Blacks is to define an enemy against which to measure the scope of your new community. From this acknowledgment of a plural singular, a difference in common from Blacks, the White person has accepted the full range of actions required to subordinate Blacks to the hierarchy that race requires. It leaves open only the question of what action is required. The fact that often Whiteness is merely perceived as innocuous, as the possibility of violence held in abeyance as a way to mark the supposed liberal political position of the White person, is not less frightening to the Black person than the White person who says directly that they dislike you as Black but can live with you.

As Wright writes in the short story "Fire and Cloud," "We gotta lie t white folks! Theys on our necks! They make us lie t them! What can we do but lie?" (171). The law was used if Blacks refused to accept these social strictures and informal White violence was insufficient to correct the behavior. The White person had to learn how to assess a challenge to the racial hierarchy; they were not born with this knowledge, just as Wright points out that Blacks had to learn the limitations of their race.

LEARNING TO BE OBEDIENT

What Wright demonstrates is how Blacks must always display an awareness of their difference from Whites, that Whites were human in ways that Blacks were not, and that any encroachment on the social privileges held by Whites was to be interpreted by Whites as a sign of a threat to their sovereign status. Blacks had to give way in their ability to frame or define the social interaction with Whites, and were instead expected to engage in cajoling, pleading, and acquiescing in turn to allow Whites to change their opinions. In the second story, "Big Boy Leaves Home," Wright describes how several young Black boys go swimming in a pond on a White farmer's land. This is someone who the kids know does not like Blacks and so will potentially do violence to them if they are caught on the property. At the same time, as they say, "The White folks got plenty swimming pools n we ain got none" (27).

As they lie there naked on the embankment drying off, they see a White woman standing on the opposite side of the pond. The boys become terrified of their situation, for, because they have been trained to view the White woman as a person to fear in particular ways, they make the mistake of trying to get their clothes instead of going into the pond or the forest to cover their nakedness. Since the clothes are near the woman, as they approach her the boys explain that they just want to get their clothes and are not there to bother her. She sees four naked Black young men approach her where she did not expect anyone to be. Instead of listening to what they say she becomes frightened and screams for her fiancé, who is nearby (30). As the White man arrives with a gun the boys are still trying to take their clothes and flee rather than run away unclothed. Two of the boys are shot and killed immediately.

After asking if she is hurt, instead of turning and taking her away with him, the White man advances on the two remaining boys to shoot them as well. In desperation and under threat of death the one called Big Boy manages to grab the rifle and wrestles it away. The other boy, Bobo, jumps on the back of the man and is thrown to the ground. As Bobo is lying on the ground the White man beats him with his fists, stopping only when Big Boy hits the White man knocking him to the ground. (31–32). Having grabbed the White man's gun, Big Boy retreats and prepares to run away. Instead of withdrawing to safety the White man charges, clearly not expecting that the Black boy will shoot. When given a chance to retreat or stop the conflict the White man in each case refuses and attacks. He is shot by Big Boy and killed as he rushes forward to take the gun away. The two boys run off leaving the White woman alone with her dead fiancé. Two young Black men and one White man are dead over the social rules of Jim Crow life.

Both boys know the inevitable result of having killed a White man and rush off separately to their homes to seek safety. For the boy of the title, Big Boy, it is arranged that he hide somewhere away from home for the night and then take a truck leaving for the North in the morning. Big Boy hides in a kiln, and hears as the mob catches Bobo nearby. After tying Bobo up and cutting off some "sourvineers," the mob pours tar on him and burns him alive (56). Throughout, the White men and women are singing, "We'll hang ever nigger t a sour apple tree" (55). After this a hunting dog comes searching for Big Boy in the kiln and Big Boy is forced to silently strangle it in his arms to avoid discovery (59). The situation that evening is summed up in the words of one of the mob, when he says, "Ef they git erway notta woman in this town would be safe" (53). Big boy manages to survive the night and leaves the next morning for the North.

Clearly the young men are wrong to go onto someone else's property, and knowing that the farmer does not like Blacks, this is clearly unwise. But what begins as a minor transgression that is considered typical for teenagers testing the social limits of their world quickly becomes something very different. The situation is really twofold. First, Big Boy is asked when he arrives home immediately after the killing, "How come yuh didn't go t school this mawnin? Didn't yo ma send you t school?" (39). For Blacks it was important not to be where you were not expected by Whites, and certainly it was not permitted to fight back and kill someone White. To be a Black teenager, such as in the case that made national news of the shooting to death of Trayvon Martin while visiting his father in a gated community in the Spring of 2012 in Florida, is to have to learn that there are no safe ways to test the limits of White authority.

As Wright demonstrates when riding in the truck in "The Ethics of Living Jim Crow," Blacks learn that even the slightest deviation from demonstrable subordination is coupled with a set of social norms that always must be obeyed. The combination of established social rules and the need to be subordinate to all Whites regardless of their actions is something that the Black adults in the story are unable to control for in their young teenagers.

The other problem is the lynching itself. Since the event could be described as a case of self-defense on the part of Big Boy, who was being rushed by someone who had just killed two of his friends, in this situation it is the fact that no legal recourse was available for both young men that is the problem. They could just as easily be lynched for being naked in the presence of a White woman as for killing the White man; at that initial point in the story the boys were completely available to the full authority of the White community, its interpretation of events, and its decision as to the type of punishment merited by the perceived transgression of White rules for Black behavior.

I described the event in some detail because Wright does a good job of showing how a series of choices by the young men bring them into riskier conditions in their environment. It makes sense for Blacks to be risk averse in the face of the increasing violation of norms that are established by Whites. The Black person can predict the response if caught transgressing a rule by an absolute White authority. This is an authority that is both generally available to all Whites and immediately located in the presence of each White individual. This problem in racial politics is not that of calling out the Black person but of calling on others to form Whiteness, a community that can then see a difference described in the Other.

This reverses the traditional model developed by Fanon (2008) in *Black Skin, White Masks*, where a young boy calls out to Fanon and identifies him as a Negro from out of the racially undifferentiated collective. Contrary to Fanon's perspective, the child is first dependent for his gesture on the idea that others accept the continued presence of something held in common with one another such that this can define a difference from the Black person. This Whiteness remains quiescent unless they are asked to use it explicitly. For example, if he had said, "Look, a Negro" in the presence of a group of Blacks, the response would have been for both child and Fanon one of asking the question of why this query mattered to the child. The assumption of Whiteness is prior to the definition of Blackness in this example, even if it serves an important racial purpose to place the responsibility on the Black person as being different, as though this difference was given. This is similar to Tracy Strong's assessment discussed in Chapter 1 that Schmitt depends too much on the definition of an enemy to define friends. The conditions for becoming White do not depend on the presence of an Other, but rather depend entirely, always, on the ambitions of members of the community. Political theorists have too often overdetermined the fact of Blackness in their study of race as a way to justify, even when critical, the idea of race as defining a different human from themselves.

STANDING ONE'S GROUND

It is unnecessary to have a perceived threat to the community to realize the authority defined by Whiteness in the US polity. The White woman at the pond need not have felt threatened to demand the punishment of the young men who were naked in her presence, when the boys had already decided to violate the property restrictions by coming onto the farmer's lands uninvited. The expectation that Blacks would run around naked in the countryside in midday and attack White women is obviously problematic in itself. The perspective requires that we avoid asking the question of why young men are naked by a swimming hole and therefore possibly demanding that the woman retreat temporarily to give them privacy. At least we could expect that had the boys been White she would merely have become embarrassed and asked them to dress and become presentable.

The events assume the idea of Whites never having to question their own presence and actions in relation to Blacks. Just as the White man twice attacks in the story rather than retreats, without any hesitation at the fact that nothing is evidently wrong with the woman, and that as he faces several young men attacking them this may not be the wisest course. The fact that the White man has already killed two of the boys and they are not charging but clearly begging not be attacked is not a deterrent to his aggression. Wright touches on something very important here, in that White social and political authority is defined most often through this idea of not retreating or changing its description of itself due to the actions of Blacks, that to give way to Blacks is against the basic idea of being White.

This idea of standing one's ground, of resisting any encroachment on the actions of Whites and the social space defined by the White community as their own was a local manifestation of the assumption that as we saw in *The Marrow of Tradition*, the US polity was described as founded for Whites and expected to reflect that fact. The idea of territorial borders to Whiteness, be it in the form of neighborhoods, areas of town, or enclaves, is a natural outgrowth of the description of distinct racial communities, as it arises from the central functions of a political entity according to Schmitt: protection and obedience (Schmitt 1996: 52). To be in the wrong area of town for a Black person has often been enough to warrant arrest, something Wright addresses briefly when the protagonist of the short story "Fire and Cloud" must run through a White section of town and is stopped by the police.

The Whites in the story "Big Boy Leaves Home" have to justify their actions to other Whites, not the Blacks they encounter. To the extent that Whites in the community have the perception that an action is justified in the punishment of racial transgressions it is considered acceptable to the polity. This is the definition of absolute sovereign authority. During Jim Crow the problem of local law enforcement and the protection of the rights of Blacks was a constant source of tension between the Black community and local government authorities who were with few exceptions members of the very community of Whites who were victimizing Blacks. Two decades after the riot in South Carolina depicted in *The Marrow of Tradition*, the Tulsa Riot, in May of 1921, occurred under similar auspices: Blacks were seeking improvements in the resources and living conditions available to them under Jim Crow segregation. Black newspapers, a growing Black elite, returning Black veterans from World War One, and a slew of grievances regarding unequal housing, education, employment as well as significant individual White violence against Blacks made for a political confrontation with a White community set against a change in the racial hierarchy. The Black community sought to use the law to establish their rights against racial discrimination as citizens (Brophy 2002: 5, 79). Against these claims for justice and the attempt to hold the government accountable to a democratic politics was set the implacable resolve of the community of Whites to demonstrate that

> This is a white's civilization and a white man's Government, and the white man is and will remain supreme. The Negro race can be and should be happy, contented, prosperous, lawabiding, and helpful to his community and to his Nation. (2002: 77)

An armed confrontation ensued under the pretext of an attempted lynching of a Black man falsely accused of raping a White woman when he slipped while leaving an elevator and grabbed her shoulder to keep from falling (24). She screamed and the Black man was arrested for attempted rape. In the riot that followed a major part of the town of Greenwood was burned and dozens of people were killed (59). The armed resistance by some Blacks was not effective in stopping the violence; instead, Blacks who took up arms were shot. The White community used airplanes as well as organized gangs of Whites to coordinate the killing of Blacks, and the looting and burning of property owned by Blacks (46).

One argument for the shift from Jim Crow to integration is the idea that the increasing violence displayed repeatedly in the media threatened the state control over the right to violence in the society. Benjamin writes, in "Critique of Violence," that "violence, when not in the hands of the law, threatens it not by the ends it may pursue but by its mere existence outside the law" (1986a: 281). The violence of the Tulsa riot belies this argument, however, as do the constant reports of lynching and everyday violence meted out by Whites on Blacks during the period.

This was the political context surrounding the actions of the Black boys in "Big Boy Leaves Home." Submission and the uncertain criteria for obedience to White authority, a condition always open to White interpretation, was preferable to White violence and the use of the local government to enforce Black subordination.

This is what makes the real-world case of Trayvon Martin in 2012 so interesting. After killing the young man, the self-proclaimed neighborhood watchman Zimmerman in the gated community was not immediately arrested by the local police department. Zimmerman was perceived by the local police as having done nothing wrong, even though he usurped their authority over legal violence. The local Black community had to appeal to the federal government, but doing so emphasized the opposition of their community to the local White community, including local law enforcement. The competing interests that exist in the case between racial communities are concealed behind the discourse on the law and its application to the situation.

The problem this case creates within the institutional provisions of the social control of Blacks under the apparatus of racial equality is that individual Whites are not supposed to take matters of racial social control in their own hands. Instead, the shift from constituted racial communities to the constitutionality of race through the instruments of the apparatus, antidiscrimination law as well as legislation such as the so called Stand Your Ground law limit individual White violence towards Blacks in lieu of police action. This distinction in violence between police and individual Whites is very important in the US today as law enforcement has much expanded its pursuit of crime within the Black community since the 1970s to implement the type of social racial control formally brought by segregation laws and the White community (Benjamin 1986a: 287; Alexander 2012). What Zimmerman has to do is prove, because of the specific description of authority over violence by the police, that he is not in fact an example of that politics of the exception, the "racist." This is how the apparatus works today.

The determination of guilt and the type of crime committed by either Trayvon, who was shot, or Zimmerman the shooter is dependent on the influence the different racial communities can bring on the actions of local law enforcement, the district attorney's office, elected officials, and others involved in the case.

This interpretation is different from one that describes the law and institutions as distinct in their discursive practices from that of any one racial community interest. It also describes a political discourse that asks the question of what about the event was racial such that it would generate this description of distinct racial communities of social interest? Within this discourse the question would be, what does race have to do with the event of this shooting such that its description would coalesce racial communities? President Obama publicly stated that if he had a son he would have looked like Trayvon Martin. That the president is suggesting that his son would be just as liable to be shot in that situation is a challenge to the apparatus of racial equality where the politics of exception defines someone who would be the president's son as exempt from normal racial practices of criminalization and violence. This is not a conflict between two racial political strategies by the White community, of on the other hand allowing some Blacks to succeed and enjoy a reprieve from the normal criminalization and social control of the Black community and on the other hand allowing for every White person to act with sovereign authority to determine the social limits of Black activity.

This event is an example of what happens at the borders of the two parts of the political model of racial equality. The determination of the exceptional Black should have exempted Trayvon from being shot; in one description he was a law-abiding, soft-spoken high-school football player. The assumption is that if he had been a violent Black criminal dealing drugs in the gated community the matter would have been different. The language of the discourse around the shooting is whether Trayvon was wrong to wear a "hoodie" as that might identify him as "bad" in contrast to a "good" Black young man. As though this article of clothing could justify the shooting of an unarmed young person with only a bag of candy, a phone, and a soda can in his possession; just as being naked at a swimming hole that is on private property justifies killing the young Black men in "Big Boy Leaves Home." At the same time, this idea of dress and behavior as denoting character and that character matters as a definition of exceptions to the accepted rule of suspicion by Whites as to the presence of a Black person in the gated community reveals the limits of a discussion of character and racial politics.

The irony is that if Zimmerman had been a police officer this would have been more unlikely to happen because of the procedures in place to identify what type of person someone is prior to shooting, procedures that are largely absent between regular citizens, even those trained as security guards or watchmen. The social practices in place to determine those Blacks who are available to the exception, as providing conditional exemption from racial violence and certain forms of social control, differentiate today from the time of Jim Crow. The statement by Obama is a perfect example of the immediacy of the politics of race in his person and how he represents the face of formal racial equality in the US. It is in this context that the recourse to federal authority to force local legal institutions to respond to the counterclaims of those critical of Zimmerman's actions reveals a local racial problem in the shooting death of Martin. Just as during Jim Crow the application today of local law depends not only on a formal structure but more importantly on the desires of political interests. That this conflict between local and federal racial politics is resolved as a problem of local corruption instead of state's rights is the difference between Jim Crow and the apparatus of racial equality today.

FALSE PROMISES

In both "Big Boy Leaves Home" and "Down By the Riverside," Wright has Blacks kill Whites in self-defense. In both stories the White individual is shot, even though in the latter, Mann, who is Black, works to save the Whites in town from the flood. As a result of his actions to secure the family and protect other members of the White community, Mann has some expectation that his claim of self-defense for his act of violence will be heard by the larger White community. The message of "Down By the Riverside" is that a promise given by a White person to someone Black does not create political obligations; Whites cannot create community with Blacks since Whites cannot promise to that which has no independent individual sovereign status. No action by Blacks can invalidate the importance of sovereign White community. The fact that Mann kills someone White cancels any obligation towards him on their part.

The definition of the sovereign human being as a thing that can promise, as a way to create contracts, obligations, and mutual dependency between individuals, which then leads to the possibility of a popular sovereign authority made up of these individuals to establish a democratic polity, does not apply to Blacks. In this politics the Black person can not become, as Nietzsche writes:

The *sovereign individual*, equal only to himself, all moral custom left far behind. This autonomous, more than moral individual (the terms *autonomous* and *moral* are mutually exclusive) has developed his own, independent, long ranged will, who dares to make promises; he has a proud and vigorous consciousness of what he has achieved, a sense of power and freedom, of absolute accomplishment. (Nietzsche 1956: 191)

That a promise is not binding for someone White with someone Black is a central component of racial politics. This absence of trust explains the desire to coerce Blacks into obedience and social control. Without some form of forced subordination the description by Whites of Blacks as those to whom they are never obligated would obviate even the relationship between White master and Black slave. This remains the case today. Without a change in the description of race as creating someone who cannot promise to another, the White person who cannot promise to the Black person, the necessity of the racial apparatus is self-evident in a society that otherwise depends on contracts and promises for its description of democratic politics (Schmitt 1996: 78).

Since in the second short story, "Big Boy Leaves Home," the Black person escapes lynching and has no opportunity to confront Whites with his account of events, Wright allows this in "Down By the Riverside." The story begins in the middle of a flood that threatens the entire town. With his wife in labor and unable to walk, Mann has someone go fetch a boat to ferry the family to safety. Unfortunately, his brother Bob steals the boat from a White family, saying that he was unable to buy a boat. Bob thought that Mann was going to row his family to the hills away from town, but instead he has to get his wife to the hospital before she dies. This sets up the basic tension of the story, as the person that Bob has stolen the boat from is, as he puts it, "Ol' man Heartfiels, n yuh know how he hates niggers. Everybody knows his boat when they see it; its white n yuh couldn't git erway wid it" (Wright 2008: 69).

Mann rows his wife, mother, and child on the flood waters through town and in the process comes too close to the Heartfield's home and the boat is recognized as theirs. In the confusion Mann shoots and kills Henry Heartfield, even though this is clearly in self-defense just like in the case of the White man and Big Boy in "Big Boy Leaves Town"; Heartfield was about to shoot Mann (80). Unable to see if he has shot Heartfield, Mann hears someone shout, "Stop nigger! *Stop!* You killed my father! You bastard! You nigger!" (81). Mann rows away from the dock only to experience the hopelessness of the situation he has gotten himself into: "All at once he was limp, nerveless; he felt that getting the boat to the hospital now meant nothing" (81).

Mann rows on until he is closer to town and gets a tow to the hospital. There his wife is declared already dead and the boat is commandeered by the military brought in to try to save the town (90). He made the trip for nothing. Mann is then forced to join the other Blacks working on building the levee to protect the town. Wright makes a point of the military, who are all White, acting as though the Blacks have no rights in contrast to those White citizens, that they are available to coercion since it is martial law (92). At the same time, no Whites are forced to work on the levee. As Mann observes, "Black men stood on the edges of the platforms and loaded bags of sand and cement into boats," and he could see "long, black lines of men weaving snake-fashion about the levee-top" (96–97). The levee goes just as Mann arrives to work, and the boat returns to the hospital. Still under their authority, Mann helps the soldiers save White patients at the hospital and is then allowed to leave in another boat with one other Black man.

As they leave, Mann is promised by the White colonel that he will have his gratitude in the future: "You did well! I wont forget you! If you get out of this, come see me, hear?" (104). The colonel hands him a paper with address of a woman and two children trapped down river and says that if he is able Mann should save them, and otherwise to make for the hills. Instead of throwing away the paper, Mann holds on to it and gives it to the other Black man, Brinkley, as they make for the house. He is unaware until Brinkley reads it that it is the address for the Heartfields. At that point Mann does think about telling Brinkley of the problem he has with the Heartfields. He knows that "Ef we take tha woman t the hills Ahm caught!" (106). As Mann puts it, "He ought to tell Brinkley. Ahm Black like he is. He oughta be willin t hep me fo he would them . . . " (106). Instead, he says nothing and climbs into the house to help the family. At one point he is wielding an axe and thinks about killing them, but the moment passes, just as did the chance to tell Brinkley of his dilemma. At both moments Mann turns away from saving himself at the expense of his moral position. Instead Mann courageously saves the Heartfield family from drowning in a dramatic scene where the house overturns and sinks into the river.

As Mann predicts, when they reach safety he is accused of murder by the boy he has just rescued (116). Mann is innocent, did not steal the boat, and shot the other man clearly in self-defense as Henry Heartfield had shot several times trying hit him before Mann got out his gun to defend himself. Mann tries to explain, but instead the Whites listen to the young boy and Mrs. Heartfield. As the boy says, "You stole our boat and killed father and left us in the flood" (119). The White men ask Mrs. Heartfield if Mann assaulted her or her daughter, but she says no. Mann is helpless in this situation, and cannot witness in his own defense. At that point the colonel, who had promised to help him, is brought in to vouch for his being at the hospital. Instead of defending him, the colonel turns away and allows the verdict to stand. Mann is dragged away by soldiers and, fearing he will be shot, runs into the trees. Mann would rather die free than be killed. "He would die before he would let them kill him. Ahll die fo they kill me! Ahll die . . . " (123).

The inability to testify against someone White and the absence of an obligation by the White colonel to support Mann because he attacked a White man converge to trap Mann in the situation. Throughout the story Wright constantly addresses the fear of Whites that exists for everyone Black and the type of relationships that exist between Blacks and Whites. The hospital staff are noticeably distant when they tell Mann that his wife is dead. The doctor says, "Well, boy its all over . . . maybe if you could have gotten her here a little sooner we could have saved her. The baby, anyway. But its all over now, and the best thing for you to do is to get your folks to the hills" (88). This is true of the soldiers as well, when the soldier asks what Mann is crying about after finding out about his wife's death, the soldier says, "Shucks, nigger! You ought to be glad youre not dead in a flood like this" (94). What type of relationship do you create with a person you are never supposed to be obligated to, for which this is impossible?

That Blacks cannot testify in their own defense is the corollary of the inability of Whites to promise to Blacks without conditions. There is no basis for Whites to trust Blacks; it is impossible for Blacks to tell the truth about their own situation or that of others. Again we can see the problem race creates with the determination by Foucault that truth is an important component of democratic politics. Nothing President Obama does will validate his statement that he is an American by birth and a legitimate president because Blacks are not a source of veridication in America.

If we recall, this condition was also true for Whites and Blacks in *Iola Leroy*. Eugene fails to uphold his promise to Marie upon his death that she will remain free and Dr. Gresham asks Iola to pretend to be White so as to be able to marry her. In *The Marrow of Tradition* it is only upon the threat to their son that the Carterets consider allowing the half-sister Janet to inherit something from her father, and the novel ends before we are certain this occurs. Instead, what the reader is left with is the idea that in spite of the sacrifices that Blacks are asked to make they can only always have the relationship of assisting in the goals that Whites have as a community. Dr. Miller is allowed to practice because he is a good Black who helps Whites. In *Plum Bun* the narrative revolves around the idea of a difference between Whites and Blacks that presupposes that Whites are not accountable for their actions. Upon discovering that one of the winning art contestants is Black, it is understood that the award can be taken away since it should not go to a Black person. The fidelity of the art competition is set aside because of race; it is understood that any honoring of a commitment by someone White is void if the person is Black.

The description of sovereign authority in the US is given by this social condition that someone White cannot be expected to uphold a promise to someone who is Black, but someone who is Black can promise to Whites and have this upheld legally; they can be contracted to work, for example, by Whites. This is the description of the politics of the exception under Jim Crow racial politics. Only individually is this a recipe for deceit and mendacity. The truth is not required for White responses to Blacks; in fact, in a situation of authority such as race describes, truth and lies are not possible. Instead, members of each community can only respond to the decision and its social effects. The description of racial politics during the period of Jim Crow allowed Whites to refuse "to fulfill the promise implied in the act of assertion, betraying the trust of the addressee" (Jay 2010: 42), and in doing so establishes a politics that does not depend on equality across communities of racial difference. As Mark Tushnet discusses in *The NAACP's Legal Strategy against Segregated Education, 1925–1950*, what the segregation statutes of Jim Crow determined was a political definition of what was considered reasonable in the society as a social description of racial differences (1987: 22).

Racial politics does not challenge the US Constitution; instead, Blacks are the exception and unable to bring into question the role of race in the description of the polity. For Whites this has meant that the inability to promise to Black citizens has been a test of what is considered reasonable given the supposed differences between the races and not a threat to the coherence of the polity itself. The use of race in the context of equal citizenship in the US requires deception at one level, for how else to get Blacks to believe in the promise of an America that is not thought theirs by Whites? The problem is that if lying is possible for Whites, why can't it be permitted for Blacks? Why would Wright complain in the short story "Fire and Cloud" about having to lie to Whites as a condition of racial politics? Certainly the possibility of mutual deception is a reality of politics (Jay 2010: 139).

Mann in the story was unable to come up with an action that would negate the effects of his killing of a White man, without betraying an ethical position that did not allow dissembling and deflection of the truth. Mann was unable even to throw away the paper before giving it to Brinkley, to abandon the random individual to the flood when all the Whites had gone. Why did he need to be the hero, to try to save those who could be saved? His effort to save his wife was what initiated the entire journey, and so the story can be thought to depict the consequences of an altruistic and cooperative citizenship for Blacks in the face of White contempt and hostility. Even the young boy whose father was killed could have admitted that Mann saved them, that his situation should be mitigated by the facts of his valiant assistance of others after the murder. In any case why would the testimony of the young child stand unchallenged against that of Mann, who declares his innocence? The question for us today is not whether things have changed but whether the political development we contrast today with that of the days of Jim Crow would lead to a different outcome for Mann. Shouldn't a politics of equality require Whites to tell the truth of race, of its importance in their lives?

With this we return to the position described earlier where Whites assert the truth of racial difference through arguing that if someone did to them what they do to Blacks they would react very differently; only a different type of person would react to racism as Blacks do. The ability to coerce is given as proof of racial difference. Whites rarely experience the type of absolute authority that Blacks experience with regard to racial politics. But this is really beside the point. What is really implied by this perspective is that not only are Blacks responsible for their own subordination; they should react differently. Blacks must be a different type of human since they allow this treatment. Blacks must be cowardly, emotional, weak, passive, dumb, or slow of wit to not fight back against overwhelming odds and absolute authority in ways that Whites *recognize*.

Mann is speechless at the end of the novella and can only claim control over the nature and time of his demise. The White soldiers are left to wonder why Mann ran, why he saved from the flood the very people who would accuse him of murder, and why Mann risked everything to bring his dying wife to the hospital. Dr. Miller in *The Marrow of Tradition* returns to his duties as a doctor, his oath to heal the sick seemingly more important than his pride. What remains unacknowledged by Whites in the stories is the ethical position of each of the Black protagonists, and their attempt to resolve the moral dilemmas they confront as a description of freedom. The problem is how to define this freedom outside of race, as

Schmitt writes, "For what would they be free?" (1996: 57). Mann is unable to kill to save himself, and therefore he cannot challenge the authority of Whites directly.

BLOOD AND SUFFERING

The "Long Black Song" is a story of a woman, Sarah, who is raped by a White traveling salesman (Wright 2008: 137). Afterwards the man leaves behind a gramophone overnight to see if Sarah and her husband Silas might want to buy it, and he takes ten dollars off the price as some form of recompense for the act, only to have her husband when he returns home question where it came from (142). The White man returns the next day in the company of another. The husband, suspecting something strange has occurred since ten dollars was taken off the price, and that Sarah is lying to him, walks outside and meets the White salesman. In the scuffle that ensues Silas shoots the salesman and kills him. His friend rides off and gets more people to eventually kill Silas.

What is striking about the story is its focus on the physicality and the internalization of Sarah's experience even as she spends the entire time caring about the other persons around her. I interpret this to be a requirement of the burden of a history of violence and terror upon Blacks that the story is referencing by its title (Baker 1990). I believe Wright is giving the reader an almost visceral exposure to this experience of living as someone available to a violence that has no end or justification; it has no reason. We are told by Wright about Sarah hearing the crickets in the fields, wiping the sweat from her forehead, fighting back the feeling of loneliness, the thought of the long gladness of summer, and her hearing the baby Ruth banging the old clock on the floor of the house, "Bang! Bang! Bang!" (2008: 126).

Sarah describes the White salesman as a little boy several times to herself as he appears not to know much about her world. He is someone out of place, who should not be there, but who does not seem dangerous as he seems easily controllable. That this proves incorrect merely emphasizes the helplessness that Sarah experiences in the events of her own life, and the unpredictability and arbitrariness of White violence against Blacks. It is not that she is passive; Sarah is not weak, but that things happen to her that have little to do with her own choices. We are left with the feeling of a deep loneliness as a type of isolation brought upon her by the constant litany of racial violence between the two communities that cannot be met except through allowing Sarah to leave the things around her. The freedom that Wright offers Blacks through the image of Sarah is one wrought from suffering and terror, and leads to the repudiation of violence as the answer by which to challenge White sovereign authority in the US.

As she escapes from the field near the burning house that has Silas inside at the end of the story, the feeling is that Sarah is also finally free to find something new, some way to avoid being confined by the desires of others. To me this is similar to the solution found by Janie in the final pages of *Their Eyes Were Watching God* (Hurston 2006), when she is finally free of the social burdens created by the expectation of marriage to men and can find a social place in an unavowable community of her own choosing. Silas is instead tied to the life he has made for himself. As Silas says as he waits for the Whites to come for him, standing on his porch, "For ten years Ah slaved mah life out t git mah farm free . . . Ef Ah run erway, Ah ain got nothing. It don make no difference which way Ah go" (2008: 151–52). Silas is a hardworking farmer determined to be dependent on Whites for as little as possible. The perception of violation proves too much for him, even though it was Sarah who was raped. He is constantly away in the fields working, and Sarah is left alone at home with the child Ruth. Wright gives us a powerful sense of both her loneliness and the strength of emotion with which she views her world. The White man sees her as available to rape, and she is powerless to stop him. What would she do, except what Silas does, to kill him and then be killed? As she remarks to herself, "Dimly she saw in her mind a picture of men killing and being killed. White men killed the black and black men killed the white. White men killed the black men because they could, and the black men killed the white men to keep from being killed" (147). Sarah is very conscious of the fact that, "like a red river flowing," the killing went on and on between Whites and Blacks, but that this was a choice for Silas and not her (153).

Sarah sought some solution other than violence to the problem of race. When Silas is finally dead she runs through the fields holding her child, crying, "Naw Gawd!" (156). Seen in the context of the three stories that come before, "Long Black Song" is about the failure of a Black strategy of violence to stop racism, and the inability of anyone Black to stand up alone against the actions of Whites. Silas chooses, like Josh Green in *The Marrow of Tradition*, to confront and struggle against the authority of Whites as a determinant of his life. Sarah believes that she should rather accept things as they are and find something else to value. Sarah lives to define another life for herself as Silas and the White rapist die violently, but we are left with no sense of resolution, just the failure of a strategy of violence and confrontation. Sarah has no hope for the future, no strategy except flight, and few resources with which to begin again in the aftermath of the conflagration of violence that took her husband's life.

COLLECTIVE STRATEGIES

The shift from earlier stories in describing life for Blacks under Jim Crow to a focus by Wright on strategies to address racism is apparent in "Long Black Song" and it is apparent in the next story, "Fire and Cloud." "Fire and Cloud" begins the political conversation on race where "Long Black

Song" ends. The Black minister Dan is contemplating how to hold his community together in spite of the poverty and want that is occurring in the midst of the Great Depression. The tale opens with Dan walking and singing the song "A naughts a naught . . . N fives a figger . . . All fer the white man . . . N none fer the nigger" (2008: 157). If we consider how Sarah cries at the end of the last story, "Naw Gawd!" just prior to this, Wright is clearly trying to work through the idea of a strategy to change the way Black life is under Jim Crow. In the beginning of "Fire and Cloud," the mayor, the chief of police, and industrial leader, all White, confront the Black minister about his ability to both represent and control his community as the Blacks threaten to march on city hall in protest.

The mayor says that Dan, the pastor, is a good Black and that the two of them have a long-standing relationship whereby the needs of the Black community are communicated to the mayor. The two other men suggest instead that this is of no consequence if Taylor does not tell his people to refuse to join the planned demonstration. They suggest that going along with the idea of protesting against the hunger and misery in the Black community is to stir up "race hate" (182). When Dan protests the idea that the misery of Blacks and Whites is similar, and questions the mayor's assumptions, the police chief quickly interjects that Dan has called him a liar. Instead of being able to dispute the facts of the argument, because he is Black, Dan Taylor is expected to affirm the argument of the other men. In effect the Whites expect merely to state their views and have them obeyed without question.

Once they realize that Dan Taylor, whom the police chief calls "boy" the entire time, is not willing to do their bidding and ask his congregation to stay home, the meeting is over for them. The mayor says, "I don't see why we cant get along, Dan . . . Why dont you look at this thing the right way?" Instead of backing off his claim as to why it is right for his community to protest, Dan says, "Mistah Mayor, Gawd in Heaven knows mah people is hungry" (184). The response a bit later sums up the problem succinctly. Lowe the industrialist states, "Im not going to sit here and let this Goddam nigger insult me to my face!" (185).

The result is a conversation in which it is clear that anything the Black person says is of no consequence, that he cannot witness for himself against a White person, or criticize the ideas of a White person to other Whites. Whiteness signals veracity, while Blacks are there for the use of Whites. Any form of Black speaking that does not take into account this subordination is fraught with danger. What Wright suggests is that Blacks are required to retreat in the face of White interpretations of their actions, to always be attuned to this interpretation and cater to the idea of White superiority. It was important to "stay in you place" (7).

This is more than a statement of friend and enemy, of an absolute difference of status; it is also a way of defining the truth of politics. This idea of truth is central to the persistence of race as a social force. Without locating the truth of experience, of the obligations of government, of justice, in the actions of a Black individual as well as someone White it is impossible to suggest that there is racial political equality in the society. This is not a matter of minority rights, but of the inability of the political system to account for the presence of specific types of persons as the location of political claims that can override those of others. The idea of race presupposes the priority of specific claims, resulting in the collapse of the democratic political process, rather than suggesting the creation of a mechanism for including different views of the good.

To then attribute this subordination to a lack of courage on the part of Black persons, and to suggest that somehow race reflects a subordination that occurs absent this threat of violence and social control, is to ignore the history of race in the US. As in *Plum Bun*, Blacks do not seek social equality but to escape the onus of race. Wright does not offer the solution of a new community for those without community as a recipe for Black discontent with racism.

Wright offers a continuum of events from the first to the last story in the collection *Uncle Tom's Children*. The helplessness of individual Blacks in the face of White acts of exceptional politics gradually gives way to an awareness that only by relying on the collective in "Fire and Cloud" is it possible to resist and change the actions of Whites. As Wright has Dan Taylor say after his night of being whipped after the meeting, "N theyll keep on killing us less we learn how t fight! Son, its the people we mus gid wid us! Wes empty n weak this way! The reason we cant do nothin is cause wes so much alone" (2008: 210).

As the last two stories make clear, Wright feels the answer is not Black solidarity but a solidarity of both Black and White people who suffer the injustice of poverty and the social misery that accompanies this. More than this, he argues that social protest must occur, not merely doing what White elites say is right. This can take place once people begin to think about the people as a collective, the entire community of people, and set aside their personal needs. For Dan Taylor in "Fire and Cloud," the problem was that he took responsibility for the Black community; he sought to negotiate better conditions as a speaker for them, instead of allowing his own person to merge with that of the larger community. Correctly he was not willing to be described as the sole instigator of what was defined as a declaration of war on White status, described ironically by Whites as "race hate" (2008: 176). Instead he needed the community to declare its willingness to confront race as a collective. After his special status is removed he is able to act as one of many, and marches upon the city hall with a crowd of Black and White protesters.

DIRECTING COLLECTIVE ACTION

This theme of self-sacrifice as a counter to the sacrifice of Blacks by the absolute authority of White popular sovereignty is central to the last tale as well. In "Bright and Morningstar," Wright depicts the problems of meeting to discuss politics as a part of the Communist Party organization. In a description reminiscent of the fraught nature of political meetings during slavery depicted in *Iola Leroy*, the Black and White Communist Party organizers and members that comprise the main characters in the story are hunted down, betrayed by infiltrators, and brutally killed to suppress the possibility of social change. The problem is, to quote Fanon, "When a Negro talks of Marx, the first reaction is always the same: 'We have brought you up to our level and now you turn against your benefactors. Ingrates! Obviously nothing can be expected of you' " (2008: 23). What is different in the narrative is that Blacks and Whites are perceived as working together to organize as a group against Jim Crow. Wright makes it clear that even though the idea of "Reds," communists, provides the umbrella term for the political movement that he describes, race remains a problem in determining the ability of the organization to succeed politically.

Those hunting the location and membership of the meeting are White, and the quisling who betrays the group in the end is White as well. Wright has one of the Black characters say in response to the realization that someone has told the sheriff of the location of the meeting, "It wuznt nona our folks . . . The folks Ah know jus don open they dos n ast death t walk in!" (233–34). This is in contrast to her son, the communist, who is wrong about who is responsible when he says, "Ah cant see white n Ah cant see Black . . . Ah sees rich men n Ah sees po men" (234).

The critique that Wright brings up is not against the Communist Party but against White sovereignty as a constant problem for any formal party organization that is available to its inspection. The action in the story focuses almost exclusively on the problem of surveillance and betrayal, secrecy and organization. The important role of the Communist Party in mobilizing Black labor and farm interests in the South in the 1930s and 1940s is documented (Kelley 1990). The Communist Party allowed Black members to gain organizational experience and also to address some Black community needs when few organizational alternatives existed and there was no recourse to the law for local grievances. Communist Party activity was a problem for local White political and economic interests as it threatened to bring together Blacks within a complex political program for social change (Kelley 1990; Cruse and Couch 2005). What Wright points to is the difficulty for Blacks in working through this type of party structure with meetings that provided a focus for White sovereign interests in the form of the law and exceptional politics. It was through the meetings that White law enforcement and White citizens were able to locate and discourage Black party membership. As Wright points out in both "Fire and Cloud" and "Bright and Morningstar," eventually the White membership in the party made it impossible for Blacks to continue to be members and use the party as a tool to organize the political interests of their community (2008: 261).

CONCLUSION

The brutality of White exceptional acts of violence during Jim Crow is very much in evidence in Wright's stories. What stands out is the way Blacks begin to organize against the constant explicit threat of elimination. This is not merely *ressentiment*, a desire for social equality with the terms of relationships intact, but an attempt to refigure the terms of politics in the face of absolute authority. Wright gives examples throughout of how the direct confrontation of White authority always results in death, and as a result only collective sacrifice is the possible response to the politics of the exception in Jim Crow. To kill everyone, to have to kill everyone who is Black, is to eliminate race just as surely as protesting individually against the decision to race. Therein lay the source of the political force for the movement of Black nonviolent collective action that was to come shortly after Wright published *Uncle Tom's Children*. As Benjamin points out, the key to nonviolent political action is that it concerns the law and objects of the law, and not "man against man" (1986a: 289). In "Fire and Cloud" the object of the political protest was to acquire the food and resources needed to survive, as a test of the ability of local Whites to sustain the system of Jim Crow resource distribution. As we have seen, the dilemma this poses for White social control once Blacks protest en masse eventually leads to White popular sovereignty shifting the terms of exceptional politics to that which we have today.

To have Blacks police their own exceptionalism, the violence that is necessary to enable inviolate White social status must be transferred to the law and the community as such instead of resting on the actions of individual Whites. How can you march against yourself, protest against your own racial community? You can't, and so the incorporation of the politics of the exception into the constitutional apparatus of racial equality allows for no suitable target for a nonviolent movement by Blacks. This perspective also affirms a racial description of Blacks as having their individual sovereignty in question, their self-control and the ability of the community to govern itself without the assistance of an outside force at issue (Agamben 1998: 136). The idea of Blacks as unable to govern themselves is a traditional racial politics in the US, and is the basic concept today behind the use of the police, social worker, and teacher as elements of a structure of social control for those Blacks who are not exceptions.

What are the resources that Blacks are not getting a fair opportunity to pursue and what law should be the object of protest, such that Blacks can point to a specific task to be accomplished by the state that it has not already made available through the politics of equality? Only a broad-based social movement such as the Occupy Wall Street protests has the potential to ask those basic societal questions that cannot be answered through equality legislation, since it brings into focus the basic structure of economic relations in the society.

But a Black social movement such as was witnessed in the 1960s is impossible because a political apparatus has been established that both bifurcates the Black community by creating a politics of the exception and a new norm of Black subordination and defines all Blacks as the object of injustice. Both Black elite and those unable to profit from the opportunities available are set against the idea of the law, the myth of a successful Civil Rights Movement, and the end of racism as a problem of political sovereignty. This last is true to such an extent that many Blacks are willing to see the inequalities in the society as something that could be mitigated by more money, greater assets, better class position, and proper moral choices rather than understand that this perspective allows the apparatus to maintain exactly a proper balance between the number of "equal" Blacks and those left aside in the rest of the community.

This idea of a basic Black community incapacity that always allows for its bifurcation is, however, a traditional view of racial difference; Blacks have always had some members of the community who were successful, but now this is positioned as due to the neutrality of the racial politics in the society and not a product of hard work in spite of racial opposition. I just don't see a difference at this level of analysis between Jim Crow and integration in the way Blacks are incorporated into the political process as objects of White desires for a racial democratic polity. Today the politics of race, the idea of race as a decision, is merely obscured by the idea of popular sovereignty itself, in the name of democracy and through the creation of an elaborate political apparatus of racial equality.

So what politics is available to Whites as a community in this necessary shift due to the Black popular protests that are heralded nicely by Richard Wright in this book in 1940? The government realized the importance of political change to halt this type of social mobilization against the law because, as Benjamin points out with regard to a proletarian strike, but which resonates with the ambitions of the Civil Rights Movement as well,

> For it takes place not in readiness to resume work following external concessions and this or that modification to working conditions, but in the determination to resume only a wholly transformed work, no longer enforced by the state, an upheaval that this kind of strike not so much causes as consummates. For this reason, the first of these undertakings is lawmaking but the second anarchistic. (1986a: 291–92)

For one thing, with this analysis in mind the length of time it took for the US polity to shift to that of formal racial equality now makes sense. If by the 1940s there was an awareness of the need for Black collective protest against racism rather than individual sacrifice, then it took some twenty years for the political institutions in the society to develop an answer to this threat to White sovereignty. Amongst other instruments of control, this is what required an expanded police presence in the Black community from the 1970s through the War on Drugs and other programs.

It is important to understand that there has never been a time when US political institutions addressed the concerns of the Black community as integral to its own description, rather than as something that must always be accommodated to ensure White community progress. In part this is a function of the political language of minority rights, which substitutes for the political argument for the racial composition of the basic community that defines popular sovereignty. The presumption is that claims by Blacks are not basic but secondary to the description of the polity itself. As a consequence of this, Black individual political activity is unable to generate the social interest to bring the decision of race into question. Only collective action allows for the type of political demand that can potentially change how the decision is implemented throughout the society. This option of civil protest and disobedience has been closed off in the democratic polity through the political instruments supporting the formal description of racial equality of opportunity.

It is not enough to survive the violent events used to deter Black collective political mobilization. According to Wright, what is required is an organization and a social cohesion that can only occur through the description of an absolute threat to Black social interests. If loyalty to the racial community as an idea abstracted from material conditions is believed to be necessary for political action in contrast to the real threat of violence and debilitating social conditions that made it so that Blacks were no longer able to live within Jim Crow racial politics, then it is easy to dissolve the organizational force of the political movement. Rather than elevate individual Black experience with racism to the status of a decision framed in the politics of Schmitt, as a new description of Black friendship against a common White enemy, Wright is trying to frame, in his description of Whites in the Communist Party as loyal to the Black cause, the importance of a common political interest and not a social interest in dissolving the distinction of racial communities.

The political activity Wright discusses in "Bright and Morningstar" is that of a politics across racial community descriptions, as fraught with peril as this was during Jim Crow (McMillen 1989: 313). While this is unpopular at the time because it threatens White sovereign solidarity and therefore collapses the easy description of Black politics as a problem rather than as a necessity for the polity, it is prescient. Without Whites realizing that their political interests lay with the Black nonviolent movement for civil rights there would not have been political change in the 1960s. This is exactly what happened during the Civil War when Whites in the North realized that to win it was necessary to use Blacks temporarily against their own community. In the 1960s it was necessary to allow for a change in the apparatus by which race was applied throughout the society or risk losing the Cold War and our international standing in economic markets.

What this type of political mobilization across racial communities does is challenge how the racial decision of difference is applied in society, not the social importance of the description of racial communities. This is the subject of the next chapter, when we look at the fiction of the current period of racial politics. Before moving on I would like to address the description of the consolidation of White authority that is elicited by this collection by Wright.

White Problems

In the last two stories, "Fire and Cloud" and "Bright and Morningstar," Wright offers a description of how Whites respond to the growing collective political efforts by local Blacks. Unlike the White elites attempting to build Jim Crow racial policies and institutions in *The Marrow of Tradition*, the mayor, local businessman, and sheriff in "Fire and Cloud" are unable to force consent to the social practices of subordination that define the difference between the racial communities. Dan the pastor and community leader suggests that the collapse of the apparatus of subordination is due not to outside agitators but rather a symptom of the inability of Whites to secure the minimum quality of life for Blacks. The Depression is causing the starvation of Blacks in the town and they have no way to sustain a living. The quality of life for Blacks has reached the point where they must correct the allocation of resources in the society, move, or die (Wilkerson 2011). The Jim Crow society is breaking down due to the inability of existing economic relationships to sustain the Black community.

The White response is to drag Dan away that evening and beat him severely enough to send a message that his recalcitrance will be met with violence. One of many Blacks beaten that evening, the Whites realize that violence is no longer a deterrent to Black activism when the next day the entire Black community marches on the town square. The problem for the White authorities was how to maintain the necessary social control and subordination when the threat of violence was not a deterrent. When the White race riot, lynchings, and casual use of violence everyday do not deter social protest by Blacks, the only option is to revisit the way social control is instituted over the Black community.

What we see developing is a reliance on indirect mechanisms that isolate individuals from the community rather than allow for the development of a collective political awareness. If we see the US government as always having a politics of the exception with regard to Blacks that defines one important element of its sovereignty, then it is possible to see government as struggling in its role as an extension of White community interests to define how Blacks are a problem in the society. This is not a problem of pluralism, where Blacks are a competing government interest, but an issue of how to describe the problem of the Black person within a White society (Schmitt 1996: 37). In this capacity the need to isolate Whites from Blacks to control the unequal allocation of goods and services and to immunize Whites from the effects of Black life described by the effects of racial subordination are central functions of US government.

What is breaking down today is the integration of Blacks into the existing institutional activities of the government as it functions to safeguard and improve the quality of life for its White citizens. I think what Foucault says about the role of the police in developing the seventeenth- and eighteenth-century functions of the European state is very interesting in this regard (2007: 322–28). Foucault describes how with man as it object the state developed the police as a way to bring the activities of man into conjunction with state economic and political aspirations. The police were given the authority to mediate between the state and a differentiation of the population depending on the ambitions of diverse state political projects. It was through the implementation of policing that the state was able to control its citizens as an object of the political agendas developed within the government. If we take this basic idea and apply it to the US, the way that Whites used the government to implement racial distinctions socially, economically, and politically matters a great deal in the ability of the apparatus to respond to diverse problems it encounters.

In both the last two stories we see Wright describing how Whites began changing the form of policing to accommodate the new collective action by Blacks who would not be deterred by the politics of the exception developed during Jim Crow. In "Bright and Morningstar," as the sheriff gathers local Whites and begin to torture her son, without concealing their identity since the anonymity of traditional Klan garb no longer is enough of a deterrent to Black activism, his mother, who has come looking for the quisling who has betrayed the movement, reacts to the crushing of her son's knees not by acceding to the wishes of the Whites but by turning her gun on the White man who has betrayed them. That she and her son will die a horrible death is less important than eliminating the obstacle to collective action. Personal sacrifice is a requirement of the new politics for Blacks, and so the problem for the society, for White sovereignty, is how to account for this as an issue of authority and social control.

It became important to describe Blacks as a problem of sociology in terms of employment, substance abuse, educational attainment, family structure, age, and housing arrangement. As Esposito writes about the science of eugenics and the development of anthropology, "It isn't man that is valued on the basis of his economic productivity, but economic productivity that is measured in proportion to the human type to which it pertains" (2008: 129). All aspects of the individual Black person became a political imperative for ensuring the social control of the Black community once Black collective action was a possible response to Jim Crow racial politics. What we see in the stories is that already in the 1930s the White community is made aware of the problem beginning to develop in their ability to use a general application of violence and specific forms of control such as convict leasing to force Blacks to conform to the developmental needs of the society (Blackmon 2009). Admittedly this is a crude way to view the development of US racial politics from Jim Crow to the creation of the apparatus of racial equality, but how else to explain the development of educational policies, housing instruments, policing techniques, and laws to give Blacks voting rights and employment protection? As Foucault says,

> And there will now be a sort of double system. On the one hand will be a whole series of mechanisms that fall within the province of the economy and the management of the population with the function of increasing the forces of the state. Then, on the other hand, there will be an apparatus or instruments for ensuring the prevention or repression of disorder, irregularity, illegality, and delinquency. (2007: 353)

The aim was more control, not less, over Blacks as a community. What was once Jim Crow became in the 1960s the exceptional Black, the exception of the racist, and a normal Black community that through its subordination could anchor the possible pretensions of the Black elite. Instead of a White community at fault for a lack of resources in the Black community, Blacks had only themselves to blame from within the new set of sociological techniques, instruments of law enforcement, and social measurements for any deficiencies of status.

This is the answer that the White elites in "Fire and Cloud" are looking for when they leave the meeting dissatisfied with the lack of obedience by Dan, the leader of the Black community. Dan says he is not responsible for the actions of the Blacks in town, that he can't control them. The answer being developed at the time by the state is to make Blacks "responsible citizens," responsible for their own situation, and thereby absolve Whites of any complicity in their subordination. Ideally this can even be described as a subordination that is entirely encompassed by the social and economic needs of the society so that the work of race in constantly affirming the imperative of these social instruments disappears from view for the regular citizen. The racial social segregation seemingly occurs due to economic and social choices rather than the undemocratic decision of a White authorizing sovereign community. This brings us to the discussion of racial politics today.

8 Integration

> Many years have gone by now still no sign of you . . . Where ever you are, remember me, in whatever you do, I love you . . . .
>
> —Lucky Dube, "Remember Me"

> The moral imperatives of American life that are implicit in the Declaration of Independence, the Constitution, and the Bill of Rights were a part of both individual consciousness and the conscience of those writers who created what we consider our classic novels—Hawthorne, Melville, James, and Twain; and for all the hooky-playing attitude of the twenties or the political rebelliousness of the thirties, and the reluctance of contemporary writers to deal explicitly with politics, they still are.
>
> —Ellison, *Invisible Man*

The main events of *Silver Sparrow*, by Tayari Jones, take place from the 1960s to the 1980s in Atlanta, Georgia. A tale of bigamy and social stigma, the narrative history begins when a young Black man, James, gets a young Black girl, Laverne, pregnant. She is forced to leave school and marries James at 14, whereupon she moves in with him and his "brother" Raleigh at his mother's house. Even though she ends up losing the child, Laverne decides to stay with James. James and Raleigh's subsequent successful struggle to build a limo service and Laverne a beauty salon serve as a backdrop to the main story, which revolves around James's two young girls, who are half-sisters, but Black. In the context of the description in the fiction texts from earlier periods of US political development we can see that the political framing of race as no longer a barrier to social and economic success in the new politics of racial equality allows Tayari Jones to address the same social problems of sisters and inheritance, family, and social community entirely within the Black community. Whites are no longer necessary to frame the effects of race on the Black community. Just as in the middle of the Jim Crow period such as depicted in *Plum Bun,* it was no longer necessary to remind Blacks of the social limitations of their race through overt acts of White violence, since other forms of social control were available. The difference of race can now be internalized within the description of the Black community. Instead of Dr. Miller in *The Marrow of Tradition,* who works within the community and always knows that he must bring along those who are Black around him in his every success, the successful Black person under integration is unable to bring this individual exceptionalism into convergence with the needs of the larger Black community, since the idea of community solidarity is exactly what the new racial politics seeks to attenuate.

Under the current description of racial equality Blacks are no longer accountable to their entire community since the social mechanisms of mutual dependence are no longer intact. Instead, the needs of individual Blacks are increasingly defined in terms of family resources, personal resources, and the ability to define exceptional status against the normal Black community. The Black subject is placed in a condition of seeking to describe itself against its community. This new politics of equality with Whites requires a form of amnesia on the part of the subject. It is only through the absence of the history of racism and the politics of struggle that the Black community is engaged in with Whites that the Black subject is able to define itself as "equal." To be Black is defined as merely cultural and the politics of the exceptional Black becomes that of desiring individual authenticity, a social drive towards some type of racial substance beyond the decision, and not a challenge to the idea of racial difference. In *Silver Sparrow,* instead of White sovereignty giving definition to the Black community, it is the individual Black man, James, who can now serve as the force of the decision by distinguishing between two parts of the Black community, those who live in shadow and those who are now described as equal to Whites. The ambitious Black man replaces the White sovereign individual as the authority for the decision to distinguish in the Black community between types of persons who can then be sorted according to accomplishment and resources, between those he can love and those he merely lives with. This story takes place in Atlanta, and the fact that the social segregation is absolute enough to preclude the mention of Whites except once in the story, and only when they leave Atlanta, is indicative of how the internalization of racial politics within the Black community precludes addressing the apparatus itself. The new politics does not allow Blacks to begin confronting the problem of racial hierarchy and injustice.

Without divorcing Laverne or in any way signaling to her the presence of another woman in his life, James marries Gwendolyn, whom he meets at the gift-wrapping counter in a department store. While the second wife Gwendolyn is aware of his "other" wife, Laverne is not. This act of bigamy becomes a metaphor for the racial political effect of defining two types of Black community, one of which must deny the other to sustain itself. When each house has a daughter within four months of each other the plot begins to develop, with Gwendolyn's household living in the shadow of Laverne's until the final chapters of the book. At the end of the story, to keep the first household, James is forced to give up his second wife and child. He had to make a choice between love and acceptability; his social success in the new political regime is dependent on his ability to live within the community he also is a part of.

The book ends with Dana, the "Silver Sparrow," trying to live a life without this duplicity, and also without the love of her father. It is a tragedy.

It points to the problem of the bifurcation that exists between acceptable racial social practices and the racial injustice with which we actually live today. In the story we see the love James has for his hidden daughter, and the love he has for his visible daughter. Each girl lives her life in the confines of the social space given by this dual life of the father, with one being aware of it and therefore also impoverished by the split in her relationship to James. The happiness of the legitimate daughter Chaurisse depends on not discovering that what she has been missing all her life has been an attachment to this other part of her community, personified in her other sister. Eventually this social description of difference becomes too much, and Dana tries to impinge on the other family by befriending the daughter. She refuses to accept the arrangement James and Gwendolyn set forth before her birth.

Without knowing why, Chaurisse revels in this newfound friend who is so like her, someone who can give her the sense of completeness and purpose she otherwise lacks given who she is. Chaurisse's life is a product of the aspiration to equality with Whites that was given the Black community in exchange for dropping the demand for increased political authority in the society. Subsuming the idea of racial justice to that of mere equality as Whites define it maintains the decision of race socially, and allows for a continued description by a sovereign White authority of the conditions of this description of equality. White authority remains without conditions, except as it applies strictures, in the form of the exception of the racist, to itself enable social control in the polity. The consequences for Dana of not accepting this life in shadow are severe: once cut off from her father, she is unable to go to the college she was about to attend. We see her years later with a small child, living in Atlanta, the direction of her life having been altered by the secret begun by others so many years ago.

On one level the story is about the problem of secrecy and the deceptions that people can use on themselves and others to weave together a life. Racism still requires a politics of lying and deception. That bigamy is wrong, and that this is also true of the idea of bifurcating the Black community into exceptions to the rule of race and those to which it is applied comprehensively, is the point I wish to draw from the narrative.

ON HAIR

How do we differentiate between parts of the Black community? It is not a coincidence that the politics of hair remains a constant theme throughout the *Silver Sparrow*, as Dana has natural thick, flowing hair, while the "real" daughter, Chaurisse, has hair that constantly needs a weave and additions to make her complete, the Black person who is equal to Whites. Financial success and political equality occur for Blacks only by allowing the majority of the community to live in shadow, socially connected but disavowed. At the same time, this criticism is not a demand for some type of essential social community but instead a complaint about the inability to organize politically across the community of those who experience race as Blacks today.

The problem is still racism, not that some Blacks are financially successful. This is not a class problem because the politics of the exception remains described in racial terms. It is wrong to describe the success of some as erasing the ability to address the continuing effects of race on everyone in the society. *Silver Sparrow* makes the case that the social price of this description of equality is too high, as it eviscerates the potential for political cohesion in the Black community and fails to mobilize those concerned with racism in the White community. The story is an argument for healing the rift that has been promulgated through the institutional development of racial equality.

At the end of the story, as she approaches a political solution to this problem of a split community, Dana admits that in fact the two lives of Blacks within the Black community are not very far apart. The author describes the political changes in the Black community according to the natural; the natural was replaced by the press-and-curl, and now the relaxer. "Now, you get them under the hose and the hair gets nothing but wet, and you have to content yourself with just a glimpse of the roots. You have to reach your hands down under the processed stuff" (Jones 2011: 254). Contrast this imagery by Dana to that supplied by Chaurisse: "Dana's roots under the pads of my fingers were kinky, strong like ground wire" (255). It is in this context that Dana at the end of the story remarks on her sister Chaurisse's hair: "It looks really natural" (268). The contrast is also in the dress and behavior of both girls. Dana is crude, promiscuous, and rebellious, while Chaurisse is polite, demure, and a conformist. The bigamous relationship James, as a representative of the Black community, creates to love and be successful collapses as the two parts of his life come together. Without the ability to confront the source of his bifurcation in himself, since it occurs as a consequence of racial politics over which he has no authority, James can only decide to accept the new politics of the exception and thereby avoid a life within the normal conventional limitations given by the extremes of racial subordination. That he sacrifices one for the other in the end is his choice, a choice made tragic by the requirements of the current politics of racial equality.

SISTERLY RELATIONS

The story offers a telling indictment of modern-day African American life, similar to that provided in *Plum Bun*. Raleigh, light skinned and able to pass for White, loves Gwendolyn, who rejects him to continue to live in the shadow of James's respectable public existence. Gwendolyn and Dana would rather have what little social satisfaction they get from their potential to become someday a public, proper, and successful middle-class family than assert a politics that would leave this behind for something new. They live fully outside the politics of the exception provided for Blacks who succeed within the new politics of equality. At every turn in the story Dana must concede pride of place to her "real" sister, in terms of after-school clubs, activities, choice of high school, and material possessions. Instead of giving way only to Whites, the exceptional Black is elevated and provides a buffer between the continued potential material and political success of the White community and the Black community defined even in its middle-class aspirations as racially inferior and subordinate. In counterpoint to the narratives of *Iola Leroy*, *The Marrow of Tradition*, *Plum Bun*, and *Uncle's Tom's Children*, life as a Black person in a community in spite of the decision of race, which is otherwise illustrated perfectly by Raleigh being light-skinned and "white" like Iola Leroy, is rejected by Gwendolyn for the desire to remain in a relationship to the idea of race, as an exception that is equal to Whites in name only. The book clearly rejects the possibility of this new racial *rapprochement* described by integration, describing this as chimerical and necessarily full of the secrets required to maintain the illusion of racial equality.

James desires to integrate; Gwendolyn and Dana are left to fend for themselves rather than allow for a new family to develop visibly once the bigamy is discovered. This is not a matter of accepting certain social conventions, but of having allowed the desire for social conventions to overwhelm the need for acceptance as a subject who can create attachments across specific boundaries. James loves Gwendolyn and Dana, and, unlike in the case of getting Laverne pregnant by mistake, he seeks the contact and love of Gwendolyn. This does not excuse his actions, and in fact the immorality of his choice is an important component of a critique of the current politics of racial equality. It is a statement on the difficulty of bringing together the scattered parts of a community decimated by racism, allowing all of the community to heal and grow rather than a few chosen Black subjects.

The bifurcation of the Black community was the political response by White America to the Civil Rights Movement. That the second wife Gwendolyn creates a life in its shadow, and the book begins with her leaving the viewing line to witness the dead Martin Luther King Jr. because she had to go to work, is the price of the ticket for those able to accept or take advantage of the opportunities of the new model of integration. It is important not to protest or cause problems if you want to get ahead. What her daughter shows by the intransigence of her desire to pursue her father into his other life is that this sacrifice, of some Blacks for an African American life of economic and political opportunity, is not without cost to the society, the family, and the political possibilities of the Black subject. The difficulty is to battle race not through accepting its limits, but refiguring its hold on our lives. That this entire story takes place in Atlanta is not a coincidence. Atlanta is the epicenter for African American and Black life in the US South today. It is only in places where a significant community can develop that the question of the types of sacrifices necessary to be successful in the US as a Black subject can be made visible. As the author writes, "Be careful when you leave Atlanta, because you'll end up in Georgia" (2011: 266). Even the social life of the exceptional Black is based on remaining in this place, remaining stagnant politically.

The shift in the description of Black subjectivity occasioned by the politics of the Civil Rights Movement is obvious in the story. The narrative of *Silver Sparrow* describes how after this there were no longer supposed to be barriers to career choices and professional advancement for Blacks. While in the last generation the Black Pullman porter, the funeral-home director, pastor, and store owner catering to the segregated Black community were the limits of ambition for Black youth unable to afford the few colleges available to them, from the 1960s a university education at a previously largely or completely all-White institution, private-sector employment, and government jobs became available to a degree that overwhelmed any of the traditional arguments that racism was still a part of the fabric of society. It is only half a century later that it is possible to see how this new opportunity argument addressed only the formal requirements for racial equality in the society. It did little to change the importance of race and the place of White sovereignty in the society. What happened instead was the shift of responsibility for defining the limits of racial difference in the first instance onto Blacks themselves.

By making individual Black success nominally a problem of behavior and personal choice, this occludes the presence of static social practices that define discrete communities of race. This becomes obvious if we see the changes in the 1960s as due to a need to retain the status of race in society rather than accept the popular description of this being the watershed moment of a counterdecision to no longer race persons in the society. The latter is plainly not true. The imposition of a formal requirement for racial equality in the absence of a way to resolve several hundred years of developing distinct racial communities on each side of the decision is disingenuous at best. What the Civil Rights Movement did was raise the possibility of a collapse of the social order itself. Instead of addressing the place of race in US democratic politics, what now mattered was instead a presentation of racial difference that the author describes as a politics where "you really need to work on the way you present yourself" (2011: 43).

It became important to differentiate yourself from all other Blacks to be equal to Whites, to be exceptional in ways that otherwise require that Blacks remain vulnerable as a community to practices of racial subordination. This is not the same thing as opening up the Black community to the vagaries of the economic marketplace, but instead a way to frame the choices people make within the description of Blackness as due to their relative material deprivation instead of a formal racial barrier. The reasons for the formal requirements of Jim Crow remain present today in the reproduction of Whiteness as a social community within the society. This has remained untouched by the change in political instruments used to effectuate racial differences under the equality regime in the economic and political marketplace.

LIKE SPARROWS

Author Tayari Jones has the mother Gwendolyn state her knowledge of the changes brought on by Martin Luther King Jr. and the Civil Rights Movement in this way:

> She knew how much things had changed, and she was grateful for it, Lord knew that she was thankful for these new opportunities. Still, she hadn't fought for them, and now the man was dead. It would have been difficult to explain her shame even if she had anyone to explain herself to. (2011: 18)

That this is described in contrast to a difficult family life is not a coincidence. The application for admission to racial economic equality of opportunity was granted on condition that the social conditions of racial inequality remain intact. Gender politics must remain largely occluded by this desire for material success. Gwendolyn does not take up the mantle of the political struggle which the author describes has been dropped at her feet by the death of King. She instead decides to live within the confines of what has been given by Whites to reconcile Black community demands for racial equality. She tries to become the exception and the part of the Black community that always remains uncertain and expectant in their problematic attachment to Blackness. This is because this exception is contrived in response to the political desires of the White community.

The latent political potential of the 1960s was not a magical process, but a concrete requirement of a politics where a Democratic president pushed forward a legislative agenda designed to restore social order in a society reeling from riots, civil unrest, and mass political movements. The decision of race today remains obscured behind the full weight of Black and White community life and the formal instruments of racial equality. It would be a mistake to confuse the shift in how the decision is applied in society, similar to that which occurred with the collapse of formal slavery and the period of transition to Jim Crow, with a claim that race no longer exists as a problem of similar weight today in society.

When, for example, people suggest that African American fiction today should not be thought of as African American in the same tradition as the social realist novels of, say, Harper, Chesnutt, or Wright, they confuse both the absence of formal racial requirements in the law with the absence of racial instruments in the society, and the description of the writer as an exception to normal Black subjectivity in ways that an author such as John Wideman refuses to endorse (Warren 2011). The critic remains wedded to the description of the new politics of racial equality as having erased the problem of race and therefore also the continuous struggle against race that today still defines a Black community. This accepts the politics which would conceal the political work of race under the argument, for example, of Black relative economic deprivation and individual political apathy.

It is as though the image of the chain gang, the ditchdigger, and the cotton-picking slave remains the measure that is used to assess racial progress, without understanding that with economic development these are no longer representative jobs of the very poor in US society. Of course those images no longer occur on a regular basis, and so the society learns to ignore the plight of those working two or three jobs part time and cleaning and cooking for others in something now given the title of "the Service Industry." The millions of Black poor remain underemployed or on welfare in conditions that would be immediately recognizable to their ancestors under Jim Crow. Rather than "taking in laundry or sewing," being "the help," or a "handyman" for the White folks in their neighborhood, society has developed and the place of the lowest remains filled with the "new" African American, who is told that he or she should be "grateful" for the little government support he or she receives. That this support has to be given as a form of compensation for the effects for racism in housing, employment, and education is left unstated, and therefore these become labeled "entitlements" as a way to further deepen the reach of the apparatus within the individual households of the Black poor. To then classify these Black poor as victims of class politics is to misunderstand the role that race plays in US welfare-state policies (Griffin and Newman 2008).

It seems like we are confused by the Black cashier at the bank, the Black police officer, the Black professor, or even a Black president into thinking that race is unimportant. Each of these people will tell you that his or her race has always been an important issue throughout his or her life. Framing race as a social problem for the community, a matter of authenticity and culture, of presentation and behavior is just how the new politics of racial equality works. The new politics requires that this framing is described as having nothing to do with Whites or with that original decision to reproduce a community of persons who are White. Instead, Blacks are asked to divide themselves, literally in the case of James, as the measure of racial equality.

At the same time, the warning described by Fauset in *Plum Bun* of reducing the struggle to change the distinction of race to one of social equality resonates strongly in the context of contemporary racial politics. By erasing the political importance of antiracism for that which describes race as a social problem, the decision to race seems on its face to be merely a social inconvenience, a retrograde social behavior addressed best by more information on the social construction of race and courses on diversity training. This perspective is inaccurate and deceptive.

THE SERIALIZATION OF BIGAMY

It is clear from the events described both in *Plum Bun* and *Uncle Tom's Children* that the desire to not merely survive on the part of Blacks but thrive, to be free of the social constraints of Jim Crow, would overwhelm any politics in the community that sought to reassess the conditions of the apparatus of racial equality. As in the period after Slavery, to question the way that Whites and the US government incorporated the newly freed citizens into the society is to open up the entire racial apparatus to inspection. This is unacceptable to both Whites and Blacks within the politics that rewards complicity. The historical trauma of each period of racial politics blocks access, therefore, to the political forces that led to the changes in the institutional framework of race in the society. It is just easier to suggest from within the racial-equality apparatus that the shared trauma of race during Jim Crow makes it imperative to exclude racism from our everyday lives. Race becomes something that can no longer be taken up, because it describes a trauma available within our democratic society that we do not know how to address. Its presence points to a failure of the democratic experiment and a society that does not progress. As Santner writes, "Trauma could thus at some level be understood as what escapes both *narrative elaboration* and *reflexive serialization*" (2011: 201). The entire history of racial politics becomes encapsulated in the terms *slavery* and *Jim Crow*, and then society moves on within the politics of integration as the means by which to exclude an accounting that cannot occur with race. A single trauma or specific events replaces a history of racism and racial subordination of entire communities of people in the development of US democratic society (Gilroy 2006).

It is this struggle with accounting for the trauma of race, as requiring reparations, equality for those exceptional Blacks, or a democracy to come, that allows bigamy to serve as a difficult metaphor for the Black community. That it is difficult does not allow us to forget that when we write about the politics of race we are discussing events such as those in *Uncle Tom's Children*. The trauma of bigamy, of realizing that the love you thought was yours alone is also shared with another, of discovering and being discovered, of establishing the social life that sustains this decision, haunts all who are involved. How would someone White take on the burden of racial history today in the US if it is not considered sufficient to put the burden on someone who can become the "racist"? I think it is important for Whites to address directly the politics that allows for a slow march back to using race openly as the apparatus of racial equality becomes less efficacious after

President Obama. The myth of radical change that occurred to cover over the Jim Crow period for the generation of Whites born after the mid-1970s needs to be replaced with an understanding that the politics of race continues unabated (Santner 2006: 75). The White subject today remains in the midst of a developing racial history rather than looks back on a terrible past for which they are not responsible (164). That our grasp of history is always different from what actually occurred should not dissuade the development of a critical race politics that asks Whites to understand that the social basis of their community continues to depend primarily on the racial subordination of Blacks.

For Blacks a similar problem arises, and this is evident in the narrative of *Silver Sparrow*. For Gwendolyn as she works instead of attending Civil Rights protests, finding a way to conform to the new sense of possibility given by racial equality, what she sacrifices is the ability to define the basis for racial politics. She is unable to do so because of her willingness to be confined in Black Atlanta, to live within the new subjection instead of refusing the bifurcation of community and the betrayal of another woman her marriage to James incurs. Gwendolyn is fully aware of James's marriage before she agrees to go out of state to marry. These choices represent the bits and pieces of a response to the trauma of racial politics, and need to be acknowledged for the political anesthetization and paralysis this represents for the Black subject as a moment that has finally been crystallized in the election of President Obama. The ambitions of the Black community are not encompassed in the ambition to be elected president of the United States, but to improve, as Iola Leroy sought to do, the situation for all the Black freedmen and women. Gwendolyn gradually accepts that her own life as a second wife and in her career represents social progress for Blacks according to Whites, but this leaves her bereft of the very community she once knew.

If one works from within the Black community so that he or she refuses to be distinguished from others and asks why other Blacks are thought different because of grades, test scores, credit ratings, or work experience, this forms a politics that counters the easy separation of good and bad Blacks by the apparatus. It means we perhaps become once again less than stellar representatives of the race and exceptions to the rule, and must face the truth about how resources are explicitly assigned based on the possibility of distinguishing some Blacks from others as a way to erode any common political focus. To divide the political attention of the Black community by the doubling that Foucault describes, of both affirmation and protection, in the context of the traumatic history of racial politics and the constant presence of race as a social threat to the individual Black subject is to refuse Blacks the possibility of surviving as a community (2007: 353). This is the effect of the practice of bigamy; it destroys the community. This politics takes place even as the individual Black subject is available to the operations of a racial politics derived from White community sovereign interests that can only be countered by an opposing racial community.

The resolution of the problem of the bifurcation of the Black community has to be accomplished by the two sisters, who are doubles of one another even if they are physically dissimilar (Santner 2006: 194). Jones has the sisters meet much later in their lives after the main story and discover that each has found it possible to come closer to what each sought in the other; they are each more complete without the artificial distinctions of the apparatus. What race requires today is a form of body double, a constant series of choices so as to become an exception to someone else, to make sure Whites can recognize how different he or she is from those who do not succeed. This is a form of self-confirmation by Blacks of the difference that race presupposes between humans. A critique of this would demand that Blacks and Whites, the experiences a similar twin object in the form of the "racist," confront their double, that which has been split off by the apparatus of racial equality. To look on that person who is both the same and yet separated by social and political institutional forces is to see the entire apparatus. For both Blacks and Whites it raises the question of how similar each part of the community must be to allow race to remain coherent as a politics in spite of this bifurcation. This is not an affirmation of racial absolutism but a realization of the effects of race as a problem that democracy must address. The problem of the body double that race today creates is the main theme of the work of fiction addressed next.

THE PRISONER AND THE PROFESSOR

In *Brothers and Keepers* (1984), John Wideman writes about his brother's life, his own, and the way things developed differently for them both. John became a famous writer, a university professor, and moved away from home, while his younger brother Robby did not. Instead, Robby got involved in drugs and crime, and ended up with a life in prison. At one level the difference in destiny is described as one of character: John has the patience to learn the fundamentals of the game (of basketball, which serves as a metaphor for John Wideman for life), training himself to play, diligently delaying instant gratification, accepting assistance from others, until he is offered a sports scholarship to the university. Robby wants the quick fix, the easy route, and finds that people are drawn to him and his charisma in ways that count for something on an everyday basis (Wideman 1984: 219). One desires to get out of the ghetto and the other sees no way that he can accept the terms of this escape. The book is superficially about the personal consequences each brother experiences from the different choices he makes, but the substantial narrative provides an important statement on the way the current politics of integration delineates a specific path to success out of a general situation of African American racial subordination.

That this path to exceptional Black status for John is one of conformity, discipline, and luck is obvious from the story, but it also describes how the price of that success is to leave behind the militancy and agitation of the 1960s and 1970s. There is no place for the struggle against racism beyond the confines of the ghetto, and therefore personal militancy and social agitation are viewed as merely a symptom of not having succeeded in leaving its confines. Criticism of this process is described within the apparatus as a response not to racism but to *ressentiment*, which can be addressed through the individual choices given by the current politics of racial equality (1984: 114). Robby Wideman has a brief period of political activity in high school, but it leads nowhere because it has nowhere to go. The only paths to success for Blacks are in sports and music, and doing well in school. Robby was protesting the poor conditions in the schools, how they were not a vehicle for anything but continuing the status quo, and after this early moment of lucidity Robby ends up descending into a life of drugs and quick money through gangster activity. Eventually he is an accomplice to a murder when someone is killed in a botched robbery and he is sentenced to prison for life. This is a very familiar story today for the Black community and few successful African Americans do not know at least someone in their immediate family who has been imprisoned.

In *Brothers and Keepers* the death of Martin Luther King Jr. also serves as a marker for the political choices available for Robby. As he puts it, "Together was were it was at. Didn't nobody dig what King putting down. We wasn't about begging whitey for nothing and we sure wasn't taking no knots without giving a whole bunch back" (1984: 113). As with Gwendolyn in *Silver Sparrow*, Robby takes King's assassination as incidental to the political changes they feel must be made. She has to get to work, and Robby is focused on building a community of activists to change the high-school structure. Robby's brother, John Wideman, was intent on teaching African American literature at the University of Pennsylvania (111).

The author addresses the problem that the government had with the movement, in that the answer Whites developed to the activism and rebellion on the part of Blacks was to acquiesce to some parts of the political program and therefore remove the institutional focus of the social movement. This is illustrated by the author through a description of how Robby resolved the problem of his father's use of physical force to discipline him as a child. When Robby finally takes a pair of scissors to protect himself from attack, his father refuses to push forward. Instead of taking the scissors and punishing Robby, he accepts the fact of his rebellion and in doing so leaves Robby to his own devices, adrift in his own ambition. Refusing to develop or acknowledge a new politics that could accommodate the demands of the movement with the new requirement to be economically successful, Robby and John's father are forced to accept the bifurcation of the family and therein also the community. According to his father, Robby was a "rebel," and so instead of working with his desires and thereby making Robby's ambitions in life a part of the family goals, his father and society left him alone (110). This was a politics of failing alone instead of coming together to support individual initiative and an alternative vision of politics. By pretending that these consequences were a result of Robby's choices and not a refusal to accept his desire for social change, the responsibility for his imprisonment is placed not on society but on Robby himself. This is the traditional politics of race as difference reformulated for the economic current needs of the society. In the same fashion, in response to the political activism by Robby the school system implements a new regimen the next school year to limit the ability of students to protest, with police, metal detectors, and locks on the classrooms (117).

John Wideman gives the reader a description of how Black life developed in response to the politicization of the 1960s. Seen through the different lives of the two brothers, the way the schools, businesses, and police responded to the aspirations of Blacks for some answer to racial injustice was to create a series of tests or conditions for advancement into White society, all the while retaining the social distinction between races through indirect instruments of social control (Parenti 2008; Alexander 2012: 100). As the author explains, once at the university all of the Whites told John to put his past behind him, to forget his connection to the problem of race as it played out on the rest of his community in his absence. This did not mean that John became a part of their community, but that he was anointed an exception to the rules of the social discipline to which otherwise John would have been subjected as a Black person, conditional on his abiding by the explicit social rules of his racial status.

To then say that race does not exist, for John to say this, would merely be a sign that this denouement of his own person was necessary to survive, as a condition for security beyond the ghetto. For Wideman the book is a testament to the false dichotomy being offered by this politics of racial equality. It does not offer more than a temporary reprieve from specific effects of race. The author reveals this in his discourse on what it is like to visit his brother in prison, how it feels to reenter the walls of the community of Blackness allowed by Whites today under integration. He writes, "In order to live with myself and manage my life in the intervals between visits I had learned to shut my brother out of my mind. I could deal with his plight only by brutal compartmentalization" (1984: 221). On the one side you have the African American, "the image of dependency and helplessness," and on the other you have the successful hardworking Black professor who has done all the right things to get ahead in life.

NOT MY PROBLEM, I'M WHITE

John Wideman struggles to not in turn exploit the story of his brother for personal gain, from the outside of that part of the community looking in. He has to work to avoid turning his family and what remains of this aspect of the Black community into something to prove the veracity of the description of race as equality today. This is a description of race as something that burdens African Americans and not Whites, as a matter of individual social and cultural choices and not as a political decision defining distinct communities of racial difference (200). What John has to work against as a strategy of production is the idea that in the community of Blacks, the African American can be divided by a politics that allows the acknowledgment of the exceptional circumstances of some to the detriment of all others in the community (Shelby 2005: 153–60). The definition of success for Blacks requires merely this willful blindness, or at best an awkward silence or complicity around the facts of the bifurcation of the community into those who are financially and politically integrated with the White middle class and elite as exceptions, and those who increasingly live in poverty, economic uncertainty, and political abjection as prisoners and victims of drugs and crime (Davis 2003; Oliver and Shapiro 2006; Parenti 2008; Alexander 2012: 188).

In response to his brother's incarceration, John turns away. As Wideman puts it,

> I forced myself to forget, become as deaf and dumb as the blocks of stone walling him away . . . It was a trick I'd learned early on. A survival mechanism as old as slavery. If you're born black in America you must quickly teach yourself to recognize the invisible barriers disciplining the space in which you move. (1984: 221)

In the story "The Ethics of Living Jim Crow," Richard Wright describes a situation where a Black woman is beaten bloody in front of him by the store owner and the son for whom Wright works. Instead of stopping them, or asking what they are doing, he keeps wiping the brass ornamentation, watching out of the corner of his eyes at what unfolds (2008: 8). The difference between Jim Crow and integration is a politics that encouraged and required Whites to act exceptionally as individuals and collectively to control Blacks, and the contemporary period that demands a response of self-censorship of the Black community. This is a form of acquiescence by Blacks to the politics of social control necessary to support White sovereign authority. That the current definition of racial politics describes how Robby eventually ends up in prison as a matter of poor personal choices should not obscure the fact that under Jim Crow the politics of race required an identical turning away by the Black community from the effects of race on individuals. For Blacks the equation of race is explicit. Wright writes that afterwards the store owner and son made the distinction between him and the woman very clear: "They would not beat me if I knew enough to keep my mouth shut" (1984: 8). That this relationship of silence and fear is still true today gives the story *Brothers and Keepers* its poignancy as a story about two brothers.

The most dramatic difference in racial politics today from that of Jim Crow is in the location of the political requirement for Whites, not in its continual ordering of the Black subject. For Whites, the new era of racial equality before the law has meant the ability to leave racial social control up to the courts and other institutional processes, instead of demanding individual exceptional activity to control the social activities of Blacks. Only in cases where Blacks do not pay attention to the limited description of success being provided in the apparatus does the discourse of White sovereign authority still arise for White individuals. Physical attacks such as during the riot described in *The Marrow of Tradition* or in the lynching in "Big Boy Leaves Home" are therefore rarely necessary today. Wideman argues that social control is now more completely in the hands of a constitutional political authority. The police, the social worker, the public-school teacher, the parole officer, and the head of human resources in a private company have become the most important way to define racial difference in the society today. This is not to say that Whites are not also poor, but instead that Blacks as a community are available to a different type of social control, the expectation of a difference in treatment and resources, than Whites. Ironically, the very moment of success for legal equality was the moment that the role of government in maintaining the decision to race in society expanded.

DEFLECTION AND OBFUSCATION: LIBERAL WHITES

This is accomplished by allowing each individual White person access to a social mechanism where any onus of racial bias, of acting from the decision, is deflected onto something else, another White person, someone Black, a formal rule, or the law. Each individual White person therefore has only to shoulder a small portion of the burden of the decision and the action that occurs from it, rather than justify or defend him- or herself as fully responsible for the idea of race. This form of passing on the responsibility to a figure or idea that remains metaphysical always allows Whites to claim that they both benefit from being a member of the White community but at the same time have nothing against Blacks, that in fact they possibly do not even see race. This position is not duplicitous, but rather a function of the way race is described as something held not by persons, but a decision always existing outside of time and space, outside of the legal equality that exists, and therefore something to be constantly measured and remarked upon as unfair and yet unchangeable by individuals or the government itself. In this racial gesture there seems to be no White sovereign authority; there is only the state and its democratic processes.

This is the theoretical difficulty with the idea that the politics of race in the US is outside the purview of democratic politics, that it should be resolved as a social artifact of the former condition of slavery. The formal equality of Blacks does not resolve the problem of race in the US, but tests the ability of the law to address an issue for which the US government is already implicated. Race therefore offers a description of a situation where a democratic representative government has to accommodate a concern by Blacks that has developed outside of its original mandate, and as the discussion here portrays it, when it is complicit and dependent for its successful operation on the interests of the White community. This is why the election of an African American to the presidency is so controversial. It asks of White sovereignty that it accept the limitations on its authority given by the political expediency of the current apparatus of racial equality. The political claims of illegitimacy, anti-Americanism, and ideological socialism leveled at President Obama are important, rather than merely a function of US democratic popular culture, because these narratives define real political limits to the effects of the tenure of the first Black president on the politics of race outside of the definition of racial equality. Without these constraints, the politics of exceptional activity used during Jim Crow to support White sovereignty would occur generally in the society as a condition for Obama's presidency, and the institutional structure of formal racial equality would collapse.

The stability of the racial polity in the US is defined by this balance between the ability of Whites to maintain the distinctions of racial difference by a specific politics of the exception and the functions of democratic government. The danger of a situation such as the race riot described in *The Marrow of Tradition* or the more contemporaneous lynching party described in "Big Boy Leaves Home" occurs if this balance of recognized White personal authority without responsibility and the public control of Black political aspirations is threatened. For those Blacks who disobey the law and who refuse to accept the conditions of their impoverishment but also refuse to accept the path for exceptional success, there is only the naked apparatus of the law and its form of physical control (Alexander 2012: 98). As John describes Robby's life in prison, "The flimsiest pretext would make murdering him acceptable, he had no means of protecting himself" (Wideman 1984: 83; Alexander 2012: 61).

The slightest deviation from the conditions of Black freedom under racial equality allow for immediate action on the part of the institutions of government. That the limits of this freedom are taught young Black children at an early age is remarked upon by Harper, Wright, and Wideman, writing in different eras of racial politics in the society. An example of the degree of social control demanded of the political of racial equality is given by the events where Professor Henry Louis Gates Jr. was arrested while trying to enter his own home after having locked himself out (Zhu 2009). Even though he told the officer who he was, Gates was still arrested. In the public furor that occurred, both Gates and the arresting officer were invited to the White House for a discussion of the event by President Obama. Gates's arrest was seen by many Blacks as merely a repetition of an event that the general Black public take as an everyday condition of their movement through majority White neighborhoods and in a majority White workplace. What was remarkable was its subsequent publicity in the national press, and suggests very forcefully that instead of seeing race as a problem that is incidental to American democracy, the president and his administration were aware that addressing this event would allow for a conversation to occur in public about both the idea of a Black president and the problem of White sovereignty.

The fact that President Obama did not accuse the officer of racism but instead of overzealousness in the line of duty shows a desire to reinforce the mechanisms of the Black exception, the politics whereby certain Blacks as African Americans are different and deserve the same type of respect from the law given Whites by virtue of their racial description. What President Obama did was to make more apparent the political claims that Gates and he were making in the moment for an equality based on being exceptions to the informal rules governing the social control of Blacks, not that race was unimportant to their social and political status. That this desire for immunity from suspicion is impossible given the parameters of the decision to race is obvious, but the event at the White House can be seen as an important gesture to those opposing his presidency that Obama was able and willing to remain within the limits of his racial condition, even as president (King and Smith 2011: 216). How else to explain why a sitting president would see it as valuable to meet with Gates and the arresting officer, to expose an event of race that is repeated constantly throughout the US (Neher 2009)? Certainly its ubiquity should be taken as a signal that this description of the very conscious limits of social control is still accessible to both Black and White persons in the society. This is certainly the case as well with President Obama's response to the Trayvon Martin killing in Florida, when he said that "If I had a son he would look like Trayvon Martin" (Memoli 2012).

Without putting too much importance on the role of the presidency within the democratic institutions of government in the US, it still is disturbing that not only is it obvious to someone in that office that race is still a problem for the president just as for a Black person walking through the streets of a city in the US, but also that his mere presence in the White House is conditional in ways that race determines, and not merely according to the limits of his office. President Obama's presence in the office should be public, not personal, in ways that should prohibit the idea of race from intruding in his daily life. For Whites it still matters that President Obama is Black. For Blacks in the US, little has changed in their relationship to Whites as a community; the decision remains very much in evidence, even as the possibility of personal advancement for individual African Americans such as President Obama and Professor Gates is held forth as examples of the equality of the law and the functioning of democracy in the society.

THE POLITICS OF FEAR

The other major theme in the novel is given by Wideman's description of the fear and trauma associated with Robby's running from the law. With the license to shoot first, because he is classified as armed and dangerous, the police represent a particular danger to Robby once he leaves the scene of the murder. For three months Robby escapes the authorities, and his capture is not described in the book. While on the run the author describes how "A special watch was set upon those, like my mother, who would be hardest hit. The best was hoped for, but the worst expected; and no one could claim to know what the best might be" (Wideman 1984: 4). This idea of fear and the possibility of violence, of terror in the form of those with the authority to act with impunity to reinforce the racial social order, was an important factor in the subordination of slaves, Blacks under Jim Crow, and continues for African Americans today. But this is always connected to uncertainty and the inability for Blacks to decide when and how the form of violence and enforcement will take place. As was discussed earlier, Wright explicitly describes this condition in the tale "Down by the River" when Mann runs from the soldiers instead of letting them possibly shoot him later on their own terms. The freedom to choose how to punish is the right of the sovereign and not its victims. It is this that President Obama cannot do in his public response to Gates and the officer; he does not have sovereign authority to change the terms of the social control of Blacks in the society. President Obama is always available to the discourse of social control that comes from within the description of Whiteness in US society. This partially explains the volume of criticism President Obama receives that addresses his potentially overstepping his authority as a president and the public discourse of having to take the country back from what he may accomplish in his tenure as president. To suggest publicly, as Sarah Palin did in 2010, "that it's time to take our country back" is not only to suggest that something has been taken away from a section of the American electorate with President Obama's election, but also to warn that this portends the acceptable limit of the impact of the Black exception under the politics of racial equality. Inadvertently, perhaps, Sarah Palin has uttered a claim to want to revisit the conditions of racial equality, to return the racial politics in the US to an earlier time when Blacks were subject to a different politics of the exception.

Whether this is the idea of being revealed as passing, of fearing the capture by those seeking to return former slaves in the North to indenture in the South, or the vicissitudes of the master and local White militia patrollers, Blacks feared White censure and punishment during slavery. During Jim Crow this description of Black subjection as available to the fear of possible violence and specific forms of social control was just as much in evidence. Today this fear is described in the possible failure to become chosen by Whites as exceptional, as special and deserving of their attention as an individual symbol of racial equality. In spite of good intentions, and in fact this is itself a possibility given by the apparatus, the politics of the decision are not available to Whites as individuals. Blacks can only be conceptualized as subjects through the discursive practices that support the apparatus. Wideman remarks on this with regard to the different paths taken by both him and his brother. "We were different. The world had seized on the difference, allowed me room to thrive, while he had been forced into a cage" (1984: 77). This created an effective distance between the two brothers representing the two parts of the community.

LOOKING FROM THE OUTSIDE IN

As John Wideman puts it, "the hardest habit to break, since it was the habit of a lifetime would be listening to myself listen to him" (77). Seen from the other side of the choice of being exceptional, of trying to succeed as an African American, there is a distance from the idea of community in the accumulated habits of complicity and conformity to the authority of the decision as a choice, not merely against the grain of the human. The constant pressure to make the right choices does not make the person less Black, because the choices only occur in the context of being Black, but they do attenuate the connection to a politics of the Black community that would resist this description of exceptional and normal, as good and bad Black subjects. To turn toward the limits of Black subjection as a way to accept the conditionality of one's survival is to then create a distance to those others who either refuse or do not understand these limitations on their freedom.

For John Wideman this took the form of being outside of himself in a way that allowed him not to rebel, nor to seek immediate gratification in the absence of the possibility for success. This is a very different problem than that Iola experiences, for example, as she tries to get out of her own way, the image of being Black that stands against her freedom to define a life, or that Angela experiences as she rejects Whiteness to attempt to leave her obsession with race behind. Instead, John learned to watch himself with the gaze of the apparatus, to judge his actions based on how it would impact his chances for success within the frame provided by Whites. He learned what was acceptable to succeed, only later to realize, as did Angela, that this subjection required the abandonment of the rest of his community to a different set of circumstances. John Wideman played basketball, got a scholarship to UPenn, and from there went on to become a college professor and professional fiction writer. Because he refuses to make these same choices, Robby did not have the capacity to distance himself from the effects of race in this way, of living outside of himself; his Black subjection was all-encompassing, creaturely in a way that demanded that he fight against its confines. Robby is the modern-day version of Melville's Babo, to Whites an incomprehensibly opaque human being who is confined by the limits of his race. John Wideman ignores not the fact of his own Blackness but the idea that becoming exceptional is something he already accepts himself, as something he wants to do. He makes of the idea of his exceptional Black status his choice, rather than describing it as an unacceptable, inescapable condition of subjection defined by racism and White authority.

CHOOSING TO LEAVE

As the author explains it, this choice allows him to avoid addressing the fear that otherwise attends Black subjectivity. It does not change his availability, as Gates's case shows, to the authority of the apparatus. John does not forget but he also no longer lives with the risks attendant on being Black in the space allowed for normal Black community life. John avoids the ghetto and other areas that Blacks frequent. Once he finds out that his brother is on the run after killing someone, the author realizes that "my years of willed ignorance, of flight and hiding, had not changed a simple truth: I could never run fast enough or far enough" (1984: 4). It is not a coincidence that this sentiment is echoed by Robby, who at the time is on the run from the law.

Tayari Jones also describes the pain and inevitability of reckoning with the limits of Black subjection in *Silver Sparrow*, through the contrast between the two sisters and the father's choice of action. The difference between sisters, one White and the other Black, in *The Marrow of Tradition* also serves to move the plot forward towards the tragedy of the race riot, as does the differences between Iola and her brother, in *Iola Leroy*, the former sold into slavery by deceit, the latter remaining in the North and free. Angela, in *Plum Bun*, lives with the anxiety of paying a price for her choice of passing into Whiteness and this is juxtaposed by the condition defining the Black subjection of her sister Virginia. Together these examples describe a requirement for the Black subject to always live in a state of uncertainty and await description by a White subject. The response to this uncertainty by a Black subject is understandably one of desiring to achieve the relative safety of exceptional status and the willful forgetting of the possibilities attendant on failure. In this way the Black community is made complicit with the current politics of racial equality as much as are Whites, since its precepts offer the potential for some to avoid the full application of the institutional description of racial difference described in the areas of employment, law enforcement, housing, and education.

When the White subject is given as both available and general, as it is today, this creates a situation where individual Whites can both claim membership in a community of race but deny having any responsibility for its constant reproduction after the end of Jim Crow. Whites are only rarely viewed as responsible individually for racism, and these are described as exceptional cases. As a result, the idea of Whiteness seems to exist independent of any racial animus. The assurance of the difference of race is taught each individual White person, just as Wideman learns from childhood the limits of his aspirations as a Black person. For Whites race always just makes a difference, unless he or she decides it doesn't. What is learned is the method of attributing racial difference, of making the decision but transferring authority to make the decision to the community itself. This transfer eliminates any possibility of changing the effects of the decision, and ensures that no one person can be responsible for the social definition of race.

The entire construction whereby a person claims Whiteness and also states that he or she is not defining racial difference in his or her actions arises from this mechanism of obfuscation. The decision becomes something for which no oneclaims responsibility. It does not depend for its definition on the processes of governmentality either since the issue of White sovereignty is not defined there. The descriptions of two racial communities continue to develop alongside one another as in the past. This is the force of Tayari Jones's description of the African American community in *Silver Sparrow*, where race becomes something that casts its shadow over the Black community without a definitive source such as was available for scrutiny under Jim Crow.

There is no target for the racial limits within which lives are led; instead, the idea of a decision to succeed or fail substitutes for the old distinction of knowing your place in Jim Crow exceptional politics. In this way Blacks and Whites police the decision themselves, with the difference that only those African Americans who submit to the process of exceptional success are permitted to leave the description of Black poverty and social vulnerability that is now taken as the hallmark of the Black community by Black's themselves. The move to require authenticity in the terms of this subordination is a function of this model of racial equality, as it further allows for the distinction Wideman speaks of by defining a difference between those Blacks who rail against the decision, such as his brother Robby, and those, such as himself, who accept the conditions for success given by the White sovereign community (Shelby 2005).

The problem with this model of racial equality is that it allows individuals to compete without addressing the role of racial communities as reproducing specific practices of exclusion. Equal opportunity for Black individuals does not simply imply equality for all in the community as such, so the idea of racial equality is a misnomer. Instead, what is meant is for those who manage to figure out how or have specific resources available, there is an equal chance of competing for specific jobs, even possibly the presidency of the United States of America. But the new opportunity should not, as Tayari Jones suggests in her subtle description of two sisters, one silver and only partially visible to the Black community the other black and legitimate, be confused with the absence of race as a way to distinguish between supposedly important human differences that denote a distinction in status between persons of specific communities.

What should have been an extended community, of everyone, Black and White, sparrows all, has continued to be plagued by the desire to differentiate between persons as a way to allocate personal and material attention. As Foucault points out in his lectures of 1984, the problem for democracy is just this idea of ethical differentiation, how to distinguish between claims to truth about the experience of living in society (2008b: 62). If we assume with the fiction texts described here that the Black subject has a particular litany of claims to the truth of American democracy as a political project, then to level these claims in the name of equality of opportunity is to also erase the contribution of persons to the discourse who do suffer unduly from the political processes that persist. This definition of equality suggests that the problem of race is merely that of a majority-minority dispute over the interpretation of goods in public, not a larger problem of the development and convergence of US government with an intact description of White sovereign authority.

What is important here is that while the authority of Whites to act individually was eliminated by equality legislation and a change in custom in the 1960s, the idea of Whiteness as a status or community of which a person was a member did not change. Whites still consider themselves different from Blacks in some qualitative measure, by convention. It is the effects of this convention, its application within informal aspects of everyday life, that must now be feared by African Americans. It is critical to understand that without this type of convention to support an extralegal structure of norms of difference the idea of race would collapse. It would literally have no meaning unless taught, a White subject fashioned so it could adopt a role such that someone Black is different. Even the idea of racial difference is attenuated in the need to remove any possibility of making an individual White person responsible for what is now labeled "racism," the belief that someone of a different race is inferior.

Conclusion

> I was no longer the person my friend and his family had known and loved—I was a stranger now, and keenly aware of it, and trying hard to act, as it were, normal. But nothing *can* be normal in such a situation. They *had* known me, and they *had* loved me; but now they couldn't be blamed for feeling *he thinks he's too good for us now*.
> —Baldwin, "No Name in the Street"

> There you are, listen, I had things to say to you about the general framework of these analyses. But, well, it is too late. So, thank you.
> —Foucault, *The Courage of Truth*

ON COMMUNITY

If we truly believe that everyone is equal, then why does race remain salient socially, on the job, and in politics? As Balfour writes in reference to the work of Baldwin, "Equality thus extended to the formerly unequal leaves unaddressed the question of what allows white Americans to see black Americans as their inferiors in the first place" (Balfour 2001: 127). The answer of course is that the idea of race has become associated with the community of persons rather than an individual decision. This retreat or turn back into a community of difference, different traditions, different families, different behaviors and language is a return to the putative origins, the myth of the decision of race in the US, rather than its elimination. It cements the description of a difference that, even though potentially fungible, is immanently static and exclusionary.

In the past the idea that Blacks were different, had different customs, and different ways of thinking and behaving was a central element in describing the need for slavery and then Jim Crow. This is true as well today. What is new is the idea that the apparatus of legal equality impinges on the description of racial difference in areas outside the law, that is, everyday life. For most Blacks the idea that individual Whites could no longer legally, with impunity, adopt the authority to control them was a significant step away from the form of racial subordination most common in the society. That goods and services could not be legally denied Blacks was a significant change in the way people lived for over eighty years in the US under Jim Crow.

As *Brothers and Keepers* points out, with integration the fear of individual Whites immediately gave way to a fear of failing to succeed, of failing to escape the poverty, crime, and drugs increasingly becoming a part of Black community life, the fear of failing to take advantage of the new opportunity to improve. And yet, while the immediate fear of White individual authority was no longer legally supported, the social norm of inviolate White status and person remained intact. The fear of challenging White authority remains justified, as no change has occurred in the status of Whiteness in the society. This is identical to the message in *Iola Leroy* regarding the need for Blacks to take advantage of the new freedom from slavery. As in the period leading up to Jim Crow, in the absence of an attenuation in the efficacy of the politics of race, as a distinction that it is important to preserve, the eventual result of a shift in racial politics will lead to a sedimentation in the institutional stratification of society along racial lines (Locke 1992). Then once it is no longer seen as anything but a natural consequence of choices people make as individuals, it will be adopted into law. This process is far along at this point, more than forty years after the major successes of the Civil Rights Movement.

The key elements of the decision as a part of the apparatus of formal equality remain intact. The status of White elites is not threatened. Blacks serve as a form of leverage over the White poor in the form of a threat as well as legitimizing a model of opportunity (Olson 2004: 86). The ability of Whites to acquire jobs before Blacks is not at risk. The public attention paid to this idea, that Black equality might lead to Whites being denied jobs, that someone Black might edge out someone White for a position they deserve by virtue of their being White, is indicative of how important preserving the status of Whiteness remains in society. To suggest that someone acquired a position because they are Black is in this politics to delegitimize the process of hiring; yet at the same time to question the merit of someone who is Black when they do acquire a job or position coveted by someone White is to suggest that they could not have acquired the job except because they are Black. In this way, the African American is able to acquire status in society only so long as this is not at the expense of Whites as a community and individual Whites specifically. Exceptional Blacks are conditionally accepted because, as was pointed out, their presence confirms the justice of the system of equal opportunity and they are not able to threaten the existing structure of benefits to Whites. Whites are able to socially segregate at will, so that the idea of racial community and the ability to define its substantive content remain in their control. No law or custom violates the idea of White authority as such, none that would not have been in place during the Jim Crow or slavery eras.

While Forest in *Plum Bun* could confront the presence of Blacks in a restaurant as beneath his social dignity and therefore demand that they should be thrown out, today the absolute description of races as types of humans is given the pretense of a difference that is quantitative, not qualitative. The idea that equality is one of opportunity given different resources and personal choices removes the political onus of a general description of absolute difference of type for one of degree. This reverses the direction of causality in the social control of Blacks, but not its consequences. Nancy points out the reticence with which people talk about love, and a similar condition holds for what is usually conceived of as its opposite, the reluctance with which we speak of hate (1991: 83). The decision to race is a politics of hate. This is not anger, which requires justification, a cause, but the pure hatred of a difference that is categorical because it does not require content. In fact it demands only its defense as a decision, which can take any variety of forms but ultimately rests not on an explanation but the fact of the decision itself. The change that was enacted in the 1960s was that the categorical description of hate was concealed behind the politics of difference as a measurement of individual attributes, of a justification for treating Black and White persons individually different. This new racial equality before the law was therefore quantitative not qualitative, the measure of a person's resources supposedly concealing the politics of race. It then became possible to confuse class with race rather than understand that the discussion of class depended on the racial structure. Contrary to Hall's description of race as a modality of class, class was defined by the politics of race (Hall 1980).

The terrible duality of absolute value and difference converging in the Black and White person is evident in both a work from the 1980s such as *Brothers and Keepers* and the recently published work *Silver Sparrow*. In each, the idea of a need to strive to overcome the differences that otherwise exist, of resources, of success, of freedom of choice, of values, overwhelms the perception of the category of race as absolute that allows for the conditions within which they live. It is as though the characters in each narrative act out their lives within the confines of a game where the fact of race is unavailable to criticism. Instead, they have to justify their successes and failures as personal choices while pretending that these were not structured by the very circumstances that during Jim Crow obviously defined limits to Black life. The same few material resources, the absence of educational and employment opportunities, the criminalization of large swathes of the community, and the centrality of violence, social misery, and substance abuse are now their own responsibility. The contempt that allows for it to be considered normal and acceptable that large numbers of Black people live in poverty and social misery, and experience the frustration and constraints that lead to the life described for Robby Wideman in prison, remains firmly in place.

This politics of hate is cold, not hot; it describes merely the distinction of us and them, or friend and enemy, but does so by stating a hierarchy of value that is immutable. It suggests that Obama might be president but he is not White, and therefore this is a difference that makes all the difference. It forces questions to the fore of his suitability to lead the country politically; it questions and thereby also provides real limits to his actions in the name of supporting the decision of race itself. That equal opportunity allows someone Black to hold an office does not negate or even approach the problem of racial difference. Seen another way, even the attainment of the office of the president by someone Black did not bridge the divide that exists between the two descriptions of race: absolute difference and the politics of difference. This means that the striving that Wideman and Jones describe is futile. It merely realizes a cosmetic success, of material wealth and social efficacy, without erasing the idea of race that maintains a society of two distinct White and Black communities in the US.

Agamben's discussion of the difference between natural life and sacred life in *Homo Sacer: Sovereign Power and Bare Life* (1998: 100) provides some insight into the problem of the decision of race and the description of sovereignty that it provides. According to Agamben, the natural life and sacred life are contained in one body politics, as individual liberties and sovereign power, respectively (125). So what happens if individual liberties for a population are reduced to the point where sovereign power is coincident with bare life, so much so that, as Agamben suggests, Hitler was able to describe Jews as "lice" to be exterminated (114)? The change in liberties alters the institutional characterization of sovereign power. In contrast to a racial sovereignty that was just there, implacable in its announcement of a state of exception for Blacks during Jim Crow, the new description of White sovereign authority disappears (169). It does this through the political indetermination created by the exception of the racist. The normal Black subject is not real but a construction of White sovereign political ambitions; it is only the definition of the enemy as an imperative and not a true depiction of Black persons in their social capacity as human beings.

We who are Black are always normal in this way unless, as John Wideman points out, through the work of the instruments of education, law enforcement, and economic life that define the racial apparatus, we choose and are chosen to be the exception. The Black prisoner is, however, not the only normal Black subject within the apparatus; so too is the Black subject as welfare recipient, underemployed, the drug user, and deficient parent. It is an abject subject that is only always the work of the racial apparatus on the Black community, in contrast to a life lived in spite of this subjection.

So what we see today is a politics that leaves largely untouched the actions of the distinction of race, even though there are material benefits for Blacks who are exceptional, while absolving Whites of responsibility in its operation. In *Silver Sparrow* we see that Whites are no longer even physically necessary to reproduce the distinction between persons of the one part of the apparatus where race works to subordinate persons, that between the exceptional and normal Black subject. In *Brothers and Keepers* John Wideman is unable to do more than describe the work of the current racial apparatus on himself and his brother; there is no political efficacy within its institutionalization by which to address the decision to race that persists in the reproduction of a social White community. That this idea of the social was present as a politics of racial contempt in the 1920s, when

Schmitt was defining a concept of politics, that Blacks just want "social equality," should warn us that the description of a social White community is not innocent. The invocation of the innocent social definition of Whiteness works within the apparatus precisely because it is the opposite of the social as an idea of racial difference, of segregation and absolute distinction between racial persons, during the previous political apparatus of Jim Crow. Its invocation as a description of racial community makes it still harder to form a critique against the effects of the decision. To equate race with ethnicity, for example, or culture, is in this way merely to assist the work of race in remaining indeterminate within discursive practices (Hooker 2009).

How do we address this racial sovereignty that exists outside of the constraints of the apparatus? It is certainly not possible to do so solely within the confines of our racial subjection, because there then is only race as identities and communities of difference. The apparatus describes a White subject that is without race and a Black subject that is comprehensively raced within the society (Olson 2004; Baum 2006).

It is because of this that it becomes crucial that the politics we seek to develop is a politics of life instead of a description of our human limitations as a problem of authority and social control. I take seriously what Derrida says in *Learning to Live Finally: The Last Interview*, that "survival is an originary concept that constitutes the very structure of what we call existence, *Dasein*, if you will" (2007: 50).

The problem with approaches to the idea of racial politics in traditional political theory is that these do not provide the basis for survival but instead repeat the gesture of an existential distinction of friend and enemy, confusing the absence of symbolic representation or the acknowledgment of the idea of race as sufficient to critique the ideational structure of the movement from ontic to ontological that defines the decision of race. We can see this problem in how Agamben discusses racism in *Remnants of Auschwitz: The Witness and the Archive*. He writes of how the prisoner in the Nazi camps would through the institutional process become a type of bare life, that the biopolitics of racism had this result as its object (Agamben 1999: 153).

Agamben supports his description of racism using Foucault's well-known definition in the lectures *Society Must Be Defended* (Foucault 2007), which I discussed earlier. Agamben writes, "The biopolitics of racism so to speak transcends race, penetrating into a threshold in which it is no longer possible to establish caesuras" (Agamben 1999: 85). This description of racism, race and its politics, assumes the efficacy of the friend and enemy distinction without asking the question of how a raced subject could address the decision. Asking the question of where the idea of race comes from such that it can be described as a biopolitics does not lead to the development of a politics of life, a biopolitics against the authority of "the sovereign power to *make die*" (83). Instead, the analysis ends where it begins, stating the possibility of bare life without providing for a politics of survival beyond the institutionalization of the decision of racial difference. The problem is just this inability to understand the problem from the perspective of the person who is defined after Whiteness; as Black, the person does not wield a similar desire for social control and coercion but instead seeks to escape the description of enemy provided by the social institutions in the polity. The Black person and his or her community are not seeking a similar sovereign authority to match the idealization of persons through race that Whites have created.

For the sovereign the problem of politics appears as a concern for how many survive and under what conditions. As the object of race, the Black person instead desires a way to live in spite of the description of race, a way to dissolve the hold the decision has on life. What the politics of Jim Crow, as described in the fiction of Richard Wright, allowed for Blacks was the terms of survival as a definition of the politics of the exception. The organized mobilization of the White community in activities such as lynching and race riots, the practices of convict leasing, and the everyday racial violence and social control meted out by Whites were sufficient to allow only survival in ghettos and Black areas of cities and towns throughout the country.

Unless another perspective on race is developed, this is all we have by way of analysis, a theory that explains the abjection of Blacks as a confirmation of the passivity and opacity of this supposed type of human being. Even the *jouissance* of Black culture is in this case attributed to Whites, as able to elicit something valuable from this community through the social pressures brought to bear by racism. For someone Black this perspective erases all potential for independent political activity; it reduces everything to race.

The problem is that today for Whites and for their sovereign authority to persist, it is necessary to describe how race works as a form of taking responsibility that then supports the politics of the exception of the racist. This politics of absolution does not have any effect on the description of Blacks as absolutely different; it merely erases the culpability of Whites in the actions of their sovereign community. Whites become liberals, or colorblind, and worry only about how Blacks interpret their actions. Even the approach to race as a problem is seen as an accomplishment in beginning the gesture of reconciliation within the White community with itself, as a way to describe race as something that happens "out there," or is caused by Black social activity. It is this last issue that makes it important to understand that the original definition of Whiteness is not in terms of Blacks, but is its own device of subjection for which then an Other is established as another politics. Whiteness is defined as purity, as distinct, as special, as a politics of life (Agamben 2011a: 73).

This idea of Whiteness as merely a social community in which to live is then harnessed to a politics of human difference, a *thanatopolitics* for which racial communities are established. For Blacks it is impossible in this politics to define something Black as affirming of life, even as they remain Black. It remains possible for Whites to say affirmatively, in repetition, as Agamben does, "The simple dwelling of appearance in the absence of secrets is its special trembling—it is the nudity that, like the choirboy's 'white' voice, signifies nothing and, precisely for this reason, manages to penetrate us" (90).

For those who become victims of the biopolitics of race Agamben can offer only the use of witnessing, of the actions of the witness who testifies as a means of supposedly resolving the bifurcation of the person as a subject from a politics of life (Agamben 1999: 162). The remnant of the community that describes the subject, through witnessing to the events of the politics of race, offers the potential to cancel the effect of race on the person, to heal the wound that race creates for Blacks (164). This is what John Wideman established for the reader by bringing his brother Robby's testimony into coincidence with his own description of life as the Black exception. What we realize, however, is that merely describing the conditions that define the failure to become the exception does nothing for members of the Black community. It reminds Blacks of what is taking place upon them and between them by one or another's culpability in a conditional politics of racial equality. It does not change the decision of race or the politics of the exception that are defined therein.

What each of the protagonists in the works of fiction discussed above have in common is a desire to establish a life of social practices that is important to them, that can attenuate the descriptions of race that otherwise subject them. I think something useful can be accomplished in defining as an explicit counterweight to racial cohesiveness a community of persons that refuses to avow those practices that allow for race. That these are not obvious should not stop us from purposefully exploring the ability to leave race aside, to develop ways of measuring persons that overcome the institutional descriptions of racial difference. This is more than creating the social space for all African Americans to find common purpose, which we have seen is very effective; many did this under the auspices of the political mobilization of the Civil Rights Movement broadly conceived. What needs to occur is displayed by Angela's new description of community in *Plum Bun* but also in each of the other novels: we must refuse the terms of community defined by the current apparatus.

It is very important to develop social practices and a politics that, as Du Bois points out in *Dusk of Dawn*, challenge the division of the African American community into the exceptional and normal definitions of Blackness (Du Bois 2012a: 191–94). Tommie Shelby echoes this strategy as well. His prescription is a form of Black self-determination that relies not on a thick description of Blackness but on a definition that is as inclusive as he can make it without eroding the description of racial community itself. Everyone is welcome, so long as everyone is vulnerable to anti-Black racism and displays the form of Black political consciousness that allows for a community of trust to develop (Shelby 2005: 251). The political dimensions of "resisting, defending against, and overcoming racial oppression" define the scope of the community (253).

Within this Black community description, consideration is given to the ways that the division of the Black community, those who experience anti-Black racial social descriptions, is otherwise a diverse and variegated collection of individuals in the way that Nancy describes the collection of persons prior to the application of race (Nancy 2000: 154; Shelby 2005: 250). What characterizes Angela's actions in *Plum Bun* by refusing any longer to pass as White is a form of courage. This is a form of political action that disavows what is ready to hand. Shelby describes this as important for the Black exceptional individual (he uses the term *intelligentsia*) who seeks to engage in developing the aims of this Black self-determining community (Shelby 2005: 78–79, 182).

Where I disagree with this politics of community is in the difference between Shelby's description and that offered by Fauset when she has Angela form a community of persons that includes Whites. To work solely on Black subjectivity is to neglect the problem, as was the case for the sisters in the *Silver Sparrow*, that the basis of the entire racial apparatus lies in the constant work of White sovereignty to affirm its interests.

The solution to the politics of the apparatus is not only to form communities within the confines of race given by our experiences, to nurture the wounds of race or recognize our common suffering. I believe we need to address the problem of White sovereignty by also developing a community that can include Whites unable to live as normal or exceptional White subjects in the society (Olson 2004; Baum 2006; Wise 2011). We need to form a larger community than that which divides us into racial groups. I am advocating for a stronger politics of community development within critical race theory.

I do not think Shelby's and also Du Bois's strategic community is ineffectual or wrong. Considering the argument above on the structure of racial politics in the society, it seems apparent that without simultaneously interrogating what is meant by a White social community, a Black community, no matter how thin in conception, leaves itself open to the reformulation of the terms of racial subjection rather than a more trenchant critique of racial political development in the society.

Fauset has Angela retreat as a form of disavowal, to form a community of persons that in their acceptance of unavowed status cannot change the terms of their exile, ostracism, and vulnerability, as with Iola in *The Marrow of Tradition*, to the continuing effects of race around them. I am not suggesting that. Instead, we need to work more explicitly on the terms, as Shelby does when identifying the criteria for admission into a Black self-determining political community, on the definition of loyalty, political consciousness, and personal experience necessary to include Whites within a community that works explicitly against the current apparatus of racial politics in the society (Shelby 2005: 67–71). It is just as important to challenge Whites in their complacent belief that the apparatus leaves them color-blind.

This politics has to be developed not merely as a statement but in concrete terms that has as its goal the erosion and division of the White community as a comprehensive social entity (2005: 132). Unlike in the case of Angela, this is not primarily a personal community, the redescription of friendships as encompassing interracial social practices, but a process of first challenging the political distinction between the racist and normal White subject, and second refusing to accept the distinction between exceptional and normal Black individuals. This is not an easy task, even if at one level it seems obvious.

Rather than a return to the conditions for racial community conflict, we must, as John Wideman does in writing about the life of himself and his brother, reject the terms of our subjection by the apparatus. In other words, we need to force ourselves to develop a critical racial subjectivity that considers the definition of material success, personal choice, and political citizenship. The focus of this politics must be on developing ways to have Whites interrogate their implication in the existing racial apparatus as a requirement for participation with Blacks in a critical racial politics. I am not suggesting that Whites subjects, as they currently define themselves within the formal structure of the racial *dispositif*, are adequate partners in a critical racial politics. The task for critical race politics will be to define, as was described by Du Bois, a world for both Blacks and Whites. This critical politics has to account for the constant attempt to place Whites in the center of our analysis, because of the effects of traditional racial politics, even in the development of political alternatives. It is for this reason that the focus in the book has been on exploring the nuances of a critical Black subject through these works of fiction by African Americans.

ON DIFFERENCE

If we accept the idea of a racial-equality apparatus that lies atop our ability to survive in spite of its weight, and that this has been true for Blacks for more than three hundred years in the US, then we begin to see the facile revisionist structure of the politics we currently use to describe the problem of racial inequality. A Black subject that is seemingly always frustrated in its desire for recognition by Whites is described with contempt by Fauset in *Plum Bun*. This idea of recognition assumes that some form of seeing, of speaking, or listening to Blacks by Whites would erase the absolute categories of race, of the decision to hate and its description of inferiority. The decision is immune to suggestion in this way; it survives because it is a political idea, not a social condition. This is the contribution that Schmitt makes to our political sensibilities about race: that politics can be described as a matter of friend and enemy and in doing so defines a form of absolute sovereignty. The Black subject is not seeking recognition but the erasure of race as it currently is defined, of the erasure of a White subject the terms of which it can access. What we have in the contemporary period is a Black subject that lives under the politics of difference while trying to address the politics of the decision.

This directly mirrors the conditions for the two sisters in Tayari Jones's *Silver Sparrow*, as one sister Dana strives against the other, in opposition to, Chaurisse. All the while Chaurisse is oblivious to her sister's existence, Chaurisse merely is there in ways that Dana cannot be. One part of the Black subject questions everything as a problem of difference from norms given by White sovereign authority, and the other part questions nothing since there is nothing available but absolute categories of difference. The former is engaged in a politics of trying to approach an impossible equality. The consequence of this for the Black community is to create an individual Black subjection that is bifurcated, at odds with itself, absolutely inferior to Whites, and malleable or different at the same moment.

In his critique of Zora Neal Hurston's book *The Eyes Were Watching God*, Richard Wright describes the author as using "the minstrel technique that makes the 'white folks' laugh . . . America likes to see the Negro live: between laughter and tears" (Wright 1993: 17). Angela's laughter when she refuses to pass any longer is directed at the White press reporter, not at herself. That she would rather reject Whiteness and laugh at the confusion this generates is an act of politics very different from the pleasure Whites traditionally received from watching "African Americans" act out fantasies of racial difference. To laugh directly at someone White in the 1920s was to potentially expose oneself to both social and physical retaliation. That those in Angela's new community regularly laugh at the racist behavior of Whites is a bold act of refusal. It invites reprisal. It also describes a relationship to the practices of race that goes beyond what Wright offers in *Uncle Tom's Children*.

That Angela is described as being in New York rather than in the Jim Crow South may seem at first to excuse Wright's depiction of Sarah running away in "Long Black Song" as a safe solution to White sovereign authority, for what else can we call the actions of the White salesman who first rapes her and then comes back the next day and expects not to be blamed for it. However, as Zora Neal Hurston herself points out in the short piece "My Most Humiliating Jim Crow Experience," the social segregation was similar in the period in both the North and the South (Walker 1979: 163–64).

What is really at issue is how Angela manages to move from being Black to being White and back again while retaining elements of both social communities, such that she feels confident that she can repudiate explicit gestures of White authority without obvious repercussions. Something similar is attempted by Wright in depicting White communist organizers in the Black communities in both "Fire and Cloud" and "Bright and Morning Star," but in both stories he has the Whites ultimately refuse to stand with

Blacks in their political struggle. What Fauset is suggesting by Angela's political act is that while laughter cannot change racial politics any more than can violence against Whites, it occurs when she finally feels completely without the burden of race. That she then leaves the country to fall in love is not a coincidence.

The critical politics of race today requires something very similar, in that we have to strategically leave aside any desire for thick descriptions of racial communities so as to bring pressure on the current politics of the racial exception and normal in the US. As with Angela, this does not change the racial subjection of the members of the new community, but instead allows them to form something that changes their relationship to racial politics. In order to do this, however, we are required to address how the apparatus is designed to conceal the work that race continues to do in society. That it does this by defining a rupture between the racial practices of Jim Crow, when *Plum Bun* and *Uncle Tom's Children* were written, and the description of formal racial equality today, the impact of which we see in *Silver Sparrow* and *Brothers and Keepers,* makes it difficult to form a politics. To remove the apparatus is also to reveal to Whites that there is no respite from the description of sovereign White political authority at the center of US democracy. A half century after the Civil Rights Movement the US remains a racial polity.

Over time, as with the period after the Civil War described in *The Marrow of Tradition*, the distinction between formal equality and race hate will converge, as it did in the stories depicted under Jim Crow in *Uncle Tom's Children*, and the resources and conditions for African Americans will begin to mirror again the description of absolute difference that race requires. This is the message of *Silver Sparrow* when both daughters begin to become friends, a precursor to the collapse of the politics that allows for the split in community. The imprisonment and substance-abuse problems that plague the community of African Americans, the type of part-time and low-paying employment that is available, the economic vulnerability and social fragility of Black existence will gradually become apparent as a problem for the entire community, revealing the false promise of racial equality today. This is what happens if Whites are not included in the political conversation of critical racial community development. The question of sovereignty in the US has to be addressed.

Emphasizing racial difference is ineffectual. Becoming authentic or passing merely accepts the description given to us, as is forming an ideal outside of the work that race does socially. Instead, the idea of diversity within the Black community has to be reversed conceptually, and made the basis for our politics. As was the case with the nonviolent Civil Rights Movement, the very conditions of our confinement are what need to be the location of our politics. We need to stop resisting our diversity and embrace it. What we see as characteristics of individuals within the apparatus, sexuality, gender, class, different abilities, distinct locales, our experiences, all work to make race effective. For example, we need to work on gender politics as a Black community, instead of seeing the differences between Black feminist writings and the scholarship on race by Black men in absolutist terms (Carby 2000; Harris-Perry 2011; Smiley and West 2012). This is not more difficult than it was for people to march in the streets of Birmingham against racial segregation in the early 1960s. But making our diversity important for the entire community is one way to resist the effects of race on the community, and force a redefinition of the apparatus. This is the type of solidarity that is required to change racial politics today.

To argue instead for Black community politics on the basis of the very description of race in the apparatus, on the basis of exceptional Black status and normal Black subordination would repeat, reproduce ourselves as in *Silver Sparrow*, the conditions of our racial subjection. To suggest that the problem for the Black community is merely improving access to economic resources, better schools, or avoiding risky behavior is disingenuous and reaffirms the existing politics of race. Those whose lives are exceptional have to learn how to get out of their own way, as Wideman does when thinking about the image he has that must be rejected of his brother Robby in prison.

Get over yourself and your accomplishments within the confines of what has been given to you. This is easier said than done, and that is why I suggest we should look at this as a problem on the level of the strategies used in the Civil Rights Movement—as confronting an implacable sovereign force that seeks to divide us from one another, through violence if necessary.

ON ACTING

Refusing to be invisible, in *Silver Sparrow* Dana befriends her sister and finally confronts the division of Black life into two distinct communities. In *Plum Bun* Angela laughs in the face of Whiteness. In *The Marrow of Tradition* Dr. Miller defers to his wife on the decision to help Major Carteret after the major has caused the death of their son. In "Long Black Song," Sarah runs into the field and away from the resolution of racial conflict that results in the death of both her Black husband and several Whites. In *Iola Leroy* Iola refuses to abandon her mother and devotes her life to working within the Black community. In *Brothers and Keepers* John decides to write his brother's story.

There is not just one description of critical race subjectivity. What is important is that an awareness of racial politics is available to the individual, as a context for our understanding of events. It is the need for this awareness, and the importance of being able to step outside of our subjection within the apparatus, that led to the discussion of Schmitt in Part I, the problem of race and community in Part II, and finally the use of fiction in Part III. Why would we use only the very tools that explicitly derive from our racial subjection to describe the possibility of criticism?

Liberalism merely defines the politics available to the normal "postracial" White subject. Its description of the concept of race is explicitly designed to eliminate the political claims of African Americans on the democratic institutions in the society. This is not a problem of denied reparations, but of not describing race as a collective conflict problem at the core of US political development; only in this way could its importance be relegated to the argument for formal equality. The question we have to pose in our time is how political theorists think of race such that they can describe it as unimportant even though they are living during the time of integration?

Liberalism asks that we see our Black selves as derivative, as invisible, or misrecognized, but never answers the more complex and important question of how to remove racial politics from its place in the US polity. That we can act against our confinement in race means that rather than being pessimistic it is better to constantly challenge its description of who we are supposed to be.

Bibliography

Agamben, G. (1998) *Homo Sacer: Sovereign Power and Bare Life*, trans. D. Heller-Roazen, Stanford, CA: Stanford University Press.
———. (1999) *Remnants of Auschwitz: The Witness and the Archive*, trans. D. Heller-Roazen, New York: Zone Books.
———. (2004) *The Open: Man and Animal*, trans. K. Attell, Stanford, CA: Stanford University Press.
———. (2005) *State of Exception*, trans. K. Attell, Chicago: University of Chicago Press.
———. (2007) *Infancy and History: On the Destruction of Experience*, trans. L. Heron, New York: Verso.
———. (2009) *What Is an Apparatus? And Other Essays*, trans. D. Kishik and S. Pedatella, Stanford, CA: Stanford University Press.
———. (2011a) *Nudities*, trans. D. Kishik and S. Pedatella, Stanford, CA: Stanford University Press.
———. (2011b) *The Kingdom and the Glory: For a Theological Genealogy of Economy and Government*, trans. L. Chiesa, Stanford, CA: Stanford University Press.
Alexander, M. (2012) *The New Jim Crow: Mass Incarceration in the Age of Colorblindness*, New York: New Press.
Appiah, K.A., and A. Gutmann (1996) *Color Conscious: The Political Morality of Race*, Princeton: Princeton University Press.
Arendt, H. (1968) *Men in Dark Times*, New York: Harcourt Brace.
———. (1972) *Crises of the Republic: Lying in Politics; Civil Disobedience; On Violence; Thoughts on Politics and Revolution*, New York: Harcourt Brace.
———. (1985) *The Origins of Totalitarianism*, New York: Harcourt.
Aristotle (1999) *Nicomachean Ethics*, trans. T. Irwin, Indianapolis: Hackett Publishing.
Ayo, D. (2005) *How to Rent a Negro*, Chicago: Lawrence Hill Books.
Baker, H. (1990) *Long Black Song: Essays in Black American Literature and Culture*, Charlottesville: University of Virginia Press.
Baldwin, J. (1998) "No Name in the Street" in *James Baldwin: Collected Essays*, New York: The Library of America.
Balfour, L. (2001) *The Evidence of Things Not Said: James Baldwin and the Promise of American Democracy*, Ithaca, NY: Cornell University Press.
———. (2011) *Democracy's Reconstruction: Thinking Politically with W.E.B. Du Bois*, New York: Oxford University Press.
Baum, B. (2006) *The Rise and Fall of the Caucasian Race: A Political History of Racial Identity*, New York: New York University Press.
Bell, D. (1987) *And We Are Not Saved: The Elusive Quest for Racial Justice*, New York: Basic Books.

——. (1996) *Confronting Authority*, Boston: Beacon Press.

——. (2004) *Silent Covenants: Brown v. Board of Education and the Unfulfilled Hopes for Racial Reform*, New York: Oxford University Press.

Benhabib, S. (1996) *The Reluctant Modernism of Hannah Arendt*, London: Sage Publications.

Benjamin, W. (1969a) *Illuminations: Essays and Reflections*, H. Arendt (ed.), trans. H. Zohn, New York: Schocken Books.

——. (1969b) "Theses on the Philosophy of History," in *Illuminations: Essays and Reflections*, trans. H. Zohn, New York: Schocken Books, pp. 253–64.

——. (1986a) "Critique of Violence," in *Reflections: Essays, Aphorisms, Autobiographical Writings*, trans. E. Jephcott, New York: Schocken Books, pp. 277–300.

——. (1986b) *Reflections: Essays, Aphorisms, Autobiographical Writings*, trans. E. Jephcott, New York: Schocken Books.

Bergson, H. (2008) *Laughter: An Essay on the Meaning of the Comic*, Rockville, MD: Arc Manor.

Blackmon, D.A. (2009) *Slavery by Another Name: The Re-Enslavement of Black Americans from the Civil War to World War II*, New York: Anchor.

Blanchot, M. (1988) *The Unavowable Community*, trans. P. Joris, Barrytown, NY: Station Hill Press.

Blight D.W. (2002) *Race and Reunion: The Civil War in American Memory*, Cambridge: Harvard University Press.

Bloom, H. (1997) *The Anxiety of Influence: A Theory of Poetry*, New York: Oxford University Press.

Bogle, D. (2001) *Toms, Coons, Mulattoes, Mammies, and Bucks: An Interpretive History of Blacks in American Films*, New York: Continuum.

Boxill, B.R. (1992) *Blacks and Social Justice*, New York: Rowman & Littlefield.

Branch, T. (1989) *Parting the Waters: America in the King Years 1954–63*, New York: Simon & Schuster.

Brophy, A.L. (2002) *Reconstructing the Dreamland: The Tulsa Riot of 1921/Race, Reparations, and Reconciliation*, New York: Oxford University Press.

Brown, M.K., Carnoy, M., Currie, E., Duster, T., Oppenheimer, D.B., Shultz, M.M., and Wellman, D. (2005) *Whitewashing Race: The Myth of a Color-Blind Society*, Berkeley: University of California Press.

Brown v. Board of Education of Topeka (1954) 347 U.S. 483.

Brown, W. (2001) *Politics out of History*, Princeton: Princeton University Press.

Browning, C.R. (1993) *Ordinary Men: Reserve Police Battalion 101 and the Final Solution in Poland*, New York: Harper Perennial.

Campbell, T. (2011) *Improper Life: Technology and Biopolitics from Heidegger to Agamben*, Minneapolis: University of Minnesota Press.

Carby, H.V. (2000) *Race Men (W.E.B. Du Bois Lectures)*, Cambridge: Harvard University Press.

Caruth, C. (ed.) (1995) *Trauma: Explorations in Memory*, Baltimore: Johns Hopkins University Press.

——. (1996) *Unclaimed Experience: Trauma, Narrative, and History*, Baltimore: Johns Hopkins University Press.

Chesnutt, C.W. (1993) *The Marrow of Tradition*, New York: Penguin.

Christian, B. (1980) *Black Women Novelists: The Development of a Tradition, 1892–1976*, Westport, CT: Praeger.

——. (1985) *Black Feminist Criticism: Perspectives on Black Women Writers*, New York: Teachers College Press.

Civil Rights Act of 1964 (1964) Pub. L. No. 88-352, 78 Stat. 241.

Clear, T.R. (2009) *Imprisoning Communities: How Mass Incarceration Makes Disadvantaged Neighborhoods Worse*, New York: Oxford University Press.

Cohen, C.J. (2010) *Democracy Remixed: Black Youth and the Future of American Politics*, New York: Oxford University Press.

Cohen, W. (1991) *At Freedom's Edge: Black Mobility and the Southern White Quest for Racial Control 1861–1915*, Baton Rouge: Louisiana State University Press.

Collins, P.H. (2009) *Another Kind of Public Education: Race, Schools, the Media, and Democratic Possibilities*, Boston: Beacon Press.

Cole, D. (1999) *No Equal Justice: Race and Class in the American Criminal Justice System*, New York: The New Press.

Conley, D. (1999) *Being Black, Living in the Red: Race, Wealth, and Social Policy in America*, Berkeley: University of California Press.

Cooper, A.J. (1988) *A Voice from the South*, New York: Oxford University Press.

Cruse, H., and Crouch, S. (2005) *The Crisis of the Negro Intellectual: A Historical Analysis of the Failure of Black Leadership*, New York: NYRB Classics.

Dahl, R.A. (1972) *Polyarchy: Participation and Opposition*, New Haven: Yale University Press.

Davis, A. (2003) *Are Prisons Obsolete?*, New York: Seven Stories Press.

Deleuze, G. (1988) *Foucault*, trans. S. Hand, Minneapolis: University of Minneapolis Press.

DeMott, B. (1996) *The Trouble with Friendship: Why Americans Can't Think Straight about Race*, New York: Atlantic Monthly Press.

Derrida, J. (1989) *Memoires for Paul de Man, Revised Edition*, trans. C. Lindsay, J. Culler, E. Cadava, and P. Kamuf, New York: Columbia University Press.

———. (1997) *Politics of Friendship*, trans. G. Collins, New York: Verso.

———. (1998) *Monolingualism of the Other; or the Prosthesis of Origin*, trans. P. Mensah, Stanford, CA: Stanford University Press.

———. (2003) *The Work of Mourning*, P.-A. Brault and M. Naas (eds.), Chicago: University of Chicago Press.

———. (2005) *Rogues: Two Essays on Reason*, trans. P.-A. Brault and M. Naas, Stanford, CA: Stanford University Press.

———. (2007) *Learning to Live Finally: The Last Interview*, trans. P.-A. Brault and M. Naas, Brooklyn: Melville House.

Derrida, J., and Dufourmantelle, A. (2000) *Of Hospitality*, trans. R. Bowlby, Stanford, CA: Stanford University Press.

de Tocqueville, A. (2003) *Democracy in America*, I. Kramnick (ed.), trans. G. Bevan, New York: Penguin Classics.

Drake, S.C., and Cayton, H.R. (1962) *Black Metropolis: A Study of Negro Life in a Northern City/Volume 1*, New York: Harper & Row.

Dred Scott v. Sandford (1857) 60 U.S. 393.

Du Bois, W.E.B. (1962) *Black Reconstruction in America: An Essay toward a History of the Part Which Black Folk Played in the Attempt to Reconstruct Democracy in America 1860–1880*, New York: World Publishing Company.

———. (1996) *The Philadelphia Negro: A Social Study*, Philadelphia: University of Pennsylvania Press.

———. (2012a) *Dusk of Dawn: An Essay toward an Autobiography of a Race Concept*, New Brunswick, NJ: Transaction Publishers.

———. (2012b) *The Souls of Black Folk*, New York: Tribeca Books.

DuRocher, K. (2011) *Raising Racists: The Socialization of White Children in the Jim Crow South*, Lexington: University Press of Kentucky.

Dworkin, R. (1978) *Taking Rights Seriously*, Cambridge: Harvard University Press.

———. (1985) *A Matter of Principle*, Cambridge: Harvard University Press.

Dyzenhaus, D. (ed.) (1998) *Law as Politics: Carl Schmitt's Critique of Liberalism*, Durham, NC: Duke University Press.

———. (1999) "Putting the State Back in Credit," in C. Mouffe (ed.) *The Challenge of Carl Schmitt*, New York: Verso, pp. 75–91.
Edelman, P. (2012) *So Rich, So Poor: Why It's So Hard to End Poverty in America*, New York: The New Press.
Ellison, R. (1965) *The Invisible Man*, New York: Penguin Books.
———. (1987) *Going to the Territory*, New York: Random House.
———. (1998) "A Party Down at the Square," in *Flying Home and Other Stories*, New York: Vintage, pp. 3–11.
Esposito, R. (2008) *Bios: Biopolitics and Philosophy*, trans. T. Campbell, Minneapolis: University of Minnesota Press.
———. (2010) *Communitas: The Origin and Destiny of Community*, trans. T. Campbell, Stanford, CA: Stanford University Press.
———. (2011) *Immunitas: The Protection and Negation of Life*, trans. Z. Hanafi, Cambridge, MA: Polity Press.
Fanon, F. (2008) *Black Skin, White Masks*, trans. R. Philcox, New York: Grove Press.
Farias, V. (1991) *Heidegger and Nazism*, Philadelphia: Temple University Press.
Fauset, J. R. (1990) *Plum Bun*, Boston: Beacon Press.
Faye, E. (2009) *Heidegger: The Introduction of Nazism into Philosophy in Light of the Unpublished Seminars of 1933–1935*, trans. M.B. Smith, New Haven, CT: Yale University Press.
Felman, S., and Laub, D. (1992) *Testimony: Crises of Witnessing in Literature, Psychoanalysis, and History*, New York: Routledge.
Ferguson, A. A. (2001) *Bad Boys: Public Schools in the Making of Black Masculinity*, Ann Arbor: University of Michigan Press.
Fleming, C. G. (1998) *Soon We Will Not Cry: The Liberation of Ruby Doris Smith Robinson*, Lanham, MD: Rowman & Littlefield.
Foner, E. (ed.) (1970) *America's Black Past: A Reader in Afro-American History*, New York: Harper & Row.
Foucault, M. (1980) *Power/Knowledge: Selected Interviews and Other Writings 1972–1977*, C. Gordon (ed.), trans. C. Gordon, L. Marshall, J. Mepham, and K. Soper, New York: Pantheon Books.
———. (1982) "The Subject and Power," reprinted in J. Faubion (ed.) (2000) *Michel Foucault: Power, Volume Three*, New York: The New Press.
———. (1990) *The Use of Pleasure: Volume 2 of The History of Sexuality*, trans. R. Hurley, New York: Vintage.
———. (1994) *The Birth of the Clinic: An Archaeology of Medical Perception*, trans. A. M. Sheridan Smith, New York: Vintage.
———. (1995) *Discipline and Punish*, trans. A. M. Sheridan, New York: Vintage.
———. (2003) *"Society Must Be Defended": Lectures at the College de France 1975–1976*, trans. D. Macey, New York: Picador.
———. (2005) *The Hermeneutics of the Subject: Lectures at the College de France 1981–1982*, trans. G. Burchell, New York: Palgrave Macmillan.
———. (2007) *Security, Territory, Population: Lectures at the College de France 1977–1978*, trans. G. Burchell, New York: Palgrave Macmillan.
———. (2008a) *The Birth of Biopolitics: Lectures at the College de France 1978–1979*, trans. G. Burchell, New York: Palgrave Macmillan.
———. (2008b) *The Courage of Truth (The Government of Self and Others II): Lectures at the College de France 1983–1984*, trans. G. Burchell, New York: Palgrave Macmillan.
———. (2009) *History of Madness*, trans. J. Murphy and J. Khalfa, New York: Routledge.
———. (2010) *The Government of Self and Others: Lectures at the College de France 1982–1983*, trans. G. Burchell, New York: Palgrave Macmillan.

Gabodo-Madikizela, P. (2004) *A Human Being Died That Night: A South African Woman Confronts the Legacy of Apartheid*, Boston: Houghton Mifflin.
Gadamer, H.-G. (1994) *Heidegger's Ways*, trans. J.W. Stanley, Albany: State University of New York Press.
———. (2004) *Truth and Method*, trans. J. Weinsheimer and D.G. Marshall, New York: Continuum.
Gates, H.L. Jr. (2010) *Tradition and the Black Atlantic: Critical Theory in the African Diaspora*, New York: Basic Civitas.
Gilman, S.L. (1985) *Difference and Pathology*, Ithaca, NY: Cornell University Press.
Gilroy, P. (2000) *Against Race: Imagining Political Culture beyond the Color Line*, Cambridge: Harvard University Press.
———. (2006) *Postcolonial Melancholia*, New York: Columbia University Press.
Glazer, N., and Moynihan, D.P. (1970) *Beyond the Melting Pot, Second Edition: The Negroes, Puerto Ricans, Jews, Italians, and Irish of New York City*, Cambridge: MIT Press.
Glenn, E.N. (2004) *Unequal Freedom: How Race and Gender Shaped American Citizenship and Labor*, Cambridge: Harvard University Press.
Goethe, J.W.V. (1959) *The Sorrows of Young Werther*, trans. V. Lange, New York: Rinehart & Company.
Goldhagen, D.J. (1997) *Hitler's Willing Executioners: Ordinary Germans and the Holocaust*, New York: Random House.
Goodheart, A. (2011) *1861: The Civil War Awakening*, New York: Vintage Books.
Gooding-Williams, R. (2009) *In the Shadow of Du Bois: Afro-Modern Political Thought in America*, Cambridge: Harvard University Press.
Gordon, M.M. (1964) *Assimilation in American Life: The Role of Race, Religion and National Origins*, New York: Oxford University Press.
Grene, D., and Lattimore, R. (eds.) (1958) *The Complete Greek Tragedies: Euripides III, Hecuba, Andromache, The Trojan Women, Ion*, trans. W. Arrowsmith, J.F. Nims, R. Lattimore, and R.F. Willetts, Chicago: University of Chicago Press.
Griffin, F.J. (1995) *"Who Set You Flowin'?": The African-American Migration Narrative*, New York: Oxford University Press.
Griffin, J.D., and Newman, B. (2008) *Minority Report: Evaluating Political Equality in America*, Chicago: University of Chicago Press.
Grosrichard, A. (1998) *Sultan's Court*, trans. L. Heron, New York: Verso
Gutmann, A., and Thompson, D. (1996) *Democracy and Disagreement*, Cambridge: Harvard University Press.
Habermas, J. (1989) *The New Conservatism: Cultural Criticism and the Historians' Debate*, trans. S.W. Nicholsen, Cambridge: MIT Press.
Hale, G.E. (1999) *Making Whiteness: The Culture of Segregation in the South, 1890–1940*, New York: Vintage Press.
Hall, S. (1980) "Race, Articulation and Societies Structured in Dominance," in UNESCO, *Sociological Theories: Race and Colonialism,* Paris: UNESCO.
Harper, F. (2010) *Iola Leroy, Or, Shadows Uplifted*, Mineola, New York: Dover Publications.
Harris, L. (ed.) (1999) *The Critical Pragmatism of Alain Locke: A Reader on Value Theory, Aesthetics, Community, Culture, Race, and Education*, New York: Rowman & Littlefield.
Harris-Perry, M.V. (2011) *Sister Citizen: Shame, Stereotypes, and Black Women in America,* New Haven, CT: Yale University Press.
Hartman, S. (2007) *Lose Your Mother: A Journey along the Atlantic Slave Route*, New York: Farrar, Straus & Giroux.

Headley, C. (1999) "Alain Locke: A Sociocultural Conception of Race," in L. Harris (ed.) *The Critical Pragmatism of Alain Locke: A Reader on Value Theory, Aesthetics, Community, Culture, Race, and Education*, New York: Rowman & Littlefield, pp. 199–208.
Hegel, G.W.F. (1977) *Phenomenology of Spirit*, trans. A.V. Miller, New York: Oxford University Press.
Heidegger, M. (1977) "The Age of the World Picture," in *The Question Concerning Technology and Other Essays*, trans. W. Lovitt, New York: Harper & Row, pp. 115–54.
———. (1993) *Basic Writings*, D.F. Krell (ed.), London: Routledge.
———. (1997) *Kant and the Problem of Metaphysics*, 5th ed., trans. R. Taft, Indianapolis: Indiana University Press.
———. (1998) *Parmenides*, trans: A. Schuwer and R. Rojcewicz, Indianapolis: Indiana University Press.
———. (2009) *The Essence of Truth: On Plato's Cave Analogy and Theaetetus*, trans. T. Sadler, New York: Continuum.
Heidegger, M., and Fink, E. (1993) *Heraclitus Seminar*, trans. C.H. Seibert, Evanston, IL: Northwestern University Press.
Hirst, P. (1999) "Carl Schmitt's Decisionism," in C. Mouffe (ed.) *The Challenge of Carl Schmitt*, New York: Verso, pp. 7–17.
Hodes, M. (1999) *White Women, Black Men: Illicit Sex in the Nineteenth-Century South*, New Haven, CT: Yale University Press.
Honey, M.K. (1999) *Black Workers Remember: An Oral History of Segregation, Unionism, and the Freedom Struggle*, Berkeley: University of California Press.
Honig, B. (1993) *Political Theory and the Displacement of Politics*, Ithaca, NY: Cornell University Press.
Hooker, J. (2009) *Race and the Politics of Solidarity*, New York: Oxford University Press.
Huffington Post (2012) "Sarah Palin Tells Sean Hannity that Obama Wants to Take America Back to Days 'Before the Civil War,' " *Huffington Post* <http://www.huffingtonpost.com/2012/03/09/sarah-palin-obama-civil-war-_n_1335017.html> (accessed 19 April 2012).
Hurston, Z.N. (2006) *Their Eyes Were Watching God*, New York: Harper Perennial.
———. (2008) *Mules and Men*, New York: Harper Perennial.
Husserl, E. (1973) *Experience and Judgment: Investigations in a Genealogy of Logic*, trans. J.S. Churchill and K. Ameriks, Evanston, IL: Northwestern University Press.
Ignatiev, N. (2008) *How the Irish Became White*, New York: Routledge.
Jaketapper (2008) "Michelle Obama: 'For the First Time in My Adult Lifetime, I'm really Proud of My Country,' " *ABC News* <http://abcnews.go.com/ blogs/politics/2008/02/michelle-obam-1-2> (accessed 19 April 2012).
James, C.L.R. (1989) *The Black Jacobins: Toussaint L'Ouverture and the San Domingo Revolution*, New York: Vintage.
Jaspers, K. (2001) *The Question of German Guilt*, trans. E.B. Ashton, New York: Fordham University Press.
Jay, M. (2010) *The Virtues of Mendacity: On Lying in Politics*, Charlottesville: University of Virginia Press.
Jones, T. (2011) *Silver Sparrow*, Chapel Hill, NC: Algonquin Books of Chapel Hill.
Kalyvas, A. (2008) *Democracy and the Politics of the Extraordinary: Max Weber, Carl Schmitt, and Hannah Arendt*, New York: Cambridge University Press.
Kantorowicz, E.H. (1997) *The King's Two Bodies: A Study in Mediaeval Political Theology*, Princeton: Princeton University Press.

Kateb, G. (1994) *The Inner Ocean: Individualism and Democratic Culture*, Ithaca, NY: Cornell University Press.
Kelley, R.D.G. (1990) *Hammer and Hoe: Alabama Communists During the Great Depression*, Chapel Hill: University of North Carolina Press.
———. (2003) *Freedom Dreams: The Black Radical Imagination*, Boston: Beacon Press.
Kettner, J.H. (1978) *The Development of American Citizenship, 1608–1870*, Chapel Hill: University of North Carolina Press.
King, D.S., and Smith, R.M. (2011) *Still a House Divided: Race and Politics in Obama's America*, Princeton: Princeton University Press.
Kozol, J. (1992) *Savage Inequalities: Children in America's Schools*, New York: Harper Perennial.
Kymlicka, W. (1996) *Multicultural Citizenship: A Liberal Theory of Minority Rights*, New York: Oxford University Press.
———. (1998) *Finding Our Way: Rethinking Ethnocultural Relations in Canada*, New York: Oxford University Press.
LaCapra, D. (1996) *Representing the Holocaust: History, Theory, Trauma*, Ithaca, NY: Cornell University Press.
———. (1998) *History and Memory after Auschwitz*, Ithaca, NY: Cornell University Press.
———. (2009) *History and Its Limits: Human, Animal, Violence*, Ithaca, NY: Cornell University Press.
Lewis, D.L. (1981) *When Harlem Was in Vogue*, New York: Oxford University Press.
Lewis, J. (1998) *Walking with the Wind: A Memoir of the Movement*, New York: Harcourt Brace.
Leydet, D. (1998) "Pluralism and the Crisis of Parliamentary Democracy," in D. Dyzenhaus (ed.) *Law as Politics: Carl Schmitt's Critique of Liberalism*, Durham, NC: Duke University Press, pp. 109–30.
Lipsitz, G. (2006) *The Possessive Investment in Whiteness: How White People Profit from Identity Politics*, Philadelphia: Temple University Press.
Litwack, L.F. (1980) *Been in the Storm So Long: The Aftermath of Slavery*, New York: Vintage.
Locke, A.L. (1992) *Race Contacts and Interracial Relations: Lectures on the Theory and Practice of Race*, J.C. Stewart (ed.), Washington DC: Howard University Press.
———. (1999) *The New Negro: Voices of the Harlem Renaissance*, New York: Touchstone.
Loewen, J.W. (2005) *Sundown Towns: A Hidden Dimension of American Racism*, New York: Simon & Schuster.
Lupton, J.R. (2000) "Creature Caliban," *Shakespeare Quarterly* 51(1), pp. 1–23.
Marx, W. (1971) *Heidegger and the Tradition*, trans. T. Kisiel and M. Greene, Evanston, IL: Northwestern University Press.
Massey, D., and Denton, N. (1993) *American Apartheid: Segregation and the Making of the Underclass*, Cambridge: Harvard University Press.
McCormick, J.P. (1998) "The Dilemmas of Dictatorship: Carl Schmitt and Constitutional Emergency Powers," in D. Dyzenhaus (ed.) *Law as Politics: Carl Schmitt's Critique of Liberalism*, Durham, NC: Duke University Press, pp. 217–251.
McKnight, U. (1996) *Political Liberalism and the Politics of Race: Beyond Perfectionism and Culture*, Lund, Sweden: Lund University Press.
———. (2010) *The Everyday Practice of Race in America: Ambiguous Privilege*, New York: Routledge.
McMillen, N. (1989) *Dark Journey: Black Mississippians in the Age of Jim Crow*, Champaign: University of Illinois Press.

Melville, H. (1961) *Billy Budd and Other Tales*, New York: The New American Library.
Memoli, M.A. (2012) "Obama: 'If I Had a Son, He Would Look Like Trayvon' Martin," *Los Angeles Times* <http://articles.latimes.com/2012/mar/23/news/la-pn-obama-comments-trayvon-martin-20120323> (accessed 19 April 2012).
Miles, R. (1993) *Racism after "Race Relations,"* New York: Routledge.
Mills, C. (1997) *The Racial Contract*, Ithaca, NY: Cornell University Press.
———. (2003) *From Class to Race: Essays in White Marxism and Black Radicalism*, Lanham, MD: Rowman & Littlefield.
Morley, D., and Chen, K.-H. (eds.) (1996) *Stuart Hall: Critical Dialogues in Cultural Studies*, London: Routledge.
Morrison, T. (1993) *Playing in the Dark: Whiteness and the Literary Imagination*, New York: Vintage.
Mouffe, C. (1998) "Carl Schmitt and the Paradox of Liberal Democracy," in D. Dyzenhaus (ed.) *Law as Politics: Carl Schmitt's Critique of Liberalism*, Durham, NC: Duke University Press, pp. 159–75.
———. (1999) "Carl Schmitt and the Paradox of Liberal Democracy," in C. Mouffe (ed.) *The Challenge of Carl Schmitt*, New York: Verso, pp. 38–53.
———. (ed.) (1999) *The Challenge of Carl Schmitt*, New York: Verso.
———. (2006) *Return of the Political*, New York: Verso.
———. (2009) *The Democratic Paradox*, New York: Verso.
Myrdal, G. (1995) *An American Dilemma: The Negro Problem and Modern Democracy, Volume One*, Piscataway, NJ: Transactions Publishers.
Nagorski, A. (2012) *Hitlerland: American Eyewitnesses to the Nazi Rise to Power*, New York: Simon & Schuster.
Nancy, J.-L. (1991) *The Inoperative Community*, trans. P. Connor, L. Garbus, M. Holland, and S. Sawhney, Minneapolis: University of Minnesota Press.
———. (1993) *The Experience of Freedom*, trans. B. McDonald, Stanford, CA: Stanford University Press.
———. (1997) *The Sense of the World*, trans. J.S. Librett, Minneapolis: University of Minnesota Press.
———. (2000) *Being Singular Plural*, trans. R.D. Richardson and A.E. O'Byrne, Stanford, CA: Stanford University Press.
———. (2010) *The Truth of Democracy*, trans. P.-A. Brault and M. Naas, New York: Fordham University Press.
Nancy, J.-L., and Lacoue-Labarthe, P. (1992) *The Title of the Letter: A Reading of Lacan*, trans. F. Raffoul and D. Pettigrew, Albany: State University of New York Press.
Neher, J. (2009) "Obama Meeting with Gates, Crowley Was Productive, Jarrett Says," *Bloomberg* <http://www.bloomberg.com/apps/news?pid=newsarchive&sid=avrqlnAAG04A> (accessed 19 April 2012).
Ngai, M.M. (2005) *Impossible Subjects: Illegal Aliens and the Making of Modern America*, Princeton: Princeton University Press.
Obama, B. (2004) *Dreams from My Father*, New York: Three Rivers Press.
Oliver, M., and Shapiro, T. (eds.) (2006) *Black Wealth/White Wealth: A New Perspective on Racial Inequality*, New York: Routledge.
Olson, J. (2004) *The Abolition of White Democracy*, Minneapolis: Minnesota University Press.
Ott, H. (1994) *Martin Heidegger: A Political Life*, trans. A. Blunden, London: Fontana Press.
Parenti, C. (2008) *Lockdown America*, New York: Verso.
Patocka, J. (2002) *Plato and Europe*, trans. P. Lom, Stanford, CA: Stanford University Press.

Pinkard, T.P. (1996) *Hegel's Phenomenology: The Sociality of Reason*, New York: Cambridge University Press.
Pippen R.B. (2010) *Hegel on Self-Consciousness: Desire and Death in the Phenomenology of Spirit*, Princeton: Princeton University Press.
Plato (2002) *Five Dialogues: Euthyphro, Apology, Crito, Meno, Phaedo*, trans. G.M.A. Grube. Indianapolis: Hackett Publishing.
——. (2003) *The Symposium*, trans. C. Gill (ed.), New York: Penguin Classics.
Plessy v. Ferguson (1996) 163 U.S. 537.
Rawls, J. (1972) *A Theory of Justice*, New York: Oxford University Press.
——. (1993) *Political Liberalism*, New York: Columbia University Press.
Read, A. (ed.) (1996) *The Fact of Blackness: Franz Fanon and Visual Representation*, Seattle: Bay Press.
Rex, J. (1982) *Race Relations in Sociological Theory*, New York: Routledge.
Ricoeur, P. (2004) *Memory, History, Forgetting*, trans. K. Blamey and D. Pellauer, Chicago: University of Chicago Press.
Roediger, D.R. (2006) *Working toward Whiteness: How America's Immigrants Became White: The Strange Journey from Ellis Island to the Suburbs*, New York: Basic Books.
——. (2007) *The Wages of Whiteness: Race and the Making of the American Working Class*, New York: Verso.
Rothman, J. (2007) *Notorious in the Neighborhood: Sex and Families across the Color Line in Virginia, 1787–1861*, Durham: University of North Carolina Press.
Sacks, M. (2011) "Clarence's Questions, Part 1: The Case of the Burning Cross," *Huffington Post* <http://www.huffingtonpost.com/2011/10/07/clarence-thomas-questions-cross-burning-case_n_1000569.html> (accessed 19 April 2012).
Said, E.W. (1979) *Orientalism*, New York: Vintage.
Santner, E.L. (2006) *On Creaturely Life: Rilke/Benjamin/Sebald*, Chicago: University of Chicago Press.
——. (2011) *The Royal Remains: The People's Two Bodies and the Endgames of Sovereignty*, Chicago: University of Chicago Press.
Scheuerman, W.E. (1999) *Carl Schmitt*, New York: Rowman & Littlefield.
Schmitt, C. (1988) *The Crisis of Parliamentary Democracy*, trans. E. Kennedy, Cambridge: MIT Press.
——. (1996) *The Concept of the Political*, trans. G. Schwab, Chicago: University of Chicago Press.
——. (2005) *Political Theology: Four Chapters on the Concept of Sovereignty*, trans. G. Schwab, Chicago: University of Chicago Press.
——. (2008) *The Leviathan in the State Theory of Thomas Hobbes: The Meaning and Failure of a Political Symbol*, trans. G. Schwab and E. Hilfstein, Chicago: University of Chicago Press.
Sebald, W.G. (1997) *The Emigrants*, trans. M. Hulse, New York: New Directions.
——. (2001) *Austerlitz*, trans. A. Bell, New York: Modern Library.
——. (2003) *On the Natural History of Destruction*, trans. A. Bell, New York: Modern Library.
——. (2006) *Campo Santo*, trans. A. Bell, New York: Modern Library.
Seth, V. (2010) *Europe's Indians: Producing Racial Difference, 1500–1900*, Durham, NC: Duke University Press.
Shapiro, H. (1988) *White Violence and Black Response: From Reconstruction to Montgomery*, Amherst: University of Massachusetts Press.
Shapiro, T.M. (2004) *The Hidden Cost of Being African American: How Wealth Perpetuates Inequality*, New York: Oxford University Press.
Shelby, T. (2005) *We Who Are Dark: The Philosophical Foundations of Black Solidarity*, Cambridge, MA: Belknap Press.

Shipler, D.K. (2005) *The Working Poor: Invisible in America*, New York: Vintage.
Shklar, J. (1998) *American Citizenship: The Quest for Inclusion*, Cambridge: Harvard University Press.
Smiley, T., and West, C. (2012) *The Rich and the Rest of Us: A Poverty Manifesto*, Carlsbad, CA: SmileyBooks.
Sophocles (2002) *Sophocles, The Oedipus Cycle: Oedipus Rex, Oedipus at Colonus, Antigone*, trans. D. Fitts and R. Fitzgerald, Boston: Mariner.
Soss, J., Fording, R.C., and Schram, S.F. (2011) *Disciplining the Poor: Neoliberal Paternalism and the Persistent Power of Race*, Chicago: University of Chicago Press.
Spivak, G. (2010) *Nationalism and the Imagination*, New York: Seagull Books.
Stallybrass, P., and White, A. (1986) *The Politics and Poetics of Transgression*, Ithaca, NY: Cornell University Press.
Steedman, M. (2012) *Jim Crow Citizenship: Liberalism and the Southern Defense of Racial Hierarchy*, New York: Routledge.
Sterling, D. (ed.) (1984) *We Are Your Sisters: Black Women in the Nineteenth Century*, New York: W.W. Norton & Company.
Stockett, K. (2011) *The Help*, New York: Putnam.
Strong, T. (1996) "Dimensions of the Debate around Carl Schmitt," Foreword to C. Schmitt, *The Concept of the Political*, Chicago: University of Chicago Press, pp. ix–xxvii.
———. (2005) "The Sovereign and the Exception: Carl Schmitt, Politics, Theology, and Leadership," Foreword to C. Schmitt, *Political Theology: Four Chapters on the Concept of Sovereignty*, Chicago: University of Chicago Press, pp. vii–xxxv.
———. (2012) *Politics without Vision: Thinking without a Banister in the Twentieth Century*, Chicago: University of Chicago Press.
Sundquist, E.J. (1993) "Introduction," *The Marrow of Tradition*, C.W. Chesnutt, New York: Penguin, pp. vii–xliv.
Tate, C. (1998) *Psychoanalysis and Black Novels: Desire and the Protocols of Race*, New York: Oxford University Press.
Tate, K. (2003) *Black Faces in the Mirror: African Americans and Their Representatives in the U.S. Congress*, Princeton: Princeton University Press.
Taylor, C. (1994) *Multiculturalism: Examining the Politics of Recognition*, Princeton: Princeton University Press.
———. (1995) *Philosophical Arguments*, Cambridge: Harvard University Press.
Taylor, G. (2004) *Buying Whiteness: Race, Culture, and Identity from Columbus to Hip-hop*, New York: Palgrave Macmillan
Thompson, R.F. (1984) *Flash of the Spirit: African and Afro-American Art and Philosophy*, New York: Vintage Books.
Trouillot, M.-R. (1995) *Silencing the Past: Power and the Production of History*, Boston: Beacon Press.
Tully, J. (1995) *Strange Multiplicity: Constitutionalism in an Age of Diversity*, Cambridge: Cambridge University Press.
Tushnet, M.V. (1987) *The NAACP's Legal Strategy against Segregated Education, 1925–1950*, Chapel Hill: University of North Carolina Press.
Tutu, D.M. (1999) *No Future without Forgiveness*, New York: Doubleday.
Villa, D.R. (1996) *Arendt and Heidegger: The Fate of the Political*, Princeton: Princeton University Press.
Walker, A. (1979) *I Love Myself When I Am Laughing: A Zora Neale Hurston Reader*, New York: The Feminist Press.
Walzer, M. (1982) *Obligations: Essays on Disobedience, War, and Citizenship*, Cambridge: Harvard University Press.

———. (1984) *Spheres of Justice: A Defense of Pluralism and Equality*, New York: Basic Books.
Warren, K.W. (2011) *What Was African American Literature?* Cambridge: Harvard University Press.
Wells-Barnett, I.B. (2002) *On Lynchings*, Amherst, NY: Humanity Books.
West, C. (2001) *Race Matters*, New York: Beacon Press.
———. (2005) *Democracy Matters: Winning the Fight Against Imperialism*, New York: Penguin.
White, D.G. (1999) *Ar'n't I a Woman? Female Slaves in the Plantation South*, New York: W.W. Norton & Company.
Wideman, J.E. (1984) *Brothers and Keepers*, New York: Vintage.
Wilkerson, I. (2011) *The Warmth of Other Suns: The Epic Story of America's Great Migration*, New York: Vintage.
Wilson, W.J. (1980) *The Declining Significance of Race: Blacks and Changing American Institutions*, Chicago: University of Chicago Press.
———. (1999) *The Bridge over the Racial Divide*, Berkeley: University of California Press.
Wintz, C.D. (1988) *Black Culture and the Harlem Renaissance*, Houston: Rice University Press.
Wise, T. (2011) *White Like Me: Reflections on Race from a Privileged Son*, Berkeley: Soft Skull Press.
Wittgenstein, L. (1992) *Philosophical Investigations*, trans. G.E.M. Anscombe, Cambridge: Blackwell.
Wolin, S.(1990) *Politics and Vision: Continuity and Innovation in Western Political Thought*, New York: Free Press
Wood, A.L. (2011) *Lynching and the Spectacle: Witnessing Racial Violence in America, 1890–1940*, Chapel Hill: University of North Carolina Press.
Woodward, C.V. (1966) *The Strange Career of Jim Crow*, New York: Oxford University Press.
Wright, R. (1993) [Untitled Review of *Their Eyes Were Watching God (1937)*] in H.L. Gates Jr. and K.A. Appiah (eds.) *Zora Neale Hurston: Critical Perspectives Past and Present*, New York: Penguin.
———. (2008) *Uncle Tom's Children*, New York: HarperCollins.
Zhu, P.F. (2009) "Renowned Af-Am Professor Gates Arrested for Disorderly Conduct," *The Harvard Crimson* <http://www.thecrimson.com/article/ 2009/7/20/renowned-af-am-professor-gates-arrested-for/> (accessed 19 April 2012).
Zizek, S. (1999) *Carl Schmitt in the Age of Post-Politics*, in C. Mouffe, *The Challenge of Carl Schmitt*, London: Verso, pp. 18–37.

Index

A

African Americans, *See* Black(s)
Agamben, G., 5, 40, 54, 67, 91–3, 101–3, 112, 123, 166, 189, 220, 223; *anomie*, 80, 103; nude, 101–2
American democracy, 100, 211, 216. *See also* democracy
antidiscrimination laws, 59, 61, 74, 81, 177
Apology, The, 88
apparatus, the, 2, 5, 217–28 (see also *dispositif*): critical Black subjectivity and, 119–20, 125–6, 143, 144, 148, 150, 177–9, 189–94, 196, 202–6, 209–16; definition of community and, 52, 55, 57, 72, 80–1, 105–6, 114; democratic theory and race, 18–27, 33–4, 43–7; racial equality and, 33, 43, 46, 203, 225
Arendt, H., 86, 99, 121
assimilation, 19, 31
authenticity, 45, 48, 60, 78, 122, 196, 202, 215, 227. *See also* politics of recognition
author of society, 141

B

Balfour, L., 2, 48, 66, 217
bare life, 102, 103, 166, 220, 221. *See also* Agamben
Baum, B., 2, 17, 18, 19, 221, 229
Bell, D., 27
Benito Cereno, 87–100, 141
Benjamin, W., 6, 17, 22, 27, 36, 104, 121, 176–7, 189–90
biopolitics, 221, 223. *See also* Foucault

Blanchot, M., 4, 75–8, 80, 88–9, 92, 168, 169: disavowal, 75–6, 90, 168, 224; elective community, 169; sacrifice, 76; unavowable community, 77, 92, 185
Black(s): as animals, 99, 103–4; authentic, 45, 48, 60, 78, 122, 196, 202, 215, 227 (*see also* authenticity); creaturely, 91, 92, 97–8, 104, 123, 141, 213 (*see also* Santner); desire for social equality, 164, 168–9, 187, 189, 202–3, 221 (see also *Plum Bun*); diaspora, 137; dilemma of success for, the, 160; discontent of, 21, 22, 187; endurance, 166; exceptional, the (*see* Black exception, the); exoticism, 160; haunting, 92; limited aspirations, 149, 153, 159, 160–3, 168, 197, 199, 207, 210, 215; normal, 4, 23, 47, 91, 194, 196, 214, 225, 228 (*see also* Black exception, the); opacity, 104, 123, 141, 143, 222; political mobilization, 24, 26, 44, 108, 144, 149, 150, 156, 191–2, 223 (see also *Marrow of Tradition*); President (*see* Obama, Barack); as property, 94, 134, 137–40, 155, 157; self policing, 105, 155–6, 163, 189, 215; split life, 93; subject, the normal Black, 44, 123, 202, 220; subjectivity (*see* Black subjectivity); subordination (*see* subordination); violence against Whites, 172–85, 227

Black community, 4, 6, 12, 218, 220, 223–8 (*see also* community): critical Black subjectivity and, 119–23, 126–7, 132–9, 146, 149, 151, 153, 156, 159–64, 176–8, 186–208, 213–5; definition of community, 52, 58–9, 62, 67, 77, 91–2, 95, 101, 105–6, 109, 112, 114; democratic theory and race, 18, 23–4, 27, 34, 38, 44–8

Black exception, the, 3, 4, 218, 220, 222, 223, 228 (*see also* exception, the): and critical Black subjectivity, 119, 121, 123, 130, 138, 144, 156, 158, 163, 166, 178, 182, 189–90, 192–4, 196, 199–201, 203, 205, 214–6; definition of community and, 72, 81, 105, 107 114; democratic theory and race, 20, 23–6, 45, 46–8

Black subjectivity, 3, 4, 6, 220–1, 224–6: critical, 119–23, 126, 136, 138, 141–4, 150, 155, 161, 163, 166, 196, 199–200, 202, 204, 209, 212–4, 216; definition of community and, 52, 68, 71–2, 81, 90, 92, 94–6, 101, 109; democratic theory and race, 23–4, 26, 44, 46

Boxill, B.R., 19, 32
Brophy, A.L., 145, 176
Brothers and Keepers, 120, 205–16, 217, 219, 220, 227, 228
Brown v. Board of Education, 8, 66

C

Campbell, T., 102
Chesnutt, C.W., 120–1, 145–57, 169, 201. See also *Marrow of Tradition, The*
Civil Rights Movement, 6, 9, 218, 223, 227–8: critical Black subjectivity and the,125, 190, 199–201; 58, definition of community and the, 63, 66–7, 80–2, 105; democratic theory and race, 18, 20, 24–5, 27–8, 36–7, 47
Civil War, 6, 7, 8, 227: critical Black subjectivity and the, 120–1, 124, 127–8, 131, 134, 136, 139–40, 144–6, 150, 151, 191; definition of community and the, 58, 95–6; democratic theory and race, 20, 22, 33, 37, 43, 47

Cohen, C.J., 48, 124
color problem, the, 131
communities: in conflict, 2, 6–8, 18, 23, 29, 34, 36–9, 42, 58, 60, 69, 109, 114, 128, 147–9, 225; of difference, 25, 53, 88, 90, 119, 138–42, 221

community, (*see also* communities): bifurcation, 44, 119–20, 123, 190, 192–4, 195–216, 223; confronting, 130–4; death and birth, 75–6 (*see also* Blanchot); history of, 6, 66, 91–6, 119–127; inclusion 80, 158, 162; individual, individualism and 6–8, 9, 12, 19, 74, 84, 164; internal controls 155, 163; rejecting racial, 60, 167, 168, 213, 225, 226

community member, membership, 2, 7, 11, 12, 223, 227 (*see also* community); and critical Black subjectivity, 127, 131, 148, 151, 153, 168, 170, 175, 176, 179, 182, 188, 190, 209, 214, 216; definition of community, 51–2, 57, 59, 62–3, 67, 70, 73, 75–9, 85, 87, 90, 95, 96, 108, 110; democratic theory and race, 24, 45, 47

crime and criminalization: 4, 102, 107, 121, 135, 177–8, 205, 208, 218–9
critical race politics, 18, 48, 132, 204, 225
critical race theory, 2, 3, 14, 29–32, 45, 224, 228

D

Davis, A., 13, 121, 208
decision, the. *See* sovereignty
democracy, 2, 3, 9, 13, 14, 227: critical Black subjectivity and, 143–4, 155, 157, 165, 190, 203, 205, 211, 216; definition of community and, 56–8, 61–2, 64, 78, 86, 89, 90, 91, 95, 97, 100–1, 111–2; democratic theory and race, 19, 31, 38, 41, 43–4; White mobilization, 147–50

Derrida, J., 8, 10, 42, 52, 66, 85–6, 103, 111, 113, 119, 143, 221, 233: unavowable community, 10, 66 (see also Blanchot: unavowable community)
discrimination, 8, 11, 17, 27, 58–61, 73–4, 88, 176–7
dispositif, 5, 20, 23, 26, 225. See also apparatus, the
Dred Scott v. Sandford, 9, 28, 137
Du Bois, W.E.B., 2, 12, 18, 36, 91, 96, 124, 127, 131, 134, 141, 143, 145, 147, 160, 164, 223–5

E

Ellison, R., 18, 159, 195
emancipation, 8, 22: critical Black subjectivity and, 120, 127, 132, 135, 139, 141, 147; definition of community and, 74, 92, 95, 96
equality of opportunity, 1–8, 13, 218–9: critical Black subjectivity and, 105–6, 108, 112, 119, 161, 191, 201, 215–6; definition of community and, 61–4, 67, 72, 81–2, 100; democratic theory and race, 18–23, 25–6, 33, 37–8, 45–8
Esposito, R., 4, 38, 66, 87, 112–5, 156, 193
ethic of care, 86–8, 141–3; critique of, 141–3 (see also *Iola Leroy*)
exception, the, 2–3, 12, 220, 222, 223: as distinct from the normal, 91, 150–4; created by personal choice, 205–12; critical Black subjectivity and, 119, 123, 126, 130, 138, 144, 163, 166, 177, 178, 182, 189–90, 192–4, 196–201, 210, 212; definition of community and, 72, 83, 91, 93, 103, 108, 112, 114; democratic theory and race, 20–5, 26–7, 29–30, 36, 38–40, 41–6, 48; racist, 12, 20–23, 24–25, 112, 126, 177, 197, 220, 222. See also Black exception, the; state of exception

F

Fanon, F., 46, 68, 174, 188
Farius, V., 42
Fauset, J.R., 120, 160–70, 202, 224–5, 227. See also *Plum Bun*

Faye, E. 42
fear, 217–8: critical Black subjectivity and, 129, 135, 151, 155–6, 158, 169, 173, 181, 208, 212–4, 216; definition of community and, 44, 78, 83, 98, 101, 112–3; of failure, 135, 155, 212, 214, 217–8, 223; of Whites, 135, 170–194, 208, 212–4, 216, 217–8 (see also Wright)
fiction contra facts, 127
form of life, 125. See also Santner
Foucault, M., 4, 5, 60, 67–73, 78, 85–8, 90, 102, 143, 157–8, 159, 181, 193–4, 204, 216–7, 221; ethic of care, (see ethic of care); *parrhesiast*, 67, 72–3, 143 (see also *parrhesia*); racism as illness, 87, 90

G

Gadamer, H.-G., 51, 104
Gates, H.L. Jr., 210–2, 214
gender politics, 195–203
Gilroy, P., ix, 90, 93, 203
Goldhagen, D.J., 38, 125
Gooding-Williams, R., 2
governmentality, 215

H

Hall, S., 150, 219
Habermas, J., 124
Harper, F., 120–1, 127–40, 156–7, 169, 201, 210. See also *Iola Leroy*
Harris-Perry, M.V., 228
Hartman, S., 123
hate: crime 22, 105; politics of, 29–30, 219, 225; speech, 27, 105
Hegel, G.W.F., 8, 38, 79, 83–4, 62–5, 169
Heidegger, M., 1, 42, 51–4, 83, 103, 167
Historian's debate, 125. See also Habermas; LaCapra
Holocaust, 27, 83, 125
Hooker, J., 31, 89, 221
Hurston, Z.N., 68, 127, 160, 185, 226

I

improper, impropriety, 55, 102, 115, 152
integration, 1, 6, 8, 12, 14, 217, 229: as a threat, 145 (see also *Marrow*

246 *Index*

of Tradition); critical Black subjectivity and, 120, 124, 126, 128, 131, 154, 155, 161, 163, 176, 190, 193, 195–216; definition of community and, 81, 82, 94, 96, 100, 114; democratic theory and race, 18, 19, 20, 22, 28, 31, 35, 36, 44, 46; gender and class, 195–205; legal structure, 19, 22–3; limits, 162. See also, *Brothers and Keepers*; *Silver Sparrow*
internal enemy, 37, 137
interracial relationships, 128, 137, 225 (see also *Iola Leroy*)
Iola Leroy, 90, 120, 121, 124, 127–44, 153, 155, 156, 158, 161, 166–7, 169, 182, 188, 199, 204, 214, 218, 228; ethic of care as subordination, 142; friendship and affection, 128–9, 139; Socrates and Diotima, 129, 140, 143
Ion, 4, 69–73, 78, 110

J

Jim Crow, 1–3, 6–9, 13, 217–22, 226–7: critical Black subjectivity and, 120–2, 124–6, 128, 136, 148, 150, 154–6, 159–194, 195, 201, 202, 203–4, 208–9, 210, 212, 214, 215; definition of community and, 57, 58, 62, 66, 69, 71, 74, 80, 82, 92, 93, 94, 96, 105–6, 112–4; democratic theory and race 17–23, 24, 25–6, 28, 31, 33–4, 36–40, 44, 45, 47. *See also* racism; *Plum Bun*; *Uncle Tom's Children*
Jones, T., 120, 195, 198, 201, 205, 214–5, 220, 226. See also *Silver Sparrow*

K

Kalyvas, A., 23, 38, 41–2, 110
Kelley, R.D.G., 2, 188
King, D.S., and Smith, R.M., 1, 27–9, 33, 47, 121, 126, 149, 211
King, M.L., Jr., 58, 106, 125, 199, 201, 206
Kymlicka, W., 31, 89

L

LaCapra, D., 10, 55, 125

laughter, 36, 167–71, 226, 227, 228: as a politics, 167–8, 226–7 (see also *Plum Bun*)
liberty, 19, 88, 137
Locke, A.L., 159–60, 218
love, 217, 219, 227: across the color line, 128–32; as a critical race politics, 133–4; critical Black subjectivity, 128, 130, 132, 133–5, 140–3, 165, 167, 195, 196–9, 203; definition of community and, 77, 93, 111; public opinion of, 133, 135; was not enough, 140. *See also* Derrida; Nancy; Foucault

M

Marrow of Tradition, The, 120–1, 124, 144–58, 161, 164, 166, 169–70, 175, 176, 182, 183, 185, 192, 195, 199, 209, 210, 214, 224, 227, 228
Martin, Trayvon, 174, 177–9, 211
memory, political, 18, 103, 123, 126
Mills, C., 19, 32, 57
Mouffe, C., 30

N

Nancy, J.-L., 1, 4, 30, 52, 57, 64, 75, 78–90, 109–11, 115, 129, 208, 219, 224; being-with, 82–3, 85, 89; copresence, 83–4, 88–9; freedom as evil, wickedness, 78–9, 81, 84–5, 88–9; inoperative community, 78–82, 86, 119; racism as irrational 81
N word, 55, 72, 73

O

Obama, Barack, 7, 14, 219: critical Black subjectivity and, 125, 146, 178, 182, 204, 210–12; definition of community and, 58, 61–5, 70, 89–91, 102, 114; democratic theory and race, 23, 27, 36, 42, 43–8
Oedipus Rex, 69–73, 89–90
Olson, J., 2, 10, 18, 21, 28, 218, 221, 224
Other, the: critical Black subjectivity and, 119, 129, 132, 142, 166, 169, 174; definition of community, 52–3, 66, 75–9, 81, 83, 104, 109, 115; 30, 34

P

parrhesia, 69–70, 72–3 (*see also* Foucault); citizenship, 69–70; the role of difference, 70; three types of, 70; Whites and, 69–70
partial democratic objects, 144. See *also* Santner
Plato, 90, 139
Plum Bun, 92, 120, 160–70, 182, 187, 195, 198, 199, 202, 203, 214, 218, 223–4, 225, 227, 228
political apparatus, *See* apparatus, the
politics of care, 134
politics of friend and enemy, 2, 3, 219, 221, 225: critical Black subject and the, 131, 135, 153, 156–7, 166, 186; definition of community and the, 77, 83, 94, 99, 101, 103, 109–10, 111, 113; democratic theory and race, 22, 29–30, 34, 36–7, 39, 40–3. *See also* Schmitt
politics of life, 221–3
politics of recognition, 103, 151–2, 168
postracial, 5, 229
private racial life, 114
promise of America, the, 43, 157

Q

quantitative not qualitative, 218–9. *See also* Hegel

R

race: as a test, 157; and gender politics, 166–7; learning of, 83, 132, 139, 142, 170–1, 172–5; obedience and, 38, 92, 104, 155, 171, 175, 177, 179, 194; passing 131–2, 139, 140, 160, 161–5, 167, 169, 212, 214, 227; private beliefs and, 136–7; refusing, 168, 226; rupture, 96; shared experience, 140; solidarity against, 187; wound of, 22, 23, 37, 45, 106, 223, 224
racial difference: biological, 87; dehiscence, 14, 45; hierarchical, 23, 29, 39, 64, 85, 96, 106, 112, 133, 165
racial communities, 2, 4, 6, 8–9, 12, 222, 227 (*see also* communities, community): and critical Black subjectivity, 119–21, 130, 137, 144, 161, 170, 175, 177–8, 191–2, 200, 215; definition of community, 53, 55, 57–61, 66–90, 91, 108, 113; democratic theory and race, 19, 22, 25, 29, 32–5, 41, 44
racism: definition of, 11; learning (*see* race: learning of); retaliation as ineffective, 184–5
racist, the, *See* exception, the: racist
Rawls, J., 18–9, 31–2, 35, 41, 74, 100–1, 157
Reconstruction, 145–7
reparations, 92, 121, 141, 203, 229

S

Santner, E.L., 4, 41, 91–2, 103, 105, 126, 167, 203–5
Schmitt, C., 3, 17–8, 20, 23, 27–43, 77, 83, 85, 87, 90, 91, 94, 97–115, 135, 143–4, 154, 156, 165–8, 175, 179, 184, 191–2, 221, 225, 228
Sebald, W.G., 121–3, 126
segregation, 1, 11, 12, 221, 226, 228: critical Black subjectivity and, 121, 125, 136, 146, 152–3, 156, 159, 163, 176–7, 182, 196; definition of community and, 58, 59, 60, 61, 64, 71, 74, 80, 81, 88, 105, 106–8, 113–4; democratic theory and race, 18, 22, 27, 28, 34, 38, 40; housing, 12, 17, 27, 47, 58, 59, 60, 81, 107, 110, 176, 193, 194, 202, 214, "stay in your place," 170–4
sexism, 94, 165; See also *Plum Bun*
Shelby, T., 2, 122–3, 208, 215, 223–5
Silver Sparrow, 120, 195–205, 206, 214, 215, 219, 220, 224, 226–8
slavery, 1, 6, 217, 218: critical Black subjectivity and, 119–58, 160, 163, 166, 169, 188, 201, 203, 208, 209, 212, 214; definition of community and, 88, 93, 94–6, 98, 100; democratic theory and race, 20, 27, 30, 47; economic and political development 134; the slave after, 139. See also *Iola Leroy*; *The Marrow of Tradition*
Smiley, T., and West, C., 47–8, 228
social construction, 6, 9, 12, 26, 41, 52–5, 79, 101, 203

social equality 164–8, 187, 202, 221. See also *Plum Bun*
sovereign, the decision, 4, 9, 217–28: critical Black subject and, 119–21, 125, 131–48, 154, 156–8, 161, 162–9, 189–191, 196–201, 209, 211, 213, 215; definition of community, 51–55, 77, 79–80, 84–5, 88, 90, 91–100, 103–18; democratic theory and race, 20, 22, 26, 27–8, 30, 35, 38, 39–50. *See also* Schmitt
sovereignty (*see also* White sovereignty): popular 43–4, 97, 101–2, 109–10, 112–3, 137, 141, 143–4, 154, 164–5, 167, 187, 189–91; standing one's ground, 175–9; threat to, 145
spectral materialism, 92
state entity, 33
state of exception, 21, 30, 39–40, 67, 220 (*see also* Schmitt; Agamben); Blacks, 144
Steedman, M., 19, 27
stranger, the, 30, 34
Strong, T., 20, 30–1, 42, 97, 175
subject: degraded, 135; fractured 3, 4
subjection: conditionality of, 39, 98, 213
subjectivity, *See* Black subjectivity; White subjectivity
subordination, 9, 217, 228: critical Black subjectivity and, 122–3, 128, 130, 138–9, 142, 144–5, 153, 157, 171–2, 174, 177, 179, 183, 186–7, 190, 192–4, 198, 200, 203–5, 212, 215; definition of community and, 52–7, 80–1, 91–2, 104–5, 109, 114–5; democratic theory and race, 19, 26, 27, 34, 37, 44
suture, 22, 23, 44–5, 47, 106, 121

T

Taylor, C., 31, 89. *See also* politics of recognition
truth, 4, 8, 17, 217 (see also *parrhesia*): critical Black subjectivity and, 119, 126–7, 142–3, 148, 181–3, 186, 204, 214, 216; definition of community and, 51, 54–6, 66–73, 77, 79–80, 86–90, 103, 108

truth teller, *See* Foucault: *parrhesiast*

U

Uncle Tom's Children, 120, 170–194, 203, 226–7

V

violence, 219, 222, 227, 228: critical Black subjectivity and, 135, 138, 145, 148, 152, 155–6, 165, 166, 168, 170–94, 195, 212; definition of community and, 48, 77, 89, 91, 93, 96, 98, 104–5, 110, 113; democratic theory and race, 17, 22, 27–8, 30, 37, 41–2, 46
Voting Rights Act, 8, 9, 12, 32, 66: Black vote, the 9, 19, 66, 143, 146, 155, 157, 194

W

West, C., ix, 22, 47–8, 228
White(s): accountability, 76, 179–84; exception, 12, 20–3, 24, 105, 112, 189, 224 (*see also* exception, the: racist); inability to promise, 179–84; liberal, 21, 25, 27–8, 30–1, 44, 46, 112, 172, 209–11, 222, 229; supremacy, 19, 64, 148, 154–8, (*see also* Jim Crow)
White community, 2–3, 7, 220–2, 225 (*see also* community): and critical Black subjectivity, 119, 124–8, 130, 133, 137–41, 143–53, 160–1, 172, 174–9, 191–4, 198–9, 201, 204, 209–10; definition of community, 52, 58, 60, 63, 72, 75–6, 80–1, 93, 97, 105–7, 109, 112–3; democratic theory and race, 20–2, 24–9, 32–8, 40, 43, 45–7
White man's country, 95, 134, 149, 155
Whiteness, 217–8, 221–2, 226, 228: alongside, 160; as deceit, 165; critical Black subjectivity and, 131–3, 140–2, 151–2, 159–60, 162, 164–5, 167–75, 186, 201, 212–6; definition of community and, 53–5, 57–8, 60–1, 64, 67–8, 71–2, 75–82, 92–3, 100, 102–3, 106, 110, 112; democratic theory and race,

20–3, 26–8, 35, 37, 39, 43–4, 47; gender politics and, 166–7; its limitations, 165; mendacity, 170–2, 182; refusal, 4, 17, 26, 109, 132–3, 207; as sovereign (*see* White sovereignty); as superior culture and material wealth, 24, 28, 36, 61, 63–4, 68, 84, 113, 145, 152, 153–4, 159, 162, 164, 171, 186, 220

White sovereignty, 3, 4, 9, 220, 224, 226 (*see also* sovereign, the decision; sovereignty): critical Black subjectivity and, 119, 133, 144–6, 148–156, 159, 161, 184, 188, 190–1, 193, 196, 200, 208–11, 215–6; definition of community and, 92, 95, 109; democratic theory and race, 18–21, 24–6, 28, 32, 36–7, 41, 44, 46–8

White subjectivity, 3, 221, 224–6, 229: and critical Black subjectivity, 133, 150, 154, 159, 204, 214, 216; definition of community and, 60, 76, 77, 92; democratic theory and race, 21, 25, 44

Wideman, J.E., 120, 202, 205–15, 219–20, 223, 225, 228. See also *Brothers and Keepers*

Wittgenstein, L., 83, 167: learning, 83

Wright, R., 48, 120, 160, 170–93, 201, 208, 210, 212, 222, 226. See also *Uncle Tom's Children*

For Product Safety Concerns and Information please contact our EU representative GPSR@taylorandfrancis.com
Taylor & Francis Verlag GmbH, Kaufingerstraße 24, 80331 München, Germany

www.ingramcontent.com/pod-product-compliance
Lightning Source LLC
Chambersburg PA
CBHW062132300426

44115CB00012BA/1900